Illuminate
Publishing

C000085360

WJEC A2 Religious Studies

Studies in Philosophy of Religion

Study and Revision Guide

Delyth Ellerton-Harris

Published in 2013 by Illuminate Publishing Ltd, P.O Box 1160,
Cheltenham, Gloucestershire GL50 9RW

Orders: Please visit www.illuminatepublishing.com
or email sales@illuminatepublishing.com

British Library Cataloguing in Publication Data

A catalogue record for this book is available from the British Library

ISBN   9781 908682 109

Printed by 4edge Ltd, Hockley, Essex
3.13

The publisher's policy is to use papers that are natural, renewable and recyclable
products made from wood grown in sustainable forests. The logging and manufacturing
processes are expected to conform to the environmental regulations of the country of origin.

This material has been endorsed by WJEC and offers high quality support for the
delivery of WJEC qualifications. While this material has been through a WJEC quality
assurance process, all responsibility for the content remains with the publisher.

Editor: Geoff Tuttle
Cover and text design: Nigel Harriss
Text and layout: The Manila Typesetting Company

Photograph and Illustration Credits

Alamy.com: p7 bilwissedition Ltd. & Co. KG; p17 Michael Juno; p36 Mick Sinclair; p86 Geoffrey Robinson; p103
Leo Mason; p112 INTERFOTO.

Fotolia.com: p9 Georgios Kollidas; p20 nickolae; p43 ojoimages4.

Shutterstock.com: p10 Albert H. Teich; p13 Anastasios Kandris; p17 gornjak; p23 Juriah Mosin; p25 Patryk
Kosmider; p36 ifong; p40 Volodymyr Goinyk; p40 Valentijn Tempels; p42 dedMazay; p43 Vacclav; p44 Jan Haas;
p44 Anteromite; p55 Dirk Ercken; p59 Steve Pepple; p76 Christopher Halloran; p75 Nicku; p83 Renata Sedmakova;
p106 Paul Brennan; p109 Oleg Golovnev; p120 Ase.

Modified and reproduced by Manila Typesetting Company:
p21 christttotheworld.blogspot.com/2011/04/son-of-man-will-be-delivered-into-hands.html and
commons.wikimedia.org/wiki/File:Bible_Johns_Gospel_3_16.JPG; p65 shutterstock.com by jorisvo;
p96 the-philosophy.com/skinner-behaviorism-theory; p107 www.biography.com/people/john-calvin-9235788.

Manila Typesetting Company graphics team for the rest of the images.

Acknowledgements

I am very grateful to the team at Illuminate Publishing for their professional guidance and support. Their
approachability and expertise has made this venture much easier than it otherwise would have been.

The publisher would like to thank John Summerwill for his guidance and encouragement throughout.

Bible quotations taken from:

NIV, International Bible Society, 1984; RSV, Division of Christian Education of the National Council of the Churches
of Christ in the USA, 1973.

Revised Standard Version of the Bible, Apocrypha, copyright 1957; The Third and Fourth Books of the Maccabees
and Psalm 151, copyright 1977 by the Division of Christian Education of the National Council of the Churches of
Christ in the United States of America. Used by permission. All rights reserved.

Dedications

To Peter, my rock and love of my life, whose kindness, love and support are always evident. You have made this
venture and so many other things, possible.

To Gwen and Les for always being there with love, encouragement and principles.

To all the 'A' level students I have taught for giving me so much more than I could ever give you.

Contents

How to use this book

The content of this study and revision guide is designed to guide you through to success in the WJEC 'Studies in Philosophy of Religion' (RS 3 PHIL) A2 examination. The book has been written by the Principal Examiner for this module.

There are notes on each section of the examination:

- Is religious faith rational?
- Is religious language meaningful?
- Is religious faith compatible with scientific evidence?
- Are we 'free beings'?

Knowledge and Understanding

The first section of the book covers the key knowledge required for the examination. Here you will find summary notes on all of the topics in the specification.

Also, I have tried to give additional help that will allow you to develop your revision:

- Key terms with definitions have been highlighted. Learn them and use them.
- Grade boost suggestions have been made. These give you tips on making the most of your revision and answers.
- Stretch and challenge makes suggestions for individual research.
- Quickfire questions are there to test your knowledge and understanding.
- Examination advice is given based upon examining experience.

Exam Practice and Technique

The second section of the book covers the key skills needed for examination success. You will be given tips for a good A level answer as well as being made aware of where the common weaknesses are. Then you will be given sample answers at different grades. These are not the only way to answer that question nor are they there so that you can just learn these alone and nothing else. They are to be used as a template for you to be able to see what is required of a good answer. The commentary will make this clear to you.

You must not rely solely on information given to you. This is your examination, your grade, so you need to take responsibility. Look on the WJEC website: www.wjec.co.uk. You must be extremely familiar with the specification; in fact, you really should know it bullet point by bullet point for both the 'topics' and 'issues' sections. After all, it is from this document that I take the examination questions that you will be sitting.

Get past papers and mark schemes. You really should be going into the examination knowing what all of the possible questions are and you should have given yourself the opportunity to try them all as well.

I hope your revision goes well and that you do the best you possibly could in the examination.

Delyth Ellerton-Harris

1: Is religious faith rational?

When revising 'Is religious faith rational?', you should focus on the main topics and issues. You should understand the ontological arguments for God's existence and be able to explain them fully in classical and modern forms. You will need to know the theories of faith of a variety of scholars as well as being able to explain concepts of revelation. Finally, you need to evaluate the issues arising from these topics from a variety of viewpoints, using scholarly opinion, and an informed conclusion must be reached.

Revision checklist

Tick column 1 when you have completed brief revision notes.
Tick column 2 when you think you have a good grasp of the topic.
Tick column 3 during final revision when you feel you have mastery of the topic.

			1	2	3
What is the ontological argument for God's existence?	p7	Anselm's first form			
	p8	Anselm's second form			
	p9	Descartes – triangle and mountain/valley			
	p10	Plantinga's modal argument			
Theories about the nature of faith	p12	Voluntarist views: Tennant – faith venture			
	p13	James – will to believe			
	p15	Pascal – superdominance			
	p15	– expectation			
	p16	– generalised expectation			
...and its relation to reason and revelation	p16	General ideas			
	p17	Specifics: Faith cannot be based on reason: Kierkegaard's leap of faith			
	p18	Faith must be based on reason: H.D. Lewis			
	p19	Proof of God's existence is not needed: Plantinga's non-foundationalism			
	p19	Faith seeking understanding: Augustine and Anselm			
	p20	Kant's idealism			
Propositional and non-propositional concepts of revelation	p21	Propositional – words			
	p22	Non-propositional – events			
What are the main issues that arise from 'Is religious faith rational?'	p25	What are the strengths and weaknesses of the ontological argument?			
	p28	Is the ontological argument convincing?			
	p29	Is faith more valid if based on reason rather than revelation?			
	p30	Are faith and reason contradictory or complementary?			
	p31	Is revelation an adequate basis for religious belief?			

The ontological argument for the existence of God

The ontological argument of St Anselm of Canterbury (1033–1109CE)

Key Terms

a priori = prior to experience.

Analytic = statement is true/false by definition of the words.

Deduction = reasoning by logical stages (premises) to reach a conclusion.

in intellectu = in the mind.

in re = in reality.

Ontology = the study of being.

Perfection = a property, quality, characteristic, predicate, attribute.

From Chapters II and III of *Proslogion* St. Anselm already believed in God. In his **ontological** argument he was trying to show how obvious God's existence was to him and how absurd atheism is. He had much in common with St Augustine when it came to matters concerning faith, reason and revelation. St Anselm believed that reason demonstrates what is already believed by faith.

AO2 evaluative issues on this question are on pages 25–28.

First form

The argument comes from the word 'Ontos' or 'Being'. It is an ***a priori*** argument: it relies on analysing the definition of a word. It is therefore **deductive** and **analytic**. The conclusion flows logically from the premises.

In the argument, Anselm says that existence is a **perfection**, something which you can have or lack. He also says that the predicate is contained in the subject. So, God's existence can be shown to be self-evident by analysing the word 'God'. In other words, by analysing the word God it will be obvious, says Anselm, that God exists. In 'God exists' the subject is 'God', the predicate is 'exists'.

$$(\exists x)(y)\ x{>}y \rightarrow Gx$$
$$(x)(y)\ Ex \neg Ey \rightarrow x{>}y$$
$$(\exists x)\ Gx.Ex$$

Anselm figured it all out
(or did he?)

Key Term

Necessary = cannot not be.

Grade boost

As the argument relies on setting out sets of premises to reach a conclusion, to show you truly understand the argument, you cannot leave out any of the premises. If you did there would be a leap which is unjustified. Also, be sure to use the phrases 'has the property or perfection of existence' and 'it is more perfect to have the property of existence in reality than in the understanding alone'. Rather than using only 'God exists', write that 'God has the property or perfection of existing in reality'.

quickfire

① Complete to make it analytic: 'a bachelor is...'.

② List three perfections of the God of classical theism.

Definition of God

As the argument relies on analysing a definition, clearly the definition of God is vital:

'A being than which nothing greater can be conceived.'

The fool

Psalm 14 NIV:

1 The fool says in his heart, 'There is no God'. They are corrupt, their deeds are vile; there is no one who does good.

Anselm observed that even the fool is convinced that something than which nothing greater can be conceived is in the understanding, since when he hears it he understands it. This means that even the fool has the concept of God in his understanding, in order to reject God. Similarly, I have the concept of a unicorn in my mind in order to reject it.

So after the definition of God, in logical stages, Anselm moves on to other premises. 'Greater' means 'perfect' or 'having all perfections'. 'Conceived' means 'thought of'. Existence is a perfection you can have or lack.

As 'perfection' means 'having all perfections/predicates/qualities', then, to be 'a Being than which nothing...', God must have the perfection of existence in reality or else he would not be 'a Being than which nothing greater can be conceived'.

Why? It is surely better to have the perfection of existence in reality than in understanding alone. A lottery win is surely better in reality than in my mind alone! So, if God only had the perfection of existence in the mind or understanding, then there could be another being who had the perfection of existence in reality, who would then be greater/more perfect than God, that is, would have one more perfection than God, that of existence in reality.

But, this cannot be true by definition, as God is 'a Being than which nothing...'. So, God exists.

Gaunilo was a monk from Marmoutier in France. See later under 'weaknesses of the ontological argument' for details of his criticism of the ontological argument concerning the most perfect island conceivable. He criticised this first form, mainly because the first form has existence as a predicate. Anselm's reply was that God is 'a special case' and the argument applies only to **necessary** beings and not to contingent things like islands.

Second form

Anselm attempts to show more than God exists. Here, he tries to demonstrate that God's existence is necessary. Existence seems not to be treated as a predicate. He looks at two modes of existence: contingent (could not have been) and necessary (could not not be).

In its basic form it is greater or more perfect to have necessary existence as opposed to contingent existence. Why? Contingent existence relies on another to bring it into existence. This being is therefore limited. This being cannot then be God as God is 'a Being than which nothing...'.

If God were contingent/limited, then we could conceive of another being that has the predicate/property of necessary existence and this being would then be greater/more perfect than God, as it is more perfect to have the perfection of necessary existence.

So, GOD EXISTS!!! God's existence must be necessary in order for God to match up to the definition that Anselm has given. By analysing the definition of the word God, Anselm has shown that God exists. To deny God's existence, once we have that definition of God, is contradictory.

The ontological argument of Descartes (1596–1650CE)

Key Term
Innate = in the mind, something you are born with, not learned from experience.

Descartes' version stems from two of the main parts of his philosophy:

1. The theory of innate (inbuilt) ideas.
2. The belief in clear and distinct perception (interpretation of data).

It is in the Fifth Meditation that we find the main part of his argument. For Descartes, God is a 'supremely perfect being' that has necessary existence. In its basic form the argument goes like this:

I have an idea that I perceive clearly and distinctly, of a supremely perfect being, that is, a being having all perfections. Necessary existence is a perfection. Therefore a supremely perfect being exists that has necessary existence.

Let us unpack this. Descartes would argue that as a general principle, when we consider an idea, what we perceive clearly and distinctly as belonging to it really does belong to it. I understand clearly and distinctly that necessary existence belongs to the essence of God. Therefore, existence really does belong to the essence of God. Hence, God exists.

In other words, his argument does not depend on a random definition of God but rather on an **innate** idea whose content is granted or assumed. God's existence is the logical conclusion drawn from the fact that necessary existence is contained in the clear and distinct idea of a supremely perfect being.

In fact, as we often find in other ontological arguments, at times he suggests that the 'argument' is a self-evident truth. He used two analogies.

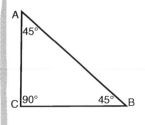

He demonstrated that necessary existence cannot be separated from the idea of God any more than three angles can be separated from the idea of a triangle. Three angles are intrinsic to the definition of a triangle just as necessary existence is intrinsic to the definition of God, a supremely perfect being. Here he is comparing his demonstration of God's existence with the very basic geometric demonstrations. We know this by instinct, directly, innately.

His second analogy is that existence can no more be separated from the essence of God than the idea of a mountain can be separated from the idea of a valley. In other words, it would be a contradiction to conceive of a mountain without a valley, as an **intrinsic** part of the definition of one entails the other. The same applies to God. It would be a contradiction to think of God, a supremely perfect being without one perfection, that of necessary existence.

Key Term

Intrinsic = belonging to a thing by its nature.

The ontological argument of Plantinga (1932CE–)

A modern version of the ontological argument

Key Terms

Modal argument = an argument which concerns claims about the possibility or necessity of God's attributes and existence.

Possible world = a way that things could be.

Questions will not be set on individual philosophers but the Specification requires familiarity with the arguments of modern philosophers. Alvin Plantinga's argument based upon '**possible worlds**' is one such modern argument. (See 'Stretch and challenge' on page 11 for a choice of others.)

Plantinga's argument is called the 'victorious' **modal argument**. It is based upon possible worlds. It runs as follows:

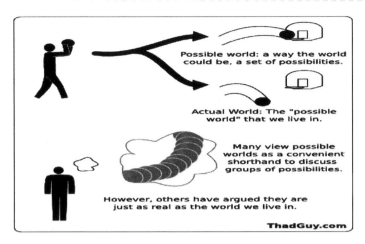

- There is an infinite number of possible worlds.
- A being can only have maximal greatness if it exists in every possible world.
- So, in every possible world there is a being which has maximal greatness.
- This being, at this point in the argument, is not God.
- In theory, there could be a being in every possible world that has more power, more knowledge and is more morally perfect than the maximally great being. After all, to be maximally great, this being only has to be in every possible world.
- So, an intrinsic part of having maximal excellence is that this being is omnipotent, omniscient and morally perfect.
- A being has maximal greatness only if it has maximal excellence in every possible world.
- Our world is a possible world.
- Hence there is a being in our world that is maximally great and therefore maximally excellent.
- This being is God.

It is a 'victorious' argument, says Plantinga, because as the premises are rational, then the conclusion is rational too, even though the conclusion may not be proven by evidence.

Stretch and challenge

Look up another discussion of a modern reformulation of the ontological argument such as that of Sobel, Malcolm or Hartshorne.

quickfire

③ Why is maximal excellence described as entailing the three attributes that it does?

④ What does it mean to say there is an infinite number of possible worlds?

Theories about the nature of faith and its relation with reason and revelation

AO2 evaluative issues on this question are on pages 29–31.

There are many theories about the nature of faith. The Specification allows the candidate to study any views of faith as a question will never be set on a specific theory. A popular choice is the voluntarist views of faith. The central feature of these theories is that faith is a voluntary act of the will, a choice, a free decision. In an examination the candidate could refer to the voluntarist view as one theory of faith and deal with it in that way. Alternatively, individual voluntarist theories of faith can be kept separate and written about as individual theories. Three such theories follow.

Key Terms

Subdoxastic = of or relating to what underlies the formation of beliefs or opinions.

Utopia = a perfect place or situation.

Voluntarist = choice, the will or voluntary action to make a decision.

quickfire

⑤ What is the difference between faith and belief?

⑥ Why is the faith-venture needed in all discoveries?

⑦ What risks may be involved in the religious faith-venture?

⑧ How is Tennant's view a **voluntarist** theory of faith?

Voluntarist views of faith 1: Tennant

F.R. Tennant (1866–1957CE): 'The faith-venture'

Tennant was an English philosophical theologian who wanted to harmonise a scientific and religious approach within an empirical (based upon sense experience or experiment) approach. His view is often called the **subdoxastic** model of faith. He takes faith to be the choosing (hence, volunteer) of a certain type of behaviour that is not based upon appeal to present facts, that involves experimenting with the possible or ideal, venturing into the unknown and taking the risk of disappointment and defeat. This can be seen with Kierkegaard, too. (See later on in this guide for information on his views of faith and its relation to reason.)

Tennant classed science and religion as similar when it comes to faith. Faith is defined as 'willing adventure' that plays a part in *all* discoveries. It reaches the 'ideally possible'. Clearly we can see the suggested comparison. Both disciplines need an element of will or choice in exercising their hypotheses. Without this choice then nothing would ever progress, no discovery would ever be made. Things would be left at the belief stage. Belief, says Tennant, involves what we already know. Faith, however, involves a voluntary act to go beyond what we already know to what we could know.

So, faith in both religion and science involves practical commitment venturing beyond evidential support. Faith is not an attempt to will something into existence but rather viewing the ideally possible as *if* it were real and then acting accordingly.

'Every machine of human invention has come about this way', said Tennant. Columbus's discovery of America is given as an example. Without his faith-venture he would have been left with belief or the fact of what was already known. America would never have been discovered. However, there is no assurance of the outcome of this 'faith-venture'. It involves risks. There may be failure. As Tennant said, if Columbus had set out to discover **Utopia**, clearly he would have been disappointed.

Voluntarist views of faith 2: James

Key Term

Passional = emotional side of our nature that we should base our decisions on.

William James (1842–1910CE): The will/right to believe

James was an American who influenced a number of thinkers across Europe and America in a number of academic disciplines. These thinkers included Edmund Husserl, Bertrand Russell, and Ludwig Wittgenstein. He delved into philosophy and psychology, which was relatively new at that time. His essay, 'The will to believe' is a controversial one. He has often been accused of recommending that people should hold irrational beliefs, as if we can believe things simply because we will to believe them. He did not intend this. He later wrote that he wished he had called the essay 'The right to believe' as what he wanted to do was to show that in certain circumstances, we are justified in having certain beliefs. This certainly includes a religious belief.

To put James' work into context, the sceptic (one who doubts) W.K. Clifford said: '*It is wrong everywhere, always and for anyone to believe on the basis of insufficient evidence.*'

James says that *no* conclusive evidence will ever arrive, so religious faith *cannot* be just a matter of the intellect. We simply *must* decide. Whatever our decision, yes, no or undecided, there is the chance of error. James accuses Clifford of risking loss of truth rather than chancing error. We also risk loss of truth.

As the decision cannot be made on intellectual grounds we are justified in deciding on '**passional**' grounds. That is, decide according to what best fits with our hopes, fears and so on. James says that this 'passional' decision will then be the one which is the most pragmatic for our own happiness and satisfaction.

An example: is there life after death? What is the most pragmatic decision?

Key Terms

Forced = has to be done.

Genuine option = real possibility.

Living = active.

Momentous = of massive significance.

Pragmatic = practical or useful.

Grade boost

Always use specific examples used by scholars in your answer. This is needed for the higher levels.

quickfire

⑨ Why do we have to make decisions based upon our passional nature?

⑩ Why should our decision be the most pragmatic?

⑪ How can we get empirical confirmation of belief in God?

Stretch and challenge

Work through the quotation by Fitz James Stephen *word by word, sentence by sentence*. Write it out in your own words. Explain how it 'fits' with James's 'will to believe' theory of faith.

James would say that this is a **genuine option**, which is **living, forced** and **momentous**. The decision cannot be made on intellectual grounds. So, we 'lawfully may' make our decision on 'passional' grounds.

If believing in life after death is the most **pragmatic** decision for me, that is, what best fits with my 'passional' nature, then this belief is justified. This is more pragmatic for me than believing that there is no life after death.

What if I remain in doubt? This is still a 'passional' decision. He says that being in doubt would be more pragmatic than not believing in life after death, but not as pragmatic as if there was a belief in life after death. He says that a religious person still gains satisfactions here and now. This comes from believing that there is a life beyond.

An atheist or agnostic does not expect a life beyond and so does not gain satisfaction from that in this life. A believer will die expecting a life beyond and will not know if they are wrong. So, it is more pragmatic for me to believe in it. Therefore, I 'will to believe' that the religious hypothesis is true. *I will also live as though it is true.* Because James believed that if I hold a belief that may itself contribute to its success; the belief may help to bring about the fact believed in. To put it in his words, 'a fact cannot come at all unless a preliminary faith exists in its coming'. Belief creates the fact.

Although religious belief does not come through empirical means, we can get empirical confirmation of the religious belief. How? We can see the positive effects of religion on a person's life. This proves the belief to be pragmatic. To those who are not willing to make that decision he would say 'live and let live' and 'go in peace'.

James concluded his 'will to believe' essay with a quote from 19th-century author, by Fitz James Stephen:

In all important transactions of life we have to take a leap in the dark... If we decide to leave the riddles unanswered, that is a choice; if we waver in our answer, that, too, is a choice: but whatever choice we make, we make it at our peril. If a man chooses to turn his back altogether on God and the future, no one can prevent him; no one can show beyond reasonable doubt that he is mistaken. If a man thinks otherwise and acts as he thinks, I do not see that anyone can prove that he is mistaken. Each must act as he thinks best; and if he is wrong, so much the worse for him. We stand on a mountain pass in the midst of whirling snow and blinding mist through which we get glimpses now and then of paths which may be deceptive. If we stand still we shall be frozen to death. If we take the wrong road we shall be dashed to pieces. We do not certainly know whether there is any right one. What must we do? Be strong and of a good courage. Act for the best, hope for the best, and take what comes... If death ends all, we cannot meet death better.

Voluntarist views of faith 3: Pascal

Key Terms

Dominate = control, rule over.

Prudence = cautious, wise.

Super = above.

Utility = useful, profitable, beneficial.

Wager = bet or gamble.

B. Pascal (1623–1662CE): his wager

In your A2 work, Pascal can be used in questions concerning 'theories about the nature of faith' AO1 as we are doing here and *also* in questions that ask 'whether faith is more valid if based on reason or revelation' AO2. Pascal's God was the God of the Bible, the God of Jerusalem, rather than the God of the philosophers, the God of Athens. This is because Pascal's God is one who reveals rather than one which is discovered through reasoned argument. Reason could never make sense of the Resurrection of Jesus in Jerusalem, for example. His God is a God who reveals enough for those who have eyes that wish to see God. Pascal is associated with referring to 'the hidden God'.

The singular name 'Pascal's Wager' is misleading, for in one paragraph of his *Pensées*, Pascal seems to present at least *three* arguments, each of which might be called a '**wager**'. It is only the final of these that is traditionally referred to as 'Pascal's Wager' and most books refer only to that argument. Here the other two arguments will also be referred to, as the ideas behind all three are linked.

1. The argument from superdominance

'God is, or He is not.' Reason can't help our decision but a consideration of the outcomes supposedly can. Since you must choose, let us see which interests you least; let's consider what the most **prudent** decision is. Let us weigh the gain and the loss in wagering that God is... If you gain, you gain all; if you lose, you lose nothing. Wager, then, without hesitation that He is.

	God exists	God does not exist
Wager for God	Eternal life	Nothing happens
Wager against God	Eternal damnation	Nothing happens

Wagering for God **superdominates** or is far more powerful than wagering against God: the worst outcome associated with wagering for God (nothing happens) is at least as good as the best outcome associated with wagering against God (nothing happens); and if God exists, the result of wagering for God is much better than the result of wagering against God. The conclusion is that rationality and prudence requires you to wager for God.

2. The argument from expectation

Here, Pascal's interest as a mathematician in gambling needs to be borne in mind. His wager has many other gambling terms such as 'stake', 'game', 'heads or tails' and so on. Also, his interest in mathematics drives his attempt to include probability theory. He says that you have to play because, as we can calculate the relative expected values of believing and not believing, it would be imprudent (unwise) not to wager for God. He says that there is a 50:50 chance of God existing. Our calculation of the expectations of the above matrix shows us that by far the most **utility** will be gained from believing in God as the expectation is for infinite reward.

Stretch and challenge

Pascal says that atheism is unreasonable as it is not a safe bet. Look up why Kierkegaard would say that it is *because* faith is not a safe bet that it is reasonable.

Find the end to Pascal's quote 'The heart has...'.

quickfire

12 Why is Pascal's God the God of the Bible, not the God of the philosophers?

13 Would Pascal agree with revelation or reason?

Key Terms

Fides = belief that – deals more with facts.

Fiducia = belief in – deals more with trust or commitment.

3. The argument from generalised expectations: 'Pascal's wager'

This now combines all of his points into a single argument. Pascal's wager has three **premises**: the first concerns the decision matrix of rewards, the second concerns the probability that you should give to God's existence, and the third is a guiding rule about rational decision making. So:

1. God exists or God does not exist; you can wager for or against God. The utilities or usefulness of the possible outcomes are shown below; all utilities but one are finite.

	God exists	God does not exist
Wager for God	(infinite)	$finite_1$
Wager against God	$finite_2$	$finite_3$

2. A rational and prudent person would choose that which gives them the greatest expected utility.
3. You should wager for God as this is the only expected outcome that will give you infinite utility.

Theism is a more sensible wager than atheism.

The relation between faith, reason and revelation

There is great debate concerning the relation between faith, reason and revelation. Basically, the debate surrounds whether faith can or should be based upon reason or revelation. It should be noted that saying that faith is not based upon reason is not thereby saying that the faith is unreasonable. Below are a number of contributors to this debate. The relation can be discussed in a number of ways. There are common general ideas to be considered which will help in essays. Some of these are:

- Is faith intellectual acceptance (reason) or an instinct, an emotional response (revelation)?
- Is it better to use your head (reason) or heart (revelation)?
- Is religious faith *fides* or *fiducia*?
- Can either give knowledge, truth, free from subjectivity?
- Positive aspects of revelation: for example, it may be clear to all.
- Negative aspects of revelation: for example, some events may be open to interpretation.
- Positive aspects of reason: for example, we can all use it.
- Negative aspects of reason: for example, it may be too intellectual.
- Can we combine rationalism and empiricism – Kant's idealism?

Specifics regarding faith and its relation to reason and revelation

An important issue here concerns **epistemology**: how do we come to know things? It is useful to learn work by having clear categories in mind.

1. Faith cannot be based on reason (but rather, faith is due to revelation)

Kierkegaard (1813–1855CE) was a Danish philosopher and theologian, born to a fairly wealthy family in Copenhagen. He was a Christian, but believed that God's existence can neither be proved nor disproved. God's existence is very different to the existence of things. Faith is not something which is based upon empirical evidence. We realise that we do not have that evidence but we have faith anyway. Faith, said Kierkegaard, is also to have doubt at the same time. He said that, 'doubt is conquered by faith, just as it is faith which has brought doubt into the world'. He likens his idea to whether or not a person deserves to be loved. Evidence for the love of someone is not needed, it simply involves a surrender to that person.

Key Terms

Epistemology = theory concerning how we know things. Philosophy recognises two ways in which humans can come to know things, namely empiricism and rationalism.

Evidentialism = solid reasons for faith.

Stretch and challenge

Research his '3Cs', further. Write another paragraph on each.

Key Term

Fideism = needs special mention. There are many strands to this term. You will see the stem of it in *fides* and *fiducia*. Fideists may say:

- Philosophical justification for God's existence is not needed.
- God's existence cannot be shown by reason, but must be accepted by faith.
- Many do not deny that reason has a place, but say that faith comes before reason.

He said that faith needs an unsupported leap into the unknown. Reason will only lead us down a blind alley. Reason is an obstacle to faith. His is the God of the philosophers and the cold logic of reason is not helpful to gaining faith. His 'leap', however, would be said by him to be a justified leap; hence it is 'reasonable'. Faith is a choice to surrender to God as opposed to reason, which is a human searching. Faith is not just not based upon reason. In fact, faith *contradicts* reason. Kierkegaard's approach would be called **fideistic**. He has '3 Cs' to his argument:

- Certainty – reason can only give us 'probably'. Religious faith needs an assurance, a certainty as faith is something that a person holds deeply. So, faith cannot be based on reason as it probably will never be enough for a faith (Approximation argument).
- Commitment – we cannot commit to reasoned argument as it is amended and revised when we get more information. We commit to something which is unchanging such as religious faith. Religious faith needs commitment so it cannot be based on reasoned argument (Postponement argument).
- Cost – to be valuable, religious faith needs to be risky, it needs to have a cost attached. The more risky, the more valuable. This means religious faith has to be improbable, in order to have a cost attached. Reasoned argument at least gives us a 'probable' so there is less cost involved. So, religious faith cannot be based on reasoned argument (Passion argument).

This is *fiducia*. Faith is like 'floating on 70,000 fathoms of water and not being afraid'.

In this category we could also include, for example, Karl Barth and Martin Buber. Also see Stretch and challenge on page 19. See other parts of this guide for their views on reason and revelation.

2. Faith must be based on reason

H.D. Lewis (1910–1992CE) says that faith, to be valid, has to be based on reason. If God revealed without the need for human reasoning, then that revelation would be unambiguous and clear to all. It is not. So humans have to use their reason in order to have a relationship with God; it must be a relationship in which humans fully use their minds.

In this category we could also put, for example, John Hick. (See Stretch and challenge on page 19.)

3. Proof of God's existence is not needed

Plantinga says that belief in God is a basic belief and therefore needs no justification or proof. This is **non-foundationalism**. It is called this as foundationalism has categories of beliefs that are said to be **basic** and **belief** in God is not one of these. The categories are:

- Things we see. I see an appendage at the end of my torso. Based upon experience rather than evidence I am justified in believing this is my leg.
- Memory reports. I had muesli this morning. I do not have to cut open my stomach to give evidence for this belief.
- Self-evident statements. It is taken for granted, obvious or needs no proof that a cabbage is not an apple.
- Analytic truths. 1+1=2. Truth or falsity is not based upon evidence.
- Firmly set beliefs. I have a toothache. I would simply believe this of myself or others.

Plantinga says that belief in God should be included as it is grounded in our experience rather than evidence.

In this category we could also put, for example, R.M. Hare's bliks and the philosophical notion of seeing-as/experiencing-as. See other parts of this guide for some information and also the Stretch and challenge task on this page.

4. Faith seeking understanding

'I do not seek to understand in order that I may believe, but I believe in order that I may understand.' This is the view of Augustine and Anselm.

For Augustine, faith comes first, the free action of trust. But, this is supplemented by divine grace. Reason does not cause faith, but supports it. Therefore, faith is rationally justifiable. Christians should use reason to understand doctrines (such as the Trinity and the Incarnation) that are given through revelation. How can this be done? Through 'divine illumination'. God illuminates the mind so that humans can understand revealed truths. Understanding is the reward of faith.

For Anselm, 'Faith seeking understanding' is often translated as 'an active love of God searching for a deeper knowledge of God'. For Anselm, reason can be used to try to understand the nature of the existence of (see his ontological argument). However, he began with revealed truths of the Bible (that there is a God) before going on to use reason to explain how this could be the case. Reason has its place in understanding revelation, but when reason faces something impossible to understand, faith can confirm the truth of it.

Key Terms

Basic belief = one that needs no justification (foundationalism).

Non-foundationalism = Plantinga's theory that belief in God is a basic belief.

Grade boost

Use the key terms in context in your essay. Use the work of at least two scholars in each of the four categories shown in the previous text regarding reason and revelation. For higher levels, bring in scholars from other parts of this topic, such as Barth, Hare, Pascal and James.

Stretch and challenge

Look up the view of one other person in the first three categories above.

Aquinas kept together revelation and reason. Look up his views and write a two-paragraph summary.

quickfire

⑭ Would *fides* be linked to reason or revelation?

⑮ Is Kierkegaard a fideist?

⑯ Why does Plantinga say that belief in God is a basic belief?

⑰ What is a 'basic belief'?

⑱ What is 'divine illumination'?

Stretch and challenge

Give two pieces of evidence that may be used to suggest we get knowledge through sense experience. Now do the same for the intellect.

Kant's Idealism

Immanuel Kant.

Kant (1724–1804) was a hugely influential philosopher. It seems that he was a man ruled by much routine. Apparently housewives would always know the precise time he was going to pass their window! He believed that his work gave a set of universal principles that would apply to all humans for all time. He wrote three 'Critiques': *Critique of Pure Reason* (1781), *Critique of Practical Reason* (1788) and *The Critique of Judgement*.

In the *Critique of Pure Reason* Kant sought to investigate the two seemingly opposing views of **empiricism** (experience) and **rationalism** (ideas). The former said that we get knowledge through sense experience; humans are '*tabula rasa*' or blank sheets, waiting to receive information. The latter said that knowledge is based upon the intellect. He observed that there was an impasse between them, no progress seemed possible. The genius of what Kant did was to say that humans get to know things from both experience *and* ideas. In other words he was synthesising two things that had been kept apart.

The essence of his Idealism was that we get information about those things that are capable of being known from our five senses. These things he called 'phenomena'. In order to make sense of this sensory data our mind then has to give a structure, an order, to this data. So our minds impose time and space as well as the 12 fundamental judgements (substance, cause/effect, reciprocity, necessity, possibility, existence, totality, unity, plurality, limitation, reality and negation) to the sense data in order to organise it as it comes in to us.

So, we can only know things in the way that our mind has organised them for us, the phenomena. Kant believed that behind the phenomena is the noumena (the reality behind the phenomena). If you like, this is 'the thing in itself' which we can never know as we always come to know something with the overlay of our mind's organisation of it. In other words, we can only see every phenomenon through our own particular tinted-colour spectacles. The reality lies behind any observation of it, so the way we observe everything may indeed not be how it really is.

Propositional and non-propositional concepts of revelation

Philosophers who say that God shows his nature and intentions to humans (as opposed to humans 'finding' God through reason) then discuss how God reveals. If God reveals, then God takes the initiative. There are two concepts of revelation.

1. Propositional

A proposition is a statement, a set of words. These are often put down in **dogmas** or **creeds**. This gives us God's revelation in words. These can be found in, for example, holy books and words of leaders within religions. For 'religions of the book', God has spoken or self-revealed in the actual words: the 'words of God'. This has big implications for holy books and leaders who are now God's mouthpiece. This generates an '**I–It**' relationship. Faith is accepting the words as being from God and therefore true: 'divinely authenticated truths'.

This view accepts that there can be *some* truths that we can know by reason (for example, that God exists) but others that can only be known through God's revelation (for example, the Trinity). Propositional is more associated with *fides* (belief that) as opposed to *fiducia* (belief in).

Stretch and challenge

Find the following Biblical references and explain what they are saying about the 'words of God':

- 2 Timothy 3 verses 15 & 16.
- Ephesians 3 verses 3–5.
- Hebrews 4 verse 12.
- Matthew 13 verse 5.
- Isaiah 40 verse 8.

Grade boost

Include examples of 'statements of belief' in your answers such as the Muslim Shahadah or Papal declarations.

Stretch and challenge

Find out more about Barth's views on Jesus as the Word of God. Write out ten points to present to your class.

If human nature is corrupted by 'The Fall', what does this mean for humans today? List five 'issues' that may arise from this.

Prepare for revision where you explain the main points of the propositional view. Start with a diagram of areas to cover:

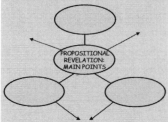

quickfire

⑲ What are 'divinely authenticated truths'?

⑳ What is Natural Theology?

㉑ Why does Barth say that humans cannot find God?

The views of Karl Barth (1886–1968CE)

In part (a) questions for Level 7 you will need to include 'where appropriate, diversity of views and/or scholarly opinion'. In part (b) questions you need for a Level 7 'different views, including where appropriate, those of scholars'. In questions on revelation and reason on the examination paper you could include people such as Luther, Calvin and Barth under 'propositional' revelation. Below is an account of the work of Karl Barth that you could use to exemplify the propositional view.

Barth's views are controversial. This is because the traditional Christian view has been that God has self-revealed in two ways. The first way is through the natural world (Natural Theology) where God has left 'clues' in nature for humans to discover. The second way is through scripture (Revealed Theology). However, Barth said that Natural Theology (which Barth redefines as the human attempt to discover God) is a misunderstanding of the *focus* of Revelation. *God* is the focus, as the revealer, *not* man as the receiver. God's revelation is in God's Word, Jesus Christ, found in the Bible and in the Church's preaching. Humans should just accept the revelation by having faith. Why does Barth have this view?

1. Human nature cannot find God as human nature has been corrupted by 'The Fall'.
2. God chose to be revealed through Jesus so this is the *only* way of knowing God.
3. Divine revelation is what is true. It is not open to trial by reason. If reason seems to go against divine revelation, then reason is wrong.

2. Non-propositional

As the name suggests, revelation is not found in the actual words of holy books or leaders. Revelation is in the event that the words are describing. The words therefore are of secondary importance. They are not the direct words of God. They are human efforts to understand the events, to grasp the meaning behind them. They are not the revelation.

An example to use in an essay = Jesus

a. There are many events involving him.
b. Different people experienced him in their everyday lives.
c. Humans wrote about him.
d. What is written depends on their experience of him.
e. So, the words are not the direct words of God.
f. The words could be various and very different, depending on the person's experience of him.

Non-propositional scholarly comments and quotes

1) Karl Rahner: 'the apostles had a global experience...lying behind propositions'.
2) Schleiermacher: 'when we feel dependent on God, this experience contains the revelation'.
3) G. Moran: revelation is a 'personal communion of knowledge, an interrelationship of God and the individual within a believing community'.
4) J. Macquarrie: 'revelation is not primarily given in the form of statements'.

Stretch and challenge

From the views of these four scholars, explain how you know that these scholars are describing a non-propositional view of revelation.

Other scholars and theories concerning non-propositional revelation

- Martin Buber (1878–1965CE): 'I and Thou.' He said revelation should be an I–Thou meeting, a meeting with another person. Contrast this with I–It, where the meeting is with an object and not a person.
- Ludwig Wittgenstein (1889–1951CE): 'Seeing as/experiencing as.' This can be shown by picture puzzles where some see them as X and others see them as Y. One event is experienced in many ways.

- Blaise Pascal: 'Hidden God.' This God shows enough of themself for those who wish to see, but will 'hide' from those who do not wish to see.

- R.M. Hare (1919–2002CE): 'bliks'. A blik is a way of seeing life. It cannot be verified or falsified; it is a way of interpreting data. Hare tells the story of the lunatic and the university dons. The lunatic, like everyone, has a blik; the lunatic's blik is that the dons wish to kill him. Religious people have a blik. Others will not have the religion blik. This is another good link to non-propositional revelation. Some see an event one way and others see it a different way. This is due to their already existing blik, which means that they see the world through their own tinted spectacles.

quickfire

㉒ What's the difference between an I–Thou and I–It relationship?

㉓ What's a blik?

Stretch and challenge

Read the whole of Hare's parable.

Consider a blik you have. Why do you have it?

Evaluative issues

These are the part (b) (AO2) questions which demand a different skill from part (a) (AO1) questions. AO2 questions will always ask the candidate to consider a quotation or a viewpoint. The candidate will be asked to assess or evaluate the validity of that quotation or statement. The aim is to give a series of arguments both in favour of and against the quotation or statement, analysing and evaluating the information.

Key things to bear in mind when answering these questions are:

- Do not just write information. That is an AO1 skill. The examiner should be able to read your work without the question in front of them and be able to tell what that question is. If you just write information it will look just like a part (a) AO1 question and, in itself, is not worth any marks.
- Instead use the information in order to evaluate effectively how valid, persuasive, strong (words used will differ depending on the wording of the question) and so on it may be.
- Aim to be synoptic in your answer. This means that in part (b) answers you should try to use information from more than one of the bulleted points specified for study in the part (a) questions as well as using material from other topics in the Specification. You can also refer to relevant aspects of your AS modules. The less isolated you make each bullet point, the greater scope you will be able to give to your answers.
- A conclusion must be given for the top levels. Otherwise you have not done what the question is asking you to do.

What follows are some examples of how you could deal with the issues in this topic. There will clearly be material that you could use in several different questions. The material given here is for guidance only. There are other, perfectly acceptable ways to answer all of these questions. You must remember that the examiner is looking for a consideration of the issue with evaluative skills which present evidence for a viewpoint. Reasoning must be used and the conclusion reached must be based upon what you have written in the main body of your answer.

Weaknesses and strengths of the ontological argument

AO1 information on this topic is on pages 7–11.

Weaknesses

Many of these involve the criticism of using 'exist' as a perfection that you can have or lack. The main point made is that 'exist' is a word that says that something is actual. It does not add anything to our description of the concept, which is what a predicate needs to do. For example, my jumper is green (predicate is green), which adds something to the description of the jumper. Saying that the jumper exists adds nothing to the description of it.

Particular scholars

1. Gaunilo (1033–1109CE) replied to Anselm's *Proslogion II*. He wrote in *On behalf of the fool* as Anselm had said that if someone did not see that God's existence is self-evident, they would be a fool. Gaunilo gave the example of an island that was the most perfect that one could conceive of.

Stretch and challenge

Make a list of 10 things that the most perfect island conceivable would have.

According to Anselm, says Gaunilo, this island must have the perfection or predicate of existence. Otherwise, it would not be the most perfect island conceivable. Why not? Because, as it is more perfect to exist in reality than in mind alone, if it didn't have the perfection of existence, then we could conceive of another island with all of the perfections of the former island but also with the perfection of existence. This island would then be the most perfect conceivable, which it cannot be as the former one has this definition!

Gaunilo's point is that Anselm's ontological argument fails as if we used his logic in other situations we would conclude that certain things exist which actually do not. I cannot go into a travel agent and book my holiday to this island. The existence of the most perfect conceivable island based upon Anselm's logic is an absurd argument and so the same applies to Anselm's argument for God's existence.

Key Term

Synthetic = statements that can be tested by the senses.

2. Aquinas (1224–1274CE) said that people have different definitions of God. Anyway, as a matter of obvious fact, not all are convinced by the argument. If it had been a very strong argument then everyone would find God's existence to be self-evident, but it is not. God's existence is **synthetic** and cannot be proved by analysing a concept. This is the same point as Hume made (see below).

3. Kant (1724–1804CE) said that, 'It would be self-contradictory to posit a triangle and reject its three angles, but there is no contradiction in rejecting the triangle together with its three angles.' It is analytically true that a triangle must have three angles.

   But one could reject the triangle along with its three angles. The same applies to a supremely perfect being. *If* there is one, then that Being must have existence but one can reject this Being with its existence without being self-contradictory. So, we can only say *if* God exists, His existence must be necessary, just as we can say *if* a wife exists, she is married.

   Anyway, Kant rejected the basic assumption that existence is a predicate. It does not add anything to the description and cannot be called a perfection. To use Kant's example, that which exists in reality contains no more than that which is in the imagination. A hundred real thalers (old German coin) does not contain one coin more than the 100 thalers in the mind. In other words 'exists in reality' is not serving the function that Anselm claims it is. Reality and in the mind give the same result.

4. B. Davies says that one cannot compare something that does not exist with something that does. There is just nothing to compare the existent thing to! Asking which is the most perfect thing, a Sunday dinner in the mind alone or a Sunday dinner in reality, makes no sense whatsoever. So, Anselm is absurd in his 'comparison' of existence in the imagination to existence in reality.

5. David Hume (1711–1776) was a Scottish philosopher who could never accept the ontological argument. He is often grouped with other British empiricists such as George Berkeley and John Locke. He has influenced economics, politics and philosophy to name but a few. In fact, Kant said that Hume was the one responsible from waking him up from his 'dogmatic slumbers!' Hume was the supreme sceptic (doubter). Certain knowledge is impossible. He criticised many of the things that humans take for granted in order for humans to lead their daily lives, for example the link between cause and effect. The knowledge that we have comes from our five senses and so it is a mistake to allow our imagination to make links before they have happened. He wanted to demolish reason as a principle.

   'Hume's fork' is an attempt to show which statements it is possible to prove true or false and thereby which of those statements are meaningful. The first type of meaningful statements is those that we can test through our senses. The second is those such as mathematical statements. If a statement is neither of these then it should be 'consigned to the flames as it is nothing but sophistry and illusion'. For further information on this see Topic 2, especially the work of the Logical Positivists.

   It is useful at this point to remind ourselves of epistemology. Epistemology is the theory of knowledge. It is suggested that there are two ways of getting to know something. One is through sense experience or experiment, empiricism. The second is through reasoning or understanding, rationalism. Hume was an empiricist, strongly opposed to rationalists before him, such as Descartes. Hume believed that all knowledge comes from the experience of our five senses. As the ontological argument is not of this nature, but rather relies on the use of reason, then he would already consider it to be a failure. He rejected the existence of innate or inbuilt ideas. In essence, Hume said that you cannot establish the truth of something by analysing it. 'However much our concept of an object may contain, we must go outside of it to determine whether or not it exists.' So, God's existence cannot be proven by analysing the word God. 'God exists' is a synthetic statement, it is either true or false and sense experience would be needed (which cannot be done) in order to determine its truth or falsity.

quickfire

24 My dog exists. My dog is brown. Which statement includes a perfection?

25 Why do critics say that existence cannot be used as a perfection?

Strengths

1. It is a deductive argument and can therefore be logically persuasive. The stages of the argument, if accepted, can entice us to reach the conclusion that 'God exists'. It is a masterpiece in how it starts with God's definition and then presents several other premises, such as 'it is better to exist in reality than in mind alone' which it is hard to argue with.

2. If existence was a perfection/predicate of a supremely perfect being, then to deny the conclusion that 'God, a supremely perfect Being exists' would be a contradiction. In fact, S. Davis says that existence *can* be a real predicate. My concept of the real 100 thalers has the predicate/perfection of *purchasing power* in the real world. My concept of 100 thalers in the imagination does not have this predicate.

3. So, the premise of 'it is more perfect to exist in reality than in mind alone' can be persuasive.

4. If Plantinga's possible worlds theory, with its premises, is accepted, it does conclude with the God of classical theism.

5. Anselm's work can be seen as a 'demonstration' of how self-evident God's existence was to him, rather than a 'proof' of God's existence.

1: 'The ontological argument is convincing.' Assess this view.

Agree

- It relies on the definition of the word 'God'. If that definition is convincing then so can the argument be.
- Things that do exist in reality are better than things that exist in the mind.

- It is convincing as a masterpiece in word play. It flows logically and is coherent.

- It uses words that are just human. We can define something as whatever we choose, but it does not mean that the thing that we have defined exists; for example 'the bogey man'.

- It is convincing to the extent that it can support the person who already has faith.

- It could be argued that it is convincing to say that 'I have existence' and therefore the use of existence as a predicate may be acceptable.

- The counter-arguments to criticisms such as Gaunilo's have been convincing in the sense that islands do not have an 'intrinsic maximum', that is that something can always be added to our definition of the greatest conceivable island. Therefore, there is no island which is the greatest conceivable. So, the ontological argument stands firm and convincing in that the argument applies to God only and not to anything other than God. Plantinga would defend Anselm in this way.

Disagree

- If, however, the definition of God is not accepted as convincing then neither will the argument be.
- However, if it is accepted that it is better to win the lottery than to just have it as an idea in the mind, that does not mean that it *has* to happen in reality.

- But, is it convincing as an argument for God's existence? Would it convince an atheist to become a theist? No.

- It is unconvincing as, rather than relying on words, the most convincing arguments look at evidence, sense experience.

- Karl Barth said that it may explain God's characteristics, but not about God's existence – it can tell what theists believe about God but not whether God exists.

- But, would it not be more convincing to say that existence is a state of being, without which we would have no predicates.

- But, the arguments against existence being a predicate are numerous and convincing. If the argument concerning God's existence cannot apply to anything else, then we could question when applied to God whether or not the argument is convincing in the first place. Anyway, if the argument is unconvincing in how it is applied in one situation then it is unconvincing in all others. Philosophers such as Kant, Russell and Frege all share Gaunilo's concerns. They all point out that 'existence' cannot be used in the same way as predicates/qualities such as 'omnipotence' and 'omniscience'.

2: 'Faith is more valid if it is based on reasoned argument rather than on revelation.' Assess this view.

Agree	Disagree
• Reason is something which all humans possess. In other areas of life, using our reason is often what decides issues.	• Reason may be too intellectual to base a faith upon. Anyway, our reasoning is often wrong.
• Faith needs to be based on a belief *that* something is true, the use of 'the head'.	• Faith requires belief in something, a commitment, the use of 'the heart'.
• Faith needs a 'secure' basis, which reason provides.	• Martin Luther said that faith must be free without security. This is echoed by Kierkegaard, who said that it is because faith is risky that it is valid.
• Aquinas had a positive attitude to reason. In his cosmological argument he demonstrates God's existence through the use of reason.	• But, Aquinas said that some things cannot be known by reason, such as the Trinity.
• St Paul said that 'we walk by faith and not by sight'. St Paul is often referred to as one who teaches that God can be known from looking at the natural world with human reason.	• The Bible takes God's existence for granted. It does not have arguments for God's existence in it. God's existence is a given reality. Take Jeremiah 5^{21+22}: 'Hear this, o foolish and senseless people....Do you not fear me? Says the Lord.' – or Jeremiah 14^9: 'He who has seen me has seen the father.'
• H.D. Lewis says that faith needs to be based on reason to be valid. Humans have to be involved if we are to have a relationship with God.	• St Ambrose said, 'It has not pleased God to save his people with arguments', suggesting that for faith to be valid it should not be based on reason.
• Augustine and Anselm both said that reason is part of a valid faith, in that it supports faith. Faith is not blind, but is rationally justifiable.	• However, for them it is not the basis of faith. Faith comes before reason and reason understands what faith believes in.

AO1 information on this topic is on pages 11–23.

3: 'Faith and reason are complementary.' Assess this view.

Agree

- James and Tennant would both say that reason is useful to a religious faith, therefore the two complement each other.

- Hick says that religious faith is rational. This means that faith is reasonable, with it being entirely rational to be a theist.

- Augustine would see no contradiction between faith and reason. He is often credited as being one of the first who felt he had to force his faith to reason. He certainly believed that reason can justify faith. When looking at the stories in the Bible, he rationalised them, drawing out their logical conclusions.

- A relationship in which we use our mind, our reach to God, is one which involves reason and this is a positive faith. It is objective and is not open to misinterpretation.

- Reason can give certainty and so complements faith.

- Plato said that knowledge comes through our intellect, our reason. So, we could use him to suggest that the knowledge we require for faith comes via reason and so faith and reason are complementary.

- Mitchell's parable of the partisan and the stranger could be used here. Religious faith and reason run alongside each other as humans do use their reason when looking at 'problems' associated with having faith and they use their reason to retain their faith, by citing good reasons for doing so.

Disagree

- Kierkegaard would say that reason and faith are contradictory rather than complementary, as reason will only lead us down blind alleys, due to the certainty, cost and commitment required by faith.

- Pascal said that faith and reason are not complementary, as reason is no path to religious faith. The God of the Bible has nothing to do with the God of the philosophers.

- However, there are still occasions when faith and reason cannot work together to establish understanding, such as the truths of The Fall or The Incarnation. So perhaps we should say that these events defy logic, with reason contradicting faith.

- Buber says that the relationship that humans should have with God is an I–Thou relationship, which is one we have with a 'person'. Natural Theology (use of reason) leads to an I–It relationship, which is one we have with an 'object'. So the kind of faith we need is not complemented by reason.

- Kierkegaard says reason cannot give the certainty needed for faith and therefore faith contradicts reason.

- Hume's views could be used to say that faith and reason are not complementary. Reason has limits and therefore cannot complement faith.

- Some would say that religious believers abandon all reason, especially when it comes to evidence that seems to count against their beliefs. Therefore faith and reason are not complementary. In fact, some would go as far as to say that faith completely abandons reason, what reason dictates is contradictory to faith.

4: 'Revelation is an adequate basis for religious faith.' Assess this view.

Agree

- Revelation is clear and unambiguous. It is an objective event, leading to its authenticity and adequacy for a religious faith.

- Propositional revelation is infallible and the words are clear, providing an adequate basis for religious faith.

- Barth would say it is the only basis for a religious faith as God has revealed through Jesus. Nothing else is needed as a basis for an adequate faith. Our reason was corrupted at 'The Fall' making revelation essential.

- Augustine and Anselm both had faith firmly rooted in revelation.

- Aquinas, despite saying that there is one Truth with two different sources, still said that revelation was superior to reason. After his religious experience, after writing volumes of 'proofs' for God's existence, he declared that everything he had written was like straw compared to what had been revealed to him. In fact, the Truth surpasses every effort of reason.

- God is so different to humans that the only adequate basis for faith is through God revealing as this is the only way to keep God's 'otherness'.

Disagree

- Revelation is open to misinterpretation. It is subjective, leading to doubts about its authenticity as a basis for religious faith.

- The words of scripture may be seen as human words – fallible. Many would see this leading to a lifeless faith, which just accepts propositions.

- This particular form of revelation would deem all religions other than Christianity as not having an adequate basis for faith. Worse than this, they would all be seen to be 'wrong'. Also, Barth's view gives a far too pessimistic view of human nature.

- Yet, it needed completion by the use of reason in their faiths.

- Yet, revelation and reason cannot contradict each other. If our use of reason is correct then it will agree with revelation. So, we could argue that revelation is not adequate in the sense that it is superior to reason, as reason provides the same knowledge as revelation does. So one is not more adequate than the other.

- Baillie said that both revelation and reason are needed for faith. Any knowledge of God is revealed to us by God. This is a two-way process with humans having a general knowledge of God and 'a searching' for God which has come about through God's revelation and a 'searching' for humans.

Summary: Is religious faith rational?

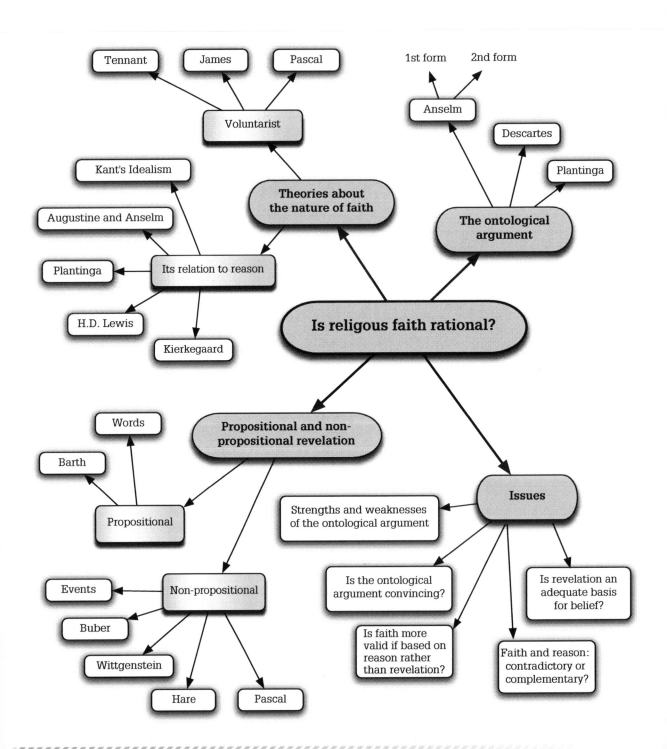

Tennant

James

Pascal

1st form 2nd form

Anselm

Descartes

Voluntarist

Plantinga

Kant's Idealism

Theories about
the nature of faith

Augustine and Anselm

The ontological
argument

Plantinga

Its relation to reason

Plantinga

H.D. Lewis

Is religous faith rational?

Kierkegaard

Words

Propositional and non-
propositional revelation

Barth

Issues

Propositional

Strengths and weaknesses
of the ontological argument

Events

Non-propositional

Is the ontological
argument convincing?

Is revelation an
adequate basis
for belief?

Buber

Wittgenstein

Is faith more
valid if based on
reason rather
than revelation?

Faith and reason:
contradictory or
complementary?

Hare

Pascal

2: **Is religious language meaningful?**

When revising 'Is religious language meaningful?' you should focus on the main topics and issues. You should identify the inherent problems of religious language, which includes the claim that it cannot be verified or falsified. The verification and falsification principles should be known in detail, including their implications for religion. Further you must be able to explain and exemplify the three stated concepts of religious language, namely analogy, symbols and language games. Finally, you need to evaluate the issues arising from these topics from a variety of viewpoints using scholarly opinion, and an informed conclusion must be reached.

Revision checklist

Tick column 1 when you have completed brief revision notes.
Tick column 2 when you think you have a good grasp of the topic.
Tick column 3 during final revision when you feel you have mastery of the topic.

			1	2	3
What are the inherent problems of religious language?	p34	Use of contradictory or abstract words			
	p34	'Ordinary' language is inadequate			
	p34	Anthropomorphism			
	p35	Verification and falsification			
What is the verification principle?	p35	Hume's contribution			
	p35	Vienna Circle – analytic			
	p35	– synthetic			
	p36	Strong verification			
	p37	Weak verification			
	p37	Implications for religion			
What is the falsification principle?	p37	Popper			
	p37	Flew			
	p39	Implications for religion			
What is the analogical concept of religious language?	p41	Aquinas – proportion			
	p41	– attribution			
	p41	Ramsey – models and qualifiers			
What is the symbolic concept of religious language?	p42	Signs			
	p42	Tillich on symbols			
What is the language games concept of religious language?	p44	Wittgenstein			
	p45	Phillips			
What are the main issues that arise from 'Is religious language meaningful?'	p47	Have the inherent problems of religious language been resolved?			
	p48	Are arguments asserting meaningfulness or meaninglessness convincing?			
	p49	Can religious language only be understood in the context of religious belief?			
	p50	Are the three concepts of religious language adequate?			
	p52	Strengths and weaknesses of the V.P. and F.P.			

Key Terms

Anthropomorphism = giving human qualities to something non-human.

Incarnation = God becoming flesh.

Metaphysical = referring to things or questions that cannot be answered in factual terms.

Omnibenevolent = all loving.

Omnipotent = all powerful.

Omniscient = all knowing.

AO2 evaluative issues on this question are on page 47.

Inherent problems of religious language

This section asks what problems does religious language contain as an inseparable part of it.

Virgin Birth	The Trinity	Omnipotent	Spirit	Eternal
Only begotten Son		Omniscient	Metaphysical	Incarnation
Timeless	Omnibenevolent		Infinite	

These are just some of the words used in religion. However, there are problems associated with religious language and this list represents just some of them:

1. Some of these words may be seen as contradictory to our logic; for example, the Virgin Birth. Also, if God is **omnipotent** then God has the power to do anything. So, God could create a human being who will never ever listen to God's words. However, if God is all powerful, God should be able to get this human to listen to God's words. This does not seem to fit with our system of logic.

2. Some of these words are abstract, metaphysical or puzzling. Many religious words or phrases may be unfamiliar or may have no physical representation. Many questions it raises cannot be answered in physical terms. For example, as we live in time, timeless can be a difficult idea. Some say that 'God is timeless' and humans can find this problematic to consider. Also, as we expect everything to have a beginning and an end, something eternal is outside of our experience. Words such as 'spirit', which have no physical representation, may cause problems, not least in that physical evidence is often called for in order to back up claims. A metaphysical question such as 'Why are we here?' is not one that can be answered by looking in a text book.

3. We only have our human, worldly language to describe that which is not 'of this world'. This may be inadequate, not being able to fully express God's majesty. It may also lead to misunderstanding and error if we take too much from worldly language and expect it to 'work' when applied to religious language.

4. Many would argue that we cannot even attempt to describe God. Synagogues do not have pictures or images of God for this reason. Therefore, are all attempts doomed to failure? Even if we can get somewhere with our language, perhaps the end result will be so partial that we are really saying nothing meaningful at all.

5. If we give God characteristics of this world, particularly human attributes, we risk **anthropomorphising** God. Examples of this would be 'God's *hand* guided me' and 'God's *eye* watched over me'.

6. We may have different understandings of words when applied to humans and worldly things; for example, 'love' is different when applied to a friend and a bar of chocolate. How much more so when applied to Jesus' love for mankind or God's love of the world. Can we really understand what these words mean?

7. Religions are full of stories that could be interpreted literally or non-literally. One such example could be Creation and The Fall in the book of Genesis. A problem may arise if people are working with different interpretations or when it is unclear which interpretation is meant in a story. Indeed, a further problem arises in terms of whether we can ever deem one interpretation to be true.

8. Some terms are used within religions which may have a slightly different meaning within each religious system, such as Karma within Buddhism and Hinduism. Also, how a word is used in a religious context may differ from how the word is used in other contexts. An example could be 'spirit'. This could mean team spirit, an alcoholic spirit a ghost-like apparition or the non-physical element that survives death.

9. Some will say that we cannot verify or falsify religious language, which brings us to our next section.

Philosophical concepts of verification and falsification

Key Terms
Meaningful = factually informative, passing on information, cognitive.

Verification = prove something true.

AO2 evaluative issues on this question are on pages 48 and 52–55.

The theme of what makes a sentence **meaningful** can be seen in the work of David Hume (1711–1776.) Hume's work states that meaningful statements are divided into two: those about ideas and those about the world. He said:

If we take in our hand any volume of divinity or school metaphysics, for instance, let us ask, does it contain any abstract reasoning concerning quantity or number? No. Does it contain any experimental reasoning concerning matter of fact and existence? No. Commit it then to the flames, for it can contain nothing but sophistry and illusion.

An Inquiry Concerning Human Understanding

A group of philosophers in the 1920s met in Vienna, and became known as The Vienna Circle. They claimed that many people spend large parts of their time talking nonsense. We may think we are making meaningful statements, but in fact, we are not saying anything factual. This group included Schlick, Carnap and Waissmann. Theirs was a picture theory of language, supported by Wittgenstein in *Tractatus*. Their work developed into Logical Positivism.

Their **verification** principle said that statements were only meaningful if capable of being shown true or false. This divided sentences into two:

1. Analytic: true or false by definition:
- A wife is married
- $1 + 1 = 2$
- X cannot be Y
- All cats are cats.

2. Synthetic: true or false through research.
- Peter has brown eyes
- Swansea City won 2-0 on Saturday
- There are three cars on her drive.

Grade boost

Remember, a synthetic statement is *still* meaningful even if it is false, as it can be *shown* to be false.

Stretch and challenge

Write out three more analytic statements and three synthetic statements.

Alfred Jules Ayer (1910–1989) was born in London. A bright and competitive atheist, he specialised in classics and at the same time began to read philosophy. He was influenced by Bertrand Russell's 'Sceptical Essays' especially where Russell said that one should not believe a statement which has no evidence for its truth. At Christ Church, Oxford he read Wittgenstein's *Tractatus* (see later on in this guide for details of this) and was influenced by it. He then went, in 1933, to Vienna and became a member of 'The Vienna Circle'. Here he worked on the main beliefs of Logical Positivism.

As Ayer said, 'If it is not analytic and cannot be tested, then best to call it **cognitively** (informatively) meaningless.' Its truth or falsity must have some experienceable difference, some difference that can be observed. If someone says 'there are twenty tables in the room', if it is true then clearly I should see something different from what I see if it is false.

Ayer's book *Language, Truth and Logic* is a classic statement of Logical Positivism. It was first published in 1939.

Strong verification

A statement is meaningful if it can be verified in practice, that is, there is conclusive verification. An example of this could be 'William has brown hair'. I would need to go and find William to check this. The problem with this is that it rules out many statements that we would class as meaningful. For example, 'every human needs to drink liquid to survive'. I am unable to conclusively verify this, as I would have to observe every person in the whole world, from the past, present and future. But surely it would be classed as meaningful.

Weak verification

A statement is meaningful if it can be verified in principle, that is, I would know what I would have to do in order to verify it. So, my above statement regarding drinking water is now meaningful. This also now allows historical statements, such as 'Mary Queen of Scots had three husbands' to be meaningful, which they would not have been under the strong principle. It should be noted that even if a statement is false it would still be meaningful if it had been open to verification.

The implications for religious language

It is claimed that language such as metaphysical language, language concerning ethics or theological language are meaningless. Religious language is meaningless as religious statements are neither analytic nor synthetic. They cannot be probable even in principle, let alone proved conclusively in practice.

A.J. Ayer would say that religious statements are conveying no information, that is, they are **non-cognitive**; at best they are '**emotive utterances**'. In fact the Logical Positivists go further than the usual criticisms of belief in God. This is because all unverifiable religious language is meaningless and so to say 'there is no God' is just as meaningless as to say 'there is a God'.

The falsification principle

Sir Karl Raimund Popper (1902–1994) was born in Vienna. He became a philosopher and professor at the London School of Economics. He is often called one of the greatest philosophers of science of the 20th century. He said that verification is not the way to test statements, but rather **falsification** is. If we have one piece of evidence against a statement, then that statement can be falsified. This makes the statement meaningful.

For example, the statement that 'all swans are white' is falsifiable, because it is possible that a swan can be found that is not white. Therefore, this statement is meaningful according to Popper.

Antony Flew (1923–2010) was a British philosopher. He was originally an atheist as he said that one should be an atheist until God's existence has empirical evidence to prove it. Later on in life there seems to have been a transformation when in 2004 he stated an inclination towards the Aristotelian God and he later wrote a book *There is a God: How the World's most notorious atheist changed his mind*.

In his atheistic days he developed Popper's ideas about falsifiability with regard to religious language. He adapted Wisdom's parable of the garden. Wisdom's parable has two people in a garden debating whether there is a gardener who comes to look after the garden. Both men physically can see the same things in the garden, but both perceive the garden differently. One focuses more on the beauty and says 'a gardener comes' whilst the other focuses more on the unpleasant parts of the garden, such as the weeds. This person says 'a gardener does not come'.

This parable has often been used to show how people view the world. The two people simply differed in how they felt about the garden (world). The way they view the garden affects whether they believe a gardener comes. The way people view the world affects whether they believe in God or not. Indeed, whether they believe in God or not affects how they view the world. Some focus on the beauty and design and say 'there is a God'; whilst others focus on evil and suffering and conclude 'there is no God'. Our conclusion depends on our perception (and our perception is generally based on our conclusion anyway!). Flew adapted Wisdom's parable into the parable of the jungle. This is an excerpt from *Theology and Falsification* (1950–51) by Flew:

> *Once upon a time two explorers came upon a clearing in the jungle. In the clearing were growing many flowers and many weeds. One explorer says, 'Some gardener must tend this plot'. The other disagrees, 'There is no gardener'. So they pitch their tents and set a watch. No gardener is ever seen. 'But perhaps he is an invisible gardener.' So they set up a barbed-wire fence. They electrify it. They patrol with bloodhounds. (For they remember how H. G. Well's The Invisible Man could be both smelt and touched though he could not be seen.) But no shrieks ever suggest that some intruder has received a shock. No movements of the wire ever betray an invisible climber. The bloodhounds never give cry. Yet still the Believer holds to his belief. 'But there is a gardener, invisible, intangible, insensible to electric shocks, a gardener who has no scent and makes no sound, a gardener who comes secretly to look after the garden which he loves.' At last the Sceptic despairs, 'But what remains of your original assertion? Just how does what you call an invisible, intangible, eternally elusive gardener differ from an imaginary gardener or even from no gardener at all?'*

> Antony Flew, *Theology and Falsification, University,* 1950–51

Stretch and challenge

Look up Wisdom's parable of the garden. List the evidence in favour of there being a gardener and the evidence against. How can this be used when talking about God?

We can see what is at work here. We have a religious believer and a sceptic both of whom are convinced that they are right. Flew is presenting the believer as one who, despite evidence against their belief (or at least no evidence in favour of it) always refuses to let their claim that 'there is a gardener' (God) be falsified.

He said that the claim 'there is a gardener' lacks any meaning (conveys no information) as the explorer will not allow anything to falsify his claim.

The implications for religious language

Flew applies this to religion and says that believers will never allow their claims to be falsified. When information is given that seems to contradict their claims, rather than giving them up, they **qualify** them, which allows them to keep their original claim. An example could be as follows:

Believer: 'God loves us as a father loves his children.'

Atheist: 'But what about the child dying of throat cancer whose earthly father is driven frantic with concern?'

Believer: 'Ah, but God's love is not the same as human love.'

Atheist: 'So, what is God's love really worth?'

This conversation could go on and on. What Flew is saying is that when evidence is given which seems to go against the believer's claim, the believer qualifies (modifies, revises) the original claim rather than give up the original claim.

He said that nothing could happen that would falsify any religious claim, therefore these claims are meaningless and die 'the death by a thousand qualifications'.

Key Term

Qualify = modify, change, limit.

quickfire

① A swearword: cognitive or non-cognitive?

② Why would 'King Henry VIII had six wives' be meaningless under the strong verification principle?

③ Why would it be meaningful under the weak?

Grade boost

So many candidates answer a question on verification and falsification with absolutely no mention of religion at all. Make sure that you put as many examples of religious statements as you can in your essay, saying why the Logical Positivists said that these statements are meaningless.

Key Terms

Analogy = comparison between two things.

Equivocal = same word, different meaning.

Univocal = same word, same meaning.

AO2 evaluative issues on the three concepts of religious language are on pages 50–52.

The concept of religious language as analogical: a non-cognitive use of religious language

Aquinas addressed the issue of how humans could talk about God. He said that we cannot speak about God **univocally**. Univocal language is when a word is applied to more than one thing and this word has the same meaning when applied to each. In a non-religious context, an example would be 'football is a game' and 'rugby is a game'. Here 'game' means the same thing. So, if we said 'Karen is wise' and 'God is wise' if speaking univocally we would be saying that Karen's wisdom is exactly the same as God's wisdom. Aquinas said that this is incorrect as there is clearly a difference between God and humans and univocal language would not show this.

Aquinas also said that we can't speak about God using **equivocal** language. Equivocal language is when the same word is used when referring to more than one thing, but the word means something entirely different in each context. In a non-religious context an example would be 'football is a game' and 'pheasant is game'. Here 'game' has an entirely different meaning. So, if we say 'Gwen is loving' and 'God is loving' if speaking equivocally we would be saying that Gwen's love and God's love are entirely different. Aquinas said that this would get us nowhere; we would never be able to say anything if God and humans are so completely different. We would know what a human's love is like but if God's is entirely different we would not be able to say anything meaningful about it.

Some have used via negativa as a way of solving the inherent problems of religious language. Via negativa is when we say what God is not, such as God is not unkind or God is not a human. This ties in with the mystical tradition where an experience of God may be said to be one which the mystics cannot explain. Others say that if we are just saying what God is not, we are getting no further forward in saying what God is.

Somewhere in between univocal and equivocal language lies **analogy**. Aquinas said we can talk about God and creatures because of a link between them, a causal link. In his view, everything goes back to God. God caused humans to be. We have wisdom, love and so on only because they are qualities which come from God. We receive what God has caused in us.

Analogy of proportion

All things have qualities in **proportion** to what they are. Humans have qualities in proportion to (what is befitting) a human; God has qualities infinitely, as that is what is befitting of God.

Analogy of attribution

Attribute can be used in two senses here. An attribute is a quality, something you can have or lack. To attribute is also to give someone the credit for something, 'I attribute my success to you'. Aquinas sees God causing, say, goodness in humans, in other words, our attribute of goodness is the result of God's attribution of goodness to us.

Aquinas said that healthy urine, the effect, is produced or caused by a healthy bull. Cause and effect are unable to be separated.

Ian Ramsey: models and qualifiers

A model is 'a situation with which we are all familiar and which can be used for reading another situation'. From this definition, you should be able to see how this is also an analogy concept. This is a typical way of explaining things in everyday life. We try to help someone to understand by using words or examples that they already understand (a model).

For example, a teacher may try to explain a religious ritual by using the model of a sportsperson who performs certain actions in the same way at all times before a race or a game. The model here is the sports ritual. The qualifier develops the model to help our understanding.

When talking about God, we may say that God is wise. 'Wise' is the model as we know what human wisdom means. We then qualify this by saying that 'God is infinitely wise'. Ramsey says that the qualifier allows us to gain some understanding about the nature of God.

> Religious discernment of depth; 'odd' words; empirical anchorage; ice breaks; light dawns; come alive; penny drops; personal; warmth; new dimension; evokes disclosure; commitment

These are key phrases in Ramsey's work. He uses these, along with many examples from everyday life to show what happens when the qualifier 'works'.

The basic idea is that there can be an impersonal situation, where a word 'odd' to that situation is heard. Because of this, the situation can change; it can become personal, take on a depth. Certainly a new dimension has been entered into. The qualifier has 'worked', we now understand, the penny has dropped. This is similar to when someone tries to explain something to you and you do not understand it. They then explain it in a different way and you then 'get it', the 'penny has dropped'. This disclosure leads to a commitment. The situation now has grounding in experience.

Key Terms

Attribution = Aquinas has been considered as using this in two ways. It can be something given to another via cause and effect and also the quality which is given.

Proportion = in ratio.

Grade boost

Refer to other parts of Aquinas' work that you are familiar with. In his cosmological argument, he makes the point that there must be a God, a first cause, or else there would be nothing. This is seen here quite clearly in analogy, the causal link. You should see that here again we have the 'cause and effect' idea of the cosmological argument. There are similarities between God and creatures, as God (cause) imposes its character on humans (the effects).

Grade boost

Include the other examples from Ramsey's book that you have found in your answer. This will really show understanding.

One example he used was of a formal setting, a High Court where we find Mr Justice Brown, wigs and ermine. The accused he finds is his best friend from his university days. The accused/friend says the 'odd' word in that setting, 'Sammy'. Can you see how the situation has now changed? This is analogous to religious language, when a model is qualified, an 'odd' word is used and eventually 'the light dawns' and we 'get it', some insight has been gained.

The concept of religious language as symbolic: a non-cognitive use of religious language

Many scholars say that as God is beyond the understanding of the **finite** world, we can't use everyday language literally in religious language. **Symbols**, myths and metaphors can help. Paul Tillich describes this as 'opening up new levels of reality that are otherwise closed to us'.

A symbol is a physical thing which represents something non-physical. An example would be that a dove is a symbol of peace. A myth is a traditional story which often contains supernatural characters and some kind of moral lesson. For example, there are many Ancient Greek myths. A metaphor is a figure of speech in which one thing is identified with another. For example, 'in that crisis, Peter was a tower of strength'. Using these concepts could allow people to talk about God meaningfully and thereby to overcome a problem of religious language which could exist if we were talking about God in a literal way.

Tillich believes that religious language is best understood as symbolic. It is not to be taken as literally true (hence, non-cognitive). He shows the similarities and differences between a 'sign', for example a traffic light, and a symbol, for example a national flag. Both signs and symbols 'point beyond themselves' and refer to the world. Both can be words, objects or actions.

But, the key difference is that signs do not participate in the reality that they point to: symbols do. He says signs are *arbitrary representations* of something. They have no 'connection' to that thing.

Key Term
Arbitrary = random.

The green light is a sign for 'go' but there is no real connection between 'green' and 'go'. Pink with purple spots could have been chosen. If a sign had to be replaced or changed, then it could; symbols can't. Symbols might have been originally chosen **arbitrarily** but they gradually become associated with the thing they represent.

An example: a national flag

How often have we seen someone, when they have won an Olympic event for example, rush to the crowd to receive the flag of their nation, drape it around themself and do a lap of honour? When they stand on the podium to receive their medal, their flag is hoisted and they cry. On television, we may also have seen scenes of people burning a nation's flag. This causes outrage. Why? When they see the flag, it is a symbol for the whole nation. It is more than a piece of cloth with a random design on it. It *points* to the nation, it is *part* of the nation, it *is the nation.*

This is what Tillich means by 'pointing beyond itself and participating in that to which it points'. It has become so much more than a flag; it has become a symbol.

For Tillich there is only one religious literal statement, that God is Being-itself. All others are symbolic. So, 'the language of faith is the language of symbols'. Religious symbols can be words, actions, objects and so on. They point to and participate in such concepts as love, repentance, peace, humility and so on.

 quickfire

④ What's the difference between a sign and a symbol?

⑤ Complete this sentence: A symbol 'points beyond itself. . .'.

Grade boost

Do not fall into the temptation of discussing symbols that are non-religious only. Use the ones suggested in the 'Stretch and challenge' to really give 'meat' to your answer. Also, do not just learn Tillich's quotations, putting them into your essay with no context. Explain them in your own words, showing how they illustrate his view of symbols.

Stretch and challenge

Find out what the following religious symbols mean to believers:

water; the Resurrection; kingdom of God; the cross; the fish; the om symbol; the Sikh 5Ks.

Within Judaism, the Star of David points to (is identified with) Judaism and it also participates in the Jewish history involving King David. The star is not separate from Judaism.

Within Christianity 'Jesus is the lamb of God' is another good example of a symbol. It clearly does not mean a cuddly thing that jumps around a field! Lamb is a traditional symbol of sacrifice and represents or symbolises Jesus' sacrifice for sins.

The concept of religious language as language games: a non-cognitive use of religious language

Stretch and challenge

Think of three games and their rules. Imagine how impossible it would be to play one using the rules of another. This could be used as an analogy for the language game theory.

L. Wittgenstein (1889–1951) was Austrian and trained as an engineer. He settled in England. He very much influenced Logical Positivism in his early years, particularly in his book *Tractatus* with its concluding sentence 'whereof one cannot speak, thereon one must be silent'. He gave up philosophy for a number of years until about 1930 when he looked anew at language in his book *Philosophical Investigations*.

In *Philosophical Investigations* he realised that there is language whose meaning is not found in picturing objects in the world. The language is simply not used in that way. Language can be non-cognitive where its function is not to give information or facts that are true or false.

How do we find its function? We look at how it is used. The words are tools. Look at their usage and we will find their meaning.

This idea is found in his language games theory, discovered whilst he was watching a game of football. He said that all language is a game, 'a form of life', and all games have rules. Words for each game are used in the context of that game; they are not to be used in another game. Otherwise, it would be like playing rugby using the rules of Monopoly!

He realised that many of the problems of religious language we looked at earlier in the book are caused by not understanding that the religious language game is for believers. It has meaning as it has use in the religious language game. By using it the believer can take part in that 'form of life'.

So, rules from games such as the 'Science' language game, which asks for 'proof', cannot be applied to the religious language game. Wittgenstein used the example of the soul. Asking for 'proof' for the existence of the soul shows a misunderstanding. 'Soul' is not part of the 'physical object' language game. A language game cannot be judged from the outside.

Language is at its worst when it is not being used or is not understood in the right context. Then it is like 'an engine idling'. If we want to get to know how the rules of a particular game are used, the best way is to 'look and see'.

The rules of how to use a word are generally agreed upon within that game. We can see this if we observe young children making up a game and deciding between them what the rules will be.

Dewi Zephaniah Phillips (1934–2006), known as D. Z. Phillips, Dewi Z, or simply DZ, was a Swansea-born supporter of Wittgensteinian philosophy of religion. He had an academic career spanning five decades, and at the time of his death he held the Danforth Chair in Philosophy of Religion at Claremont Graduate University, California, and was Professor Emeritus of Philosophy at Swansea University. Indeed it is through him that Swansea University became renowned as being a leading centre for Wittgenstein's philosophy.

In his book *The Concept of Prayer* (1965) one sees a revival of Wittgenstein's approach, which was a counter to the difficult time that religious language had endured at the hands of the Logical Positivists.

He supported Wittgenstein's view of religious language as a game. The *use* or function of religious language is non-cognitive as opposed to giving facts that are true or false.

Three examples:

1. When someone says 'I believe in God' the *real* question is what does this mean to believers, not is there actually a God or not.

2. When a person prays, it is not about presenting facts. We must ask what a person is *doing* when they pray. It may be an appeal to their inner strength, for example.

3. When a person says 'I believe in eternal life', this is not to be understood literally to mean they believe they will live for ever. They are using the words to describe the type of life that they have now.

All believers learn this language. It has meaning for them and so 'to know how to use this language is to know God'.

Grade boost

Contrast 'early' Wittgenstein, in his book *Tractatus* where he supported a picture theory of language, with 'later' Wittgenstein in *Philosophical Investigations*. His early views meant that only statements that picture facts can be meaningful. This is why his views agreed with the Logical Positivists. The fact that he then changed his views can be useful information for you to use in order to criticise the Logical Positivists.

quickfire

⑥ Why is language described as a 'tool'?

⑦ How can we get to understand the rules of a 'form of life'?

⑧ Why can one 'form of life' not judge another?

Evaluative issues

These are the part (b) (AO2) questions which demand a different skill from part (a) (AO1) questions. AO2 questions will always ask the candidate to consider a quotation or a viewpoint. The candidate will be asked to assess or evaluate the validity of that quotation or statement. The aim is to give a series of arguments both in favour of and against the quotation or statement, analysing and evaluating the information.

Key things to bear in mind when answering these questions are:

- Do not just write information. That is an AO1 skill. The examiner should be able to read your work without the question in front of them and be able to tell what that question is. If you just write information, it will look just like a part (a) AO1 question and, in itself, is not worth any marks.

- Instead use the information in order to evaluate effectively how valid, persuasive, strong (words used will differ depending on the wording of the question) and so on it may be.

- Aim to be synoptic in your answer. This means that in part (b) answers you should try to use information from more than one of the bulleted points specified for study in the part (a) questions as well as using material from other topics in the Specification. You can also refer to relevant aspects of your AS modules. The less isolated you make each bullet point, the greater scope you will be able to give to your answers.

- A conclusion must be given for the top levels. Otherwise you have not done what the question is asking you to do.

What follows are some examples of how you could deal with the issues in this topic. There will clearly be material that you could use in several different questions. The material given here is for guidance only. There are other, perfectly acceptable ways to answer all of these questions. You must remember that the examiner is looking for a consideration of the issue with evaluative skills which present evidence for a viewpoint. Reasoning must be used and the conclusion reached must be based upon what you have written in the main body of your answer.

1: 'The problems of religious language have not been overcome.' Assess this view.

Agree

- Religious language remains inadequate. We can talk about God using only 'human' language and this will never be adequate as an attempt to solve the problems of religious language. It is too restrictive and does not adequately deal with the distinctive nature of religious language.

- Some philosophers believe that we can only say what God is not (via negativa). In fact, they say that as God is outside of the empirical realm, perhaps they can do no better than this. But this method tells us nothing. For example, if you do not know what a banana is, it is no help to be told that it is not an apple.

- Metaphysical language is always going to be problematic and the fact that religious language contains so much that is not empirically verifiable means such problems cannot be overcome.

- Much religious language is myth and this causes a problem as the meaning may be unclear. The story may also not be relevant to people today as they see such stories as little more than outdated tales.

- There is the problem of anthropomorphism or giving God human characteristics. Phrases such as 'God looks after me' or 'God was with me' can give a false impression of some 'superman' and give an impression of God that many may not be happy with.

- Some words are so difficult to define, visualise or conceptualise that problems still remain. Within religion, the Trinity, soul, transubstantiation and so on may be far too baffling and confusing and therefore such language is of little relevance or use due to the problems attached to it.

Disagree

- At least using 'human' language can allow philosophers to give a partial image. This is better than no image at all. Indeed, by using a concept such as analogy, we can at least compare, for example, God's characteristics with those of humans.

- Others say that at least saying what God is not eliminates some things, which does at least lessen the vast ocean of possibilities regarding what we may say about God. If in other areas of life we work on a multiple-choice basis, at least we are getting rid of the wrong answers and by doing so, this may nudge us towards the right answers.

- Hick would disagree and said that religious language (and belief) will eventually be verified at the eschaton (the end times). Then, a statement such as 'there is life after death' will be verified if true, hence, solving the problem of religious language.

- Scholars such as Bultmann, however, believed that we can strip away or demythologise such stories in order to get to the true 'kerygma' or teaching.

- However, others may argue that using such religious language is not a problem. What such phrases do is to give a heartfelt attempt to show the reality of God in the lives of people. This is what is important and providing this has been achieved then any problem may lessen.

- Philosophers have tried to help with definitions and explanations. There are many people who can at least get some way to understanding difficult concepts. For some, as Aquinas pointed out, revelation may be needed in order to help with the concept of the Trinity. For other people, symbols help, such as showing the Trinity as H_2O, liquid, steam and ice. So the problem may be helped by the methods of revelation and symbolic use of language.

AO1 information on this topic is on pages 34&35.

2: 'Religious language is meaningless.' Assess this view.

Agree	Disagree
• Religious language does not fall into the categories established by the Logical Positivists so is meaningless. It is neither analytic nor synthetic so it cannot be held to be informative. At best, language such as 'there is a heaven' has the function of expressing emotion.	• The categories established by the Logical Positivists are arbitrary. They could equally have decided that only statements written in purple ink or spoken in English are meaningful. That would leave a lot of meaningless statements! Also the statement 'the only statements that are meaningful are those which are analytic or synthetic' is itself not verifiable. So, the verification principle could be seen to be meaningless. It could be added that expressing emotion is meaningful, it does convey information. For example if I hit my knee on the table and say 'ouch that hurt' I am telling you something.
• Under the weak verification principle so much of religious language would be classed as meaningless as it would have to be directly examined now. So, 'the Buddha was born in Lumbini' or 'Jesus had disciples' would be meaningless.	• But under the strong verification principle many religious statements can be classed as meaningful as this says that it is enough to know how this could have been verified, or what I would have to do in order for me to verify it. So, 'Muhammad had a wife' or 'David was a king' are now meaningful.
• Flew showed that believers refuse to have their beliefs falsified, thus dying a 'death by a thousand qualifications'. We see how believers keep faith in the face of the most appalling atrocities. There may seem to be no event that would make the believer give up their statements of belief. Thus religious language is meaningless as it cannot be falsified.	• Religious language is meaningful as it is not that believers refuse to hear evidence against their belief. They do, in principle, accept that their statements may be falsified. It is just that the strength of their faith is stronger than the doubts. Their statements are meaningful.
• There are so many religious statements, the very nature of which means they are unverifiable. This is because they discuss things which are metaphysical or things which by their very nature cannot be verified. Heaven by definition as a physical place entered only after death cannot be verified. It is not part of this world of physical objects that we can access via our five senses. Also, it is not something verifiable by the living so all such statements are meaningless.	• However, Hick states that religious language will be verified if true at the end times, the eschaton. If heaven and life after death are true then when we attain this we can confirm its truth, making religious language meaningful. Also many have claimed near death experiences where the 'truth' of life after death has been shown to them and they have been able to tell others about this.
• Anything that is outside of our possible observation is meaningless thus making religious statements such as 'there is a God' or 'God loves me' meaningless.	• Swinburne states that even though I cannot prove or disprove something as it is outside of my possible observation, this does not make it meaningless. So 'the toys move only when no one is watching' cannot be proved or disproved but it is still meaningful as I understand what it means to say 'the toys are moving'.

AO1 information on this topic is on pages 35–39.

- Religious language simply expresses a set of emotions and an acceptance of a certain lifestyle. It could be no more than a storybook with a magical set of beliefs that are unjustified and unverifiable. The language believers use is meaningless as it is an artificial construction which fits into their framework. It is simply the mechanism used within their framework.

- Religious language may indeed express certain feelings about things, illustrating a certain lifestyle. This way of seeing life is a blik and a blik is meaningful. It profoundly affects a person's life and so is meaningful to them. For example, I have a blik; I do not like lizards. There is no point in someone saying to me 'they are more scared of you than you are of them'. I know it will scuttle away from me, I know it will not kill me, but I still choose holiday destinations that are not renowned for lizards and would panic if I saw one. No one can falsify my belief but it is most meaningful to me.

- All three of the concepts of religious language on the Specification that religion may employ in order to talk about religion fail so religious language remains meaningless. (See later question 4.)

- The three concepts of religious language succeed. (See later question 4.)

3: 'Religious language can only be understood in the context of religious belief.' Assess this view.

In other words, 'Can religious language only be understood by believers?'

Agree

- The views of Wittgenstein show that language is a game with its own set of rules. The best way of understanding the rules is to play the game. Think of a time when you have played a game and someone does not know how to play it. They are not initially going to be as 'good' at it as you. The same applies to religion. Believers are in the best position to understand religious language as they understand the rules.

- Non-believers may not have enough information or experience to deal with the many problems of religious language. Surely it must help to have background knowledge of stories, traditions and so on in order to understand some of the teachings of religions.

- A belief, a commitment is needed in order to fully appreciate words and phrases used within religion as well as understanding the implications of them. For example, atonement is a word that requires the full reach of the believer's feeling that Jesus died for them, in order to fully understand the impact of the phrase.

Disagree

- Against this it could be said that even if you are not playing a game you can still very much understand its rules just by observing. I have never played golf but I know what the aim of it is. Equally if someone does not know the rules of a game, by observing they can come to learn. So anyone with an interest in religion can watch, learn and understand its language.

- The large numbers of students taking R.S. in 6th Forms, including those who are non-believers, seem to cope with religious language. If you are reading this and understanding it, then this is good evidence! Again religious language can be learned.

- Non-believers may not share the same feeling towards religious language as believers, but they can still understand concepts, such as atonement. The word can be known in a non-religious context and working out the logistics of its use in religion is not beyond non-believers.

- To be truly understood, religious language has to be seen as part of a dynamic whole. Words cannot hang 'mid air' they need to have a 'peg' to be hung on. Religious belief and worship is therefore necessary to provide a context for the language, which is open to believers only.

- Accepting that the words are part of a dynamic whole does not 'shut out' non-believers. They can hear and read religious language and understand its meaning.

- For some traditions knowledge of the holy book is vital and being part of that religious tradition gives the individual an advantage in terms of understanding the language of that book.

- Many theology students are staunch atheists or at least agnostics. It could be said that they have an objective view from outside the religion. Maybe they have a better chance of finding different aspects undiscovered by others with a more subjective view.

- Myth and symbol is used so much within religion that knowledge of these concepts is needed as well as an awareness of the various interpretations of it.

- In everyday life people are used to concepts such as myth and symbol. They can be identified with and understood.

- Religious language can almost be like a foreign language to non-believers. It has terms which are not used outside religion such as 'Resurrection'. Also terms are used in a religious context which have a different meaning outside of it, for example 'font'. So to get a clear understanding of how religious language is being used it is better to be part of a religion.

- Firstly, like any foreign language we can learn it. Secondly, the fact that non-believers can discuss concepts such as Resurrection shows that they have an understanding of its meaning. Thirdly, non-believers can learn the nuances of local dialect in everyday life. For example, I now know that in the Neath Valley 'tidy' does not mean 'neat' but rather, 'good' or 'I approve'. So, too, can non-believers understand the nuances of religious language and realise how usage may be different in different contexts.

4: 'The concepts of religious language are inadequate.' Assess this view.

Bear in mind that what follows are some evaluative points to consider regarding the adequacies and inadequacies of analogy, symbols and language games. The question is provocatively stating that all three are inadequate. In your answer you will need to weigh up the relative adequacies and inadequacies of each.

You may conclude that one is more adequate than another. Justify your view. Perhaps ranking them in order of adequacy would be helpful.

Agree

- If we talk about God via analogy I need to be able to present the analogy as a valid one. How would I know? If I refer to 'God the Father' on what basis have I referred to God like this? The inadequacy of this method is that I may in fact have created an analogy which has no basis in fact.

- God is transcendent, wholly other, and possibly completely unknowable. So analogy is inadequate as a method for talking about God as God cannot be compared with anything.

Disagree

- It would be an acceptable point to say 'God the Father' is a valid analogy. There is something in a believer's relationship with God which shows care and love, which is analogous to the love of a father.

- However, many say that God reveals and so is knowable. Therefore, we can get some insight into God and are justified in using analogy to express this.

- If we only compare God with something else we are only scraping the surface of what it means to talk about God. I can compare my dog's loyalty with my husband's loyalty, but I still do not really know what my dog's loyalty is.

- A comparison does give us some insight. I may not know exactly what my dog's loyalty is like but I can understand it to a degree as I know what human loyalty involves.

- Analogy only gives a partial answer. Can the phrase 'partial answer' even be used? Perhaps an answer is only rightly called that if all of the facts are fully revealed.

- Aquinas was not trying to give us a complete description of God's nature. Partial descriptions are better than no description at all.

- Analogy is inadequate as so much of what we are asked to compare is somewhat of a meaningless task. For example, being asked to compare your toothache with the painful ankle you had could be an impossible comparison. We cannot rank pain on a scale of 1–5. Pain is pain, no comparison. So, analogy may not be helpful.

- We use analogy every day. A healthy diet, a healthy complexion and healthy relationship is an example. Healthy is not used in exactly the same way, nor is it used entirely differently. It is used analogously. Also we can compare pain. I can say that my broken shoulder is not as painful as my broken leg. Analogies help.

- Symbols can change over time and have different meanings making them inadequate. For example an early Hindu symbol is very similar to a swastika.

- Not all symbols change over time. The Christian cross is and probably will remain universally a sign of Christ's death. So, they can be used adequately as a picture of something.

- God is mysterious. So, if we apply a symbol to God how do we know if it is appropriate?

- In other traditions where God is knowable then experiences of people show that they can rightly apply certain symbols to God.

- Symbols with no explanations may not 'speak' to people. The meaning may not be apparent if there is no prior understanding.

- However, surely some symbols will be obvious to many, even if there are no words to accompany them. Examples may be a crown symbolising majesty or a heart for love.

- P. Edwards said that symbols are not only inadequate but they are meaningless. This is because they do not pass on any factual information. If they do not do this, they have no purpose.

- However, others would argue that symbols do give us information. A dove tells us that peace is being referred to. A white flag would be raised for surrender. Even if facts were not being passed on via the symbol it does not mean that symbol is meaningless. It could be passing on an emotion.

- It is more adequate to give a set of information in a clear, literal way rather than through using symbols.

- Symbols are an adequate way of communicating as 'a picture paints a thousand words'. The enigmatic smile of the Mona Lisa or the love between two people captured in a photograph cannot be put into words.

- With regard to language games surely believers do intend their statements to be cognitive, that is they are giving factual information. When a person says, 'I believe in God' or 'I believe in eternal life' then surely that is what they literally mean. To claim (as language games does) that these phrases are non-cognitive is inadequate.

- However, to agree with language games there are examples of when religion is making non-cognitive statements such as 'I baptise you' or 'I love God more than you do'. The former statement is to perform a ritual and the latter cannot be proven. So language games may be adequate.

- Language games separates forms of life allowing no cross over. This is very isolationist not allowing meaningful debate to take place between different forms of life. This can lead to the claim that religious language is subjective and inadequate if referred to as a language game.

- Language games is not adequate as it does not allow for any communication between religions. They are all playing their own game with its own rules. This can be divisive.

- Language games is an adequate concept as it is appropriate to keep forms of life separate. Within religion there are specific words and concepts that are not a part of everyday language. It allows religious language to be self-sufficient and not judged according to the rules of another form of life.

- Language games recognises that religions are distinctive. One should remove shoes before entering a mosque but need not do so before entering a Church. However, if we say that 'religion' is a form of life then we can accept that religion has certain rules which unite many such as one God, worship, ritual to name a few.

AO1 information on this topic is on pages 35–39.

Strengths and weaknesses of the verification and falsification principles

Grade boost

The strengths and weaknesses of the verification and falsification principles can be used in each of the four 'issues' in the specification. Depending on the questions it will be appropriate to use them to a lesser or greater extent.

AO1 information on this topic is on pages 35–39.

Strengths

1. The Logical Positivists challenged people to give a good account of their religious language by applying some sort of test for its truth or falsity. Truth and meaning are only given to those statements which either logically fit together (analytical statements) or those statements which are factually based (empirically verifiable). This does allow us to separate sense from nonsense.

2. Religious language can be puzzling, abstract and seemingly contradictory, and these principles can be ways of making religion observe similar rules to other areas of life. After all, if I said that there was something living in my garden shed which could not be seen, touched or heard, then I doubt that you would believe me. Phrases such as God being omnipresent will strike us as odd and we may find this impossible to understand. After all, if I said that I was everywhere, I doubt you would believe me. In everyday life we are quick to pick up on people when they make a contradictory set of remarks and so this should be applied to religion, too. So, the Logical Positivists emerge as having made some strong points against religious language.

3. In everyday life we do look to verification and falsification as ways of showing meaning. For example, if I said, 'my dog is a great footballer', you would surely ask me to show you some evidence to verify this statement. Imagine that I said this in 2012. By 2025, after observation, no evidence of football skills had been found. Then my dog becomes immobile due to old age, yet I still insist that I am right. My original statement would not be considered meaningful as it has neither been verified, nor have I allowed it to be falsified.

4. The Logical Positivists base their ideas on *a posteriori* evidence. This is a strength, as many of the classical arguments for God's existence are based upon this type of argument, such as the design argument. The Logical Positivists are simply asking religion to be consistent in its use of criteria for determining meaning.

5. Some would say that some religious events defy logic, such as The Virgin Birth or the Resurrection. The Logical Positivists have a strong case when they ask for events to pass certain tests before they are considered to be meaningful. They would argue that the two events just mentioned would fail their test and are therefore meaningless. In an age of testing and logic, their views stand firm.

6. Some would agree with Flew when he said that believers will never give up their religious claims. There may be those people who we know that seem to hold beliefs (religious or not) when those beliefs defy logic, have little evidence in favour of them and a lot of evidence against them. Flew may therefore be right in his observation thus providing the Logical Positivists with another weapon in their armoury.

7. Overall, the strength of the Logical Positivists is that they leave us with a warning about being careful when we talk about God. They make religious language conform to rules that other walks of life have to conform to. This has resulted in religion providing ways of talking about God in a meaningful way.

Stretch and challenge

Explain why the Logical Positivists would say that 'the Virgin Birth' and 'the Resurrection of Jesus' are meaningless.

Weaknesses

1. The principles fail their own test. The statement 'the only statements that are meaningful are analytic or synthetic' cannot be verified or falsified.

2. Analogy, symbol and language games are successful and defeat the challenge of the principles.

3. Many philosophers argue that religious statements are non-cognitive: their intention is not to convey facts, yet they are still meaningful.

4. Swinburne's toys in the cupboard.

Key Term

Eschatological verification = confirmation (of religious beliefs) at the eschaton (end times).

This can be used to show a weakness with both the verification principle and the falsification principle. Swinburne's example suggests the idea of toys moving around and emerging from their toy cupboard. But, they only do this when there is no one watching them. So by definition we cannot prove or disprove whether toys come out of the cupboard, as the criterion for this happening is that it happens when no one is watching. However, the statement about the toys moving is still meaningful as we understand what is meant by it.

5. Mitchell's resistance worker and the stranger.

This can be used to show a weakness with the falsification principle. Mitchell said that Flew was wrong when he said that religious believers do not allow their beliefs to be falsified. He said that believers do not stubbornly block their eyes and ears, refusing to let anything falsify their beliefs. He used the example of a stranger who sometimes seems to be working for the resistance movement but sometimes against it. The evidence *is* taken seriously. However, due to the trust that exists in the stranger the resistance worker will not have his belief in the stranger falsified. The resistance worker does see the evidence against the stranger working for the resistance movement. This is taken seriously and it does raise doubts. But, there is an already existing commitment to the stranger, which overrides the doubts. In principle, therefore, the belief can be falsified even though in practice it is not falsified.

So too with God. In principle belief in God can be falsified but in practice it cannot be specified what would have to happen for the belief to be falsified. Prior commitment to belief in God overrides evidence which seems to point against God.

6. Hick's **eschatological verification**.

This can be used to show a weakness with the verification principle. He uses the parable of the Celestial City. Some statements are verifiable if true, but not falsifiable if false. Life after death is a good example. If there is one, we can verify it, but if there is not then we would have no conscious existence in order to falsify it. Along the way in life, the believer and non-believer express differing feelings over what is at the end of the 'road'. This is what happens in his parable. When we 'turn the corner' at the end, one will be right. In principle then we can verify statements about God but only after death.

7. Some religious statements are also historical statements, such as 'God made a Covenant with Abraham' or 'Jesus performed miracles'. Under the weak verification principle these are therefore meaningful as we know what we would need to do in order to verify them.

8. Davies gave an example concerning lung cancer. He said that the statement 'people with lung cancer are in danger of death' is meaningful even though we do not know what it would take to falsify this claim.

9. Hare's bliks.

This can be used to show a weakness with the falsification principle. A 'blik' is a way of seeing life. It is a belief that affects a person's life but it cannot be falsified. He gave the example of an university student who believed that the university professors wanted to kill him. No matter how many kind professors he met, he refused to give up his belief, his blik. Clearly, this blik very much affected the student's life. Hare's point was that such bliks are not making factual claims. In other words, they are non-cognitive. Their intention is not to convey facts.

Hare said that religious beliefs are bliks. They are not making factual claims. These beliefs very much affect the life of the believer and the believer will not have their religious blik falsified. Bliks are not right or wrong as they are not making factual claims. They are, however, meaningful as they affect a person's life.

quickfire

⑨ What would you need before you believed that my pet spider is a great philosopher?

⑩ Why do the verification and falsification principles fail their own test?

⑪ What's the difference between Flew and Mitchell regarding religious language?

⑫ Why are historical statements involving religion meaningful under the weak verification principle?

Summary: Is religious language meaningful?

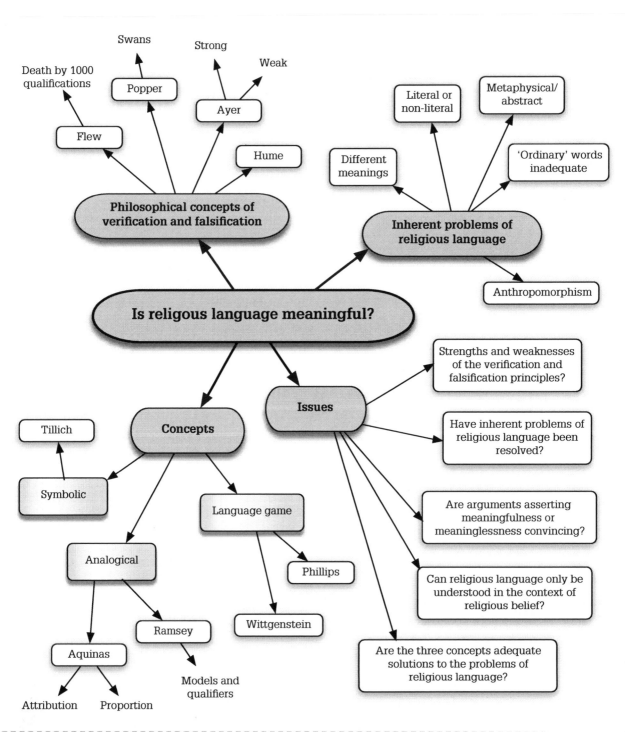

3: Is religious faith compatible with scientific evidence?

When revising 'Is religious faith compatible with scientific evidence?' you should focus on the main topics and issues. You should be familiar with a range of definitions of miracle and be able to understand why a belief in miracles is challenged. Also, you should be able to investigate the religious and scientific views of the origin of the universe and of human life. Finally, you need to evaluate the issues arising from these topics from a variety of viewpoints using scholarly opinion, and an informed conclusion must be reached.

Revision checklist

Tick column 1 when you have completed brief revision notes.
Tick column 2 when you think you have a good grasp of the topic.
Tick column 3 during final revision when you feel you have mastery of the topic.

			1	2	3
Definitions of miracles	p58	Aquinas			
	p58	Hume			
	p58	Mackie			
	p58	Swinburne			
	p59	Hick			
	p59	Holland			
	p60	Wiles			
	p60	Change for the better			
	p60	Inherent difficulties with law of nature			
Challenges to belief in miracles	p61	Hume			
	p61	Other challenges			
Arguments in the defence of miracles	p62	Various			
Religious views of the origins of the universe and of human life	p63	Jewish and Christian			
	p65	Questions raised by the Genesis accounts			
	p67	Literal or non-literal accounts?			
	p68	Creationism			
	p68	Continuous creation			
	p69	Intelligent design			
	p70	Irreducible complexity			
	p71	Hinduism			
Scientific views of the origins of the universe and of human life	p73	Continuous creation			
	p74	The Big Bang			
	p75	Evolution Darwin			
	p76	Dawkins			
What are the main issues that arise from 'Is religious faith compatible with scientific evidence?	p77	How adequate are the definitions of miracle?			
	p79	How reasonable and/or convincing is a belief? in miracles?			
	p82	Is belief in miracles essential for a religious believer?			
	p86	Can religion and science be reconciled?			

Key Terms

Deity = divine character, god, supreme being.

Interposition = placing in between objects.

Transgression = the breaking (of a law).

Violation = as transgression, but often given a more 'violent' meaning.

Volition = choice.

AO2 evaluative issues on this question are on pages 77&78.

Definitions of miracles

Aquinas has three kinds:

- Something that God has done that nature cannot do. For example, the sun going back on its course.
- Something that God has done which nature can do but not in this order. For example, someone seeing after being blind.
- Something that God has done without the working of nature, which is usually done by the working of nature. For example, an ordinary process, done by the working of nature, may be a doctor curing an illness over time. Here, the miracle is when a cure happens (instantly) without the aid of doctors.

In order to explain Aquinas' ideas further it should be noted that he distinguished between God as a Primary Cause and as Secondary Cause. Primary Cause is when God acts directly in the world (to bring about a miracle). God can do this without the need of Secondary Cause. Secondary Cause is when God acts through human agents. This is known as Double Agency. This means that God can bring about a miracle by working through human beings. Both God and the human agents are therefore involved in that miracle.

Hume: 'A **transgression** of a law of nature by a particular **volition** of the **Deity** or by the **interposition** of some invisible agent.'

Mackie: He was an Australian atheist philosopher who wrote the acclaimed *The miracle of theism*. In this book he reviews the work of Hume on miracles. He essentially agrees with Hume and his work clarifies and expands some of Hume's ideas. For Mackie a miracle would be defined as 'A **violation** of a law of nature' brought about by 'divine or supernatural intervention'. He says the laws of nature 'describe the ways in which the world, including humans, works when left to itself, when not interfered with. A miracle occurs when the world is not left to itself, when something distinct from the natural order as a whole intrudes into it.'

Swinburne: 'A violation of a law of nature by a god that is a very powerful rational being who is not a material object.' He says that if something breaks the laws of nature (which are so well established) then we should not revise our understanding of the law of nature, as some suggest we should do. This would be 'clumsy and ad hoc'. It should be classed as a break in the law of nature and therefore a miracle, providing that the two following criteria are met:

- The timescale in which it occurs should be quicker that the norm. For example, someone who recovers from polio in a minute.
- There needs to be a deeper significance, a reason for it to happen. For example, it could show God's nature to the world.

Swinburne recognises that human freedom and God's intervention may appear incompatible so he does say that such intervention does not happen too often. He asks us to bear in mind two principles when considering whether miracles could be said to occur. These principles back up his claim that miracles as he defines them can occur. They are:

- The Principle of Credulity: If it seems that X is the case, then probably X is the case. In other words what you think you have seen or think has happened probably has been seen and has happened. This is a principle of rationality. The sceptic would need to disprove the occurrence of a miracle.
- The Principle of Testimony: In the absence of good reasons to the contrary, descriptions of events are generally as people report them. In other words people generally tell the truth.

Hick says that if a miracle is a break in the law of nature then we can say *a priori* that miracles do not happen. His reason is that the laws of nature are built up on the basis of past experience. This gives us a framework and a structure necessary for going about our day-to-day life. But if tomorrow something happens that is contrary to the law of nature, we should not say that the law of nature has been broken. Instead, we say that we need to extend our current understanding of that law of nature in order to take into account the new finding.

But, he says, if a miracle is termed as an event that has religious significance, which gives a sense of the presence and activity of God, then miracles do occur.

Stretch and challenge

Suggest five things that you consider could give a sense of the presence and activity of God. For example, a beautiful sunset.

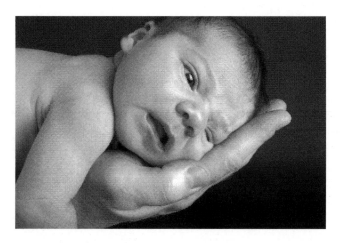

There are two ways to live your life. One is as though nothing is a miracle. The other is as though everything is a miracle.

Albert Einstein (1879–1955)

Holland: His definition does not involve a break in the law of nature either. What is seen as a miracle is all down to interpretation. He says, 'a coincidence can be taken religiously as a sign and called a miracle'.

Imagine that a child has been saved from being hit by a train due to a series of events that can be explained, even though they may be extraordinary events. Suppose that the mother says it is a miracle. Holland says that this can be termed a miracle because this is the mother's interpretation of it. Others, in a similar vein, will say that God could indeed have acted through the laws of nature to bring about this series of 'coincidences'.

Maurice Wiles (1923–2005) was Regius professor of Divinity at Oxford University for 21 years. He represented the liberal theological wing of the Church of England. He says that miracles defined as individual actions in the world do not happen. He states this in *God's action in the world* (1986). Instead he sees a miracle as there being a single act of God, which is the world as a whole. This challenges those who say that miracles are acts of God against the laws of nature.

He had this view as he said that a God who could intervene but did not on every occasion would be a God who could be rejected on moral grounds. This raises the inherent difficulty of accepting an interventionist God. Why would God act here to perform a miracle rather than there? Such a God who seems to choose miracles randomly would not, according to Wiles be a God 'worthy of worship'.

However, the lack of miracles as individual instances does not mean that connected Christian beliefs are jeopardised. Prayer, for example, still has a purpose but should not be understood as asking God to take action. Instead it should be a way of helping a group or individual to connect with God's will. Wiles said that prayer 'is the capacity to attain, however incompletely, some awareness of that intention'.

Wiles' restriction on God's action to perform miracles also applies to his action in Christ. He cannot say miracles do not happen but then allow the Incarnation and Resurrection of Jesus. Wiles claims that the doctrines of the Incarnation and Resurrection do not involve a break of the law of nature. So, the Incarnation is 'the perfection of human response to God'. The full humanity of Jesus is central and Jesus fully responded to God's grace and in doing so, incarnated God in the world.

A miracle could also be described as the *change for the better in a person*. So, from the A-Level student who now always hands essays in on time, whereas before they always had to be 'chased', to the terrorist who became a pacifist, under this definition a miracle has occurred.

Inherent difficulties with the definition of a miracle as a break in the law of nature

A miracle defined as the break in the law of nature raises serious issues. The whole point of a miracle by some definitions is that it is a one-off event. However, in order for an event to be valid from a scientific point of view it needs to be repeatable. But if it is repeatable, then it is not a miracle by the above definition, as a miracle is a 'one-off' event.

'Laws of nature' is a phrase used in science to describe the way in which past experience tells us things normally happen. If a miracle is defined as the break of a law of nature, then to be valid as a theory, science would ask for repeatability, but this cannot happen! So science will look to reassess its law of nature as now there is a new finding. So on more than one ground, the laws of nature pose a problem when it comes to defining a miracle as the breach in that law of nature.

quickfire

① Paraphrase Hume's definition of miracle.

② For Swinburne, what two criteria need to be present for a break in the law of nature to be considered a miracle?

③ Why does Hick say *a priori* that miracles as a break in the law of nature do not occur?

Challenges to belief in miracles

AO2 evaluative issues on this question are on pages 79–81.

Hume

Hume would claim that laws of nature are generalisations based on past experience. As an empiricist he weighs up the amount of empirical evidence for the laws of nature holding and for miracles occurring. In his book of 1748 *An enquiry concerning human understanding* the title of section X is 'of miracles'.

It is easier to learn his challenge to miracles in four parts:

1. Any claim should be based upon evidence. Our past experience has established laws of nature. We have a lot of evidence for them. We have very little evidence for miracles. A wise man proportions his belief to evidence. So, a wise man should believe that the laws of nature 'hold' rather than believe that miracles happen. Miracles are therefore improbable.

2. So, what do we make of the fact that people do claim miracles have happened? Hume says that their testimonies are poor in a number of ways. Firstly, they are poor as, when weighed against the amount of evidence for the laws of nature holding, the testimonies are flimsy. Secondly, the testimonies are given by people of poor quality, such as the fishermen of the New Testament or those that come from 'ignorant and barbarous nations'.

3. Further, with regard to testimony, people who claim miracles seem to abandon reason when they do so. People love superstition and wonder, and telling such tales excites them. Also, a religious person's view may be subjective and may report a miracle to 'promote a holy cause'. There may indeed be something to gain from it.

4. All religions claim miracles. He suggests that a religion's authority is grounded in its belief in miracles. As they all claim different miracles, not all can be right. Each cancels the other out. Therefore, none of them are right. This gives a 'complete triumph for the sceptic'.

quickfire

(4) For Hume, what does a wise man proportion his belief to?

(5) Why does Hume say that the 'sceptic triumphs'?

Other challenges

- Wiles (see previous section on 'Definitions of miracles') says that God does not act directly in individual circumstances in the world to cause miracles. The reason he says this is that a God who acts 'here' and not 'there' seems to be acting upon a strange, random and, in fact, morally dubious basis. A God who can act but does not act is not worthy of worship. A God who could save millions in place X but doesn't, yet turns water into wine in place Y, would have to face some pretty serious questioning. So, Wiles denies God the freedom to act in individual circumstances, but God can act in relation to the world as a whole. The world is a single act of God.

- Another challenge is that the whole idea of a miracle seems to go against the Cosmological and Design arguments. These give a picture of a structured world that shows purpose. They work on the basis of regularity. But, miracles introduce unpredictability.

- Further, a **timeless God** cannot act in time so miracles cannot happen.
- Others argue that some events claimed as miracle healings may simply be mind over matter. A person could simply believe that they are better, so no miracle has actually occurred.
- Many claimed miracles seem to be pointless. Swinburne suggests that to be a miracle there must be some deeper significance to its occurrence. This means that some things that have been called a miracle may not really deserve that title. If a statue appears to wink its eye or a face of a leader is seen in a piece of toast, we could rightly ask 'what's the point?'
- There are hundreds more challenges to miracles and also arguments in favour of their reality. You will find a worked example later under 'Evaluative issues' as well as exemplar essays at the back of this guide. From your research you will be able to add many more.

Arguments in defence of the reality of miracles

- Holy books state that miracles happen. Miracles are contained within these books which are vital to the religion. The truth of the miracle has been safeguarded over the centuries. The New Testament includes the miracles of the Virgin Birth and the Resurrection. If we accept the Bible as a literal account then these did happen. Even if these are accepted in a non-literal way such events can still defend the reality of God's power and control as a miracle. To add to this, under the weak verification principle I know what I would need to do in order to verify them and so they are meaningful accounts.
- Laws of nature can be broken as they are not set in stone. They are generalisations based upon what has happened up until now. But that does not mean that they will happen for ever. Unusual and unexpected events do happen and we are perfectly justified in saying that the law of nature has been broken.
- Ockham's razor says that the simplest explanation is the best one. If an unexpected event occurs rather than trying to find all sorts of other solutions the simplest thing to say is that 'a miracle has occurred'.
- Many will argue that it is through miracles that God reveals to humans. So to deny miracles would be to deny God that capacity to reveal. God's revelation is shown, for example, throughout the Old Testament in miracles such as in the parting of the Red Sea or in the deliverance of bread from heaven.
- Aquinas' God is a timeless God but we saw earlier on that he certainly defended the reality of miracles. This goes for other scholars and philosophers who accepted that miracles occur even if they have a different definition of miracle from Aquinas, such as Wiles and Holland.
- Others would defend the reality of miracle by saying that we may not know why God chooses to performs miracles but that does not mean that God does not perform them.

- If a miracle is defined as 'a change for the better in a person' then we can see examples of such changes in people all of the time. Under this definition then miracles are a reality.
- Many miracles are not pointless. Many act as the foundation of their faith or an event which backs up their faith. Many claimed miracles in history have had some point behind them. For example, the parting of the Red Sea allowed escape from Egypt during the time of Moses; healing miracles performed by Jesus have real significance attached to them.
- If a person sees God as an **everlasting God** (one who is in time) then God can act to perform a miracle. For this God the future really is the future and so can act to bring about a miracle tomorrow or next year.

Key Term

Everlasting God = one who is in time and so time is past, present and future for this God.

Religious views of the origins of the universe and of human life

The origins of the universe and of human life are two different things. You could be asked about either or both in the examination. However, in Creation stories you will often see them as more conflated (squashed together) than the account that is given by Science.

There are very many religious views of the origins. In this guide you are given a selection. The Specification does not demand you study any set views so you have the freedom to look in breadth or depth at the various views.

AO2 evaluative issues on this question are on pages 86–91.

Jewish and Christian

Later on in this section you can read about some important questions that are raised by the Creation stories in Genesis as well as reading about how they are interpreted differently by different people.

It must be remembered that Biblical stories are products of a time of history where the people were explaining events of their time. There are arguably two separate Creation stories. These are found in Genesis 1 and 2. One is of the six days of Creation found in Genesis 1^1–2^3. The other is of Adam and Eve found in 2^4–3^{24} (this includes the story of the Fall also).

According to modern scholarship they were written at different periods of time. Genesis 2^4–3^{24} is often dated in the 10th century BC around the time of the reign of Solomon. Israel at the time was very powerful. Genesis 1–2^3 is often dated three or four centuries later. Circumstances in the nation were very different then.

I will refer to Genesis 1–2^3 as the first creation story as it is first in the sequence in Genesis, even though it is chronologically later than the second Creation story of Genesis 2^4 onwards.

Verses used here are from the Revised Standard Version of the Bible. The two stories appear in the text to have been merged. In the first story the humans are

quickfire

⑥ How many Creation stories are there in Genesis?

⑦ What does it mean to be a steward?

not singled out with a name, whereas the second story has them as its focus. A'dam means '(every) man' and this is perhaps a play on the Hebrew word for earth or clay, 'adamah'. Eve means 'life'.

In the first Creation story 'the earth was without form and void, and darkness was upon the face of the deep; and the Spirit of God was moving over the face of the waters' (verses 2&3.) God created everything **ex nihilo** in six days and rested on the seventh. God made the heavens and the earth, light and dark, the waters, dry land and plants, different lights, birds, fish and land animals, which included humans (male and female at the same time). This was a conscious decision, a plan. Humans were the culmination of God's plan as humans were made 'in God's image'. Humans have a special place (created last) and responsibility in Creation (stewards). There is **fixity of species**.

This Creation story shows God very much as one who decrees, a God who gives an official order. God's Word is the creative force: 'God said ... and it was so' is a phrase used several times. This was a common device used in writing and also a common belief whereby God's Word becomes personified (God's Word as opposed to word) and has a power which comes forth from God. God is a transcendent God, one who is beyond the realm of humans, one who is 'other'. Throughout it is clear that God is pleased with Creation 'God saw that it was good'.

In 1[28] when referring to humans it says God 'blessed them and God said to them, 'Be fruitful and multiply, and fill the earth and subdue it'. When God looked around at all of Creation God declared in verse 31 that 'it was very good'.

In contrast to the first story where life began in the waters, the second creation story begins with a desert. Verses 4 and 5 say 'In the day that the Lord God made the earth and the heavens, when no plant of the field was yet in the earth and no herb of the field had yet sprung up – for the Lord God had not caused it to rain upon the earth, and there was no man to till the ground.'

In this story humans are the focus of the story. There is a suggestion that humans have a spiritual nature in 2[7] 'and God breathed life-giving spirit into the man' after God had formed man 'of dust from the ground'. Bear in mind that at this point it is 'the man' that is the title given rather than being named as Adam (this did not happen until 3[17]). Also, there is no woman until 2[23]. She is an afterthought. She is made as a 'helper fit for him' (verse 18). The woman was made from Adam's rib. She was called 'woman' in Hebrew 'issa' as she was taken from man, which in Hebrew is the word 'is'.

In contrast to the first Creation story where humans are made after animals, in this second story it seems that animals were made after humans (2[19]). However, see later under 'What questions may be raised by the Genesis accounts?' for a different reading of the text. It is in this account that the Garden of Eden is named. God has made a perfect Creation. The tree of knowledge of good and evil was there, which the man was commanded not to eat from.

This Creation story shows God very much as one who 'fashions', for example humans and the Garden. This contrasts with the God who decrees in the first story. Here God is immanent, present within and throughout the world. This God is one who walks and talks with Adam and Eve. He is thus given human characteristics (anthropomorphism).

At this stage 'the man and his wife were naked and were not ashamed' (2^{25}). However, the serpent tempted the woman to eat from the forbidden tree and she likewise tempted her husband to do the same. Once they had eaten the fruit they realised they were naked and covered themselves up. God knew what they had done as they had covered up their nakedness; God knew they had discovered the forbidden knowledge of good and evil.

Because of this they were punished by God. The serpent was made to travel on its belly, the woman would have pain in childbirth and her husband would 'rule over you' (3^{16}). Adam (as he is now named) will have to work hard until he dies. God drove the man out of the garden.

What questions may be raised by the Genesis accounts?

The two stories offer us different views of humanity and gender differences. Genesis 1 has male and female created at the same time, both in 'God's image' whereas Genesis 2 has the man being made first with the woman being reliant upon the man for her creation as well as being his helper. In Genesis 3 Adam names his wife. He also named the animals. This may also suggest superiority as in the ancient world to know someone's name was to have power over them. This rings true today also as it is far more effective to call a name 'James, stop right there' rather than shouting 'Oi you…'.

In the second account the woman is seen as the temptress, as the one who lures the poor, unsuspecting man into sinning. Humanity is cursed: 'To the woman he said, "I will greatly multiply your pain in childbearing"' (verse 16). She will also be ruled over by Adam. So the second account really does give an inferior

Grade boost

A possible examination question is 'Examine the differences between religious and scientific views of the origins of the universe and/ or of human life'. When you revise always note down where religion says one thing but science says another.

picture of women. Adam is told 'cursed is the ground because of you; in toil you shall eat of it all the days of your life' (verse 17).

As said earlier, in the second account God is much more anthropomorphic, immanent and involved with Creation. For example, in Chapter 3 God is heard walking in the garden among the trees 'in the cool of the day'. God speaks to the man and woman 'who told you that you were naked?' (verse 11) and subsequently talks directly to both of them as well as the serpent to tell them of their fate.

There is the claim that as well as the above giving very different views of humanity and of gender differences, there is also a glaring contradiction. In Chapter 1, man and woman are created at the same time *after* the creation of the animals. In Chapter 2 it seems that the animals are created *after* people.

This apparent contradiction is best illustrated by looking at Genesis 2[19]: 'So out of the ground the Lord God formed every beast of the field and every bird of the air, and brought them to the man to see what he would call them.'

The language appears to suggest that God made the animals after making the man and then He brought the animals to the man. However, in Genesis 1, we have an account of God creating animals *and then* creating man and woman.

The difficulty with Genesis 2[19] lies with the use of the word *formed*.

Some versions of the text have a subtly different translation which lends itself to a different version of events:

'Now the Lord God had formed out of the ground all the beasts of the field and all the birds of the air. He brought them to the man to see what he would name them.'

This suggests a different way of viewing the first two chapters of Genesis. Genesis 2 does not suggest a chronology. That is why some versions, for example the New International Version, suggests using the style 'the Lord God *had formed* out of the ground all the beasts of the fields.' Therefore, the animals being brought to the man had already been made and were not being brought to him immediately after their creation.

Another interesting discussion on whether there is contradiction or whether the accounts can be complementary is to discuss whether each account has a purpose that can be complementary even though the style and format is different.

Genesis 1 gives a comprehensive overview – a day-by-day chronological account of Creation week. It gives us the 'big picture' and outlines in summary form what God did on each day. It is much like a day-by-day log of a trip or project, almost a diary account. We are given just enough detail to ignite our curiosity and to give us a feeling of God's creative power and plan. Humans are the high point of Creation but other aspects are given mention, too.

In Genesis 2, the style changes and the account homes in on one aspect of God's creative work. This is God's focus, main purpose, or favourite part, the creation of Adam and Eve. Here the author may not be very concerned about the chronology. The author is concerned about the details of the creation of mankind, showing God's personal involvement and purpose in every step. The approach in the two accounts is similar to the difference between writing an account of something that has happened and writing about something that you care for passionately.

Stretch and challenge

Read the two creation stories in Genesis. Note down any other questions that can be raised by these accounts.

This literary technique is common, not only in Hebraic writing, but even in writing today. It is common to first give a broad overview, and then focus in on one aspect of particular importance or interest. Genesis 1 and 2 in this sense are then not conflicting reports but, rather, are complementary, each with a specific purpose and style.

Literal or non-literal accounts?

Literal

For some Christians and Jews the Genesis stories are true accounts, word for word. This would be the case for **Young Earth Creationists** (see 'Creationism'). This is often referred to as 'Fundamentalism', which you may have heard about in the news. Fundamentalism refers to followers of the 'religions of the book' (Judaism, Christianity and Islam) who accept their holy book as being literally true.

So, God did make the whole world and all its inhabitants from nothing in six days and rested on the seventh. Adam was made from the dust of the ground and Eve was made from his rib. They were tempted by the serpent and they did suffer punishment as a result of their sin.

Non-literal

Since Victorian times the view of both Reform Jews and mainstream Christianity has been that the Genesis stories are myths. So, the accounts are not word for word true but do contain important truths. Non-literalists may differ in their views in terms of how they interpret the accounts, but what unites them is that they are human words expressing ideas but not in a literal way. This would be the case for **Old Earth Creationists** (see 'Creationism').

Some emphasise that the writers of the accounts were expressing, without the knowledge that we have today, what they believed could explain the universe they lived in. Others look to the poetic nature of the accounts. Indeed, some scholars believe the author of the second creation story to be a 'poet priest'. The mythical nature of the account is never far from the non-literalist's explanation either. Creation myths have always been popular in the ancient world and it would not be surprising to have written these accounts as myths.

What truths could be found in Genesis 1–3? Many have noted what could be symbolic elements in the accounts which are listed below:

- Garden of Eden, originally a paradise made by God – the world in its original form.
- Adam – every human.
- Eve – mother, giver of life.
- The tree of knowledge – temptation.
- Creation of everything – God's power.
- Stewardship – human dominance.
- Serpent – devil/temptation to disobey.

Key Terms

Old Earth Creationism = the belief that the earth is much older than believed by Young Earth Creationists.

Young Earth Creationism = the belief that God created the world in six days, literally. The world is between 6000 and 10,000 years old.

Stretch and challenge

Explain whether you believe Creation stories are literal or non-literal. Give clear reasons for your view.

- Nakedness – original innocence.
- Eating the apple – giving in to temptation/sin.
- Covering up nakedness – shame and guilt, loss of innocence.
- Punishment from God – a changed world, now not innocent.
- Expulsion from Garden – the Fall from God's grace.

Creationism

This is the title which is generally given to the belief that everything in the world was created by God. In the 17th century, Archbishop Ussher tried to calculate the exact moment of Creation by working back from the flood at the time of Noah and adding up the supposed length of lives of the people before the flood. He concluded that it happened at 9pm on 23 October 4004 BCE.

Young Earth Creationism, which accepts Genesis literally, says that the Earth is between 6000 and 10,000 years old. Old Earth Creationism accepts a non-literal view of Genesis. Old Earth Creationists generally accept geological findings. For them the Earth is very much older, therefore, than for Young Earth Creationists.

Many Creationists point to gaps in the fossil records to back up their beliefs. For example, they may say that if evolution is correct, then why are there not fossil records for every incomplete life form along the way, such as a half-winged creature?

Continuous creation

The original thrust of **continuous creation** was scientific but it deserves a mention here. Many believe it is a religious doctrine. They say that continuous creation is the same as God's preservation, which is an established religious doctrine. God continuously creates everywhere and is thereby preserving everything. Arthur Peacocke and John Polkinghorne can be associated with this view.

The Reverend Canon Arthur Robert Peacocke (1924–2006) was a British theologian and biochemist. He believed that science can deepen our understanding of matters relating to God. He recognised that for some Christians it is hard to give up cherished beliefs. He also realised that today Creation is 'a problem'. Science, said Peacocke, is not just about what happened in the past but it is still ongoing, all of the time. Similarly, God is still creating now through the evolutionary process. God creates through the processes that science unveils.

Just as a composer, Peacocke suggests, is present in the music that the performers make through their own interpretation and talent, so God is not only present in the compositional elements God created but also in the music the world creates. God, said Peacocke, is **immanent**, embedded in the world. He saw no conflict between evolution and Christianity as evolution as a continuous process reveals God's activity.

The Reverend John Charlton Polkinghorne 1930– is an English theoretical physicist, theologian, writer, and Anglican priest. He was professor of Mathematical physics at the University of Cambridge from 1968 to 1979, when he resigned his chair to study for the priesthood, becoming an ordained

Anglican priest in 1982. Polkinghorne is the author of books on physics, and on the relationship between science and religion.

He accepts evolution and believes that God has given the world the freedom to make itself and that God is present in this process. The freedom that the creation displays in its God-given operations (evolution as a continuous process) is fully in agreement with God's purposes and ends. He gives examples such as the stars and the raw materials needed for life to back up his acceptance of the anthropic principle (God made the conditions necessary for evolution to continue). Such things are so finely tuned that they could not happen by chance.

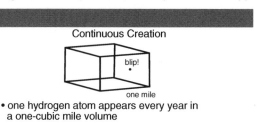

Continuous Creation

blip!

one mile

• one hydrogen atom appears every year in a one-cubic mile volume

Intelligent Design (ID)

As a result of Darwin's findings, there was an alternative to Creationism. In some countries, notably the USA, there was a considerable battle against the upsurge in the teaching of evolution. We then see the development of the ID movement.

Evolution was not in many US text books until the 1960s. When it did appear, several US states passed laws that forbade its teaching. In fact, some books had the relevant pages glued together! Some schools in the UK have taught creationism alongside evolutionary theories.

The Scopes trial of 1925 illustrates the situation well. John Scopes (1900–1970), a high school biology teacher, was prosecuted in Tennessee for teaching evolution. The press mimicked him and his was known as the 'monkey trial'. He was fined 100 dollars. The law that allowed his trial was in force until 1967.

ID has its background in the ancient design argument, which was developed by people such as Paley, who said that the universe is too complex to have come about through chance. However, due to scientific evidence and findings the soil was fertile for theories to be consolidated by science. Supporters of ID say that their observations come from scientific discovery; most would accept the Big Bang and evolution.

However, they say that these theories *on their own* cannot account for the complexity of certain biological systems and living creatures. A higher intelligence must be responsible for their complexity.

In the 1980s the work of Phillip E. Johnson contributed greatly to the debate. He wrote the book *Darwin on Trial*, which challenged evolution without intelligence behind it. He said that evolution alone can't explain, for example, how new species could be developed out of older ones.

Many supporters of ID say that it should be taught as part of the science curriculum. Critics of it say that it is just creationism by another name or creationism in a lab coat.

Key Term

Intelligent Design = the theory that the universe and life cannot have arisen by chance and was designed by some intelligent entity.

Stretch and challenge

Research the findings of the 'Dover Trial' of 2004 with regard to ID and Creationism (T. Kitzmiller *et al.* versus Dover Area School District *et al*).

Irreducible complexity

This term can be associated with Michael Behe. He said that there are some things which work just as they are; they cannot be reduced any further (irreducible) to a previously less complex state where they functioned (complexity). Evolution, of course, suggests that things do have a previously less complex state which functions and develops into more complex states. **Irreducible complexity** says that if one part of the evolutionary process were not there, that system would just not function. This then casts a doubt on evolution. There are two classic examples:

1. The mousetrap

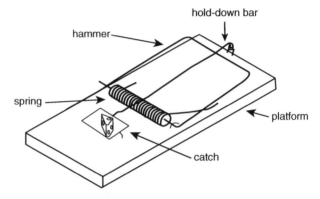

If one part, for example the spring, was removed, the device would not be a mousetrap; it simply would not work. So, it is irreducibly complex.

2. The blood-clotting system

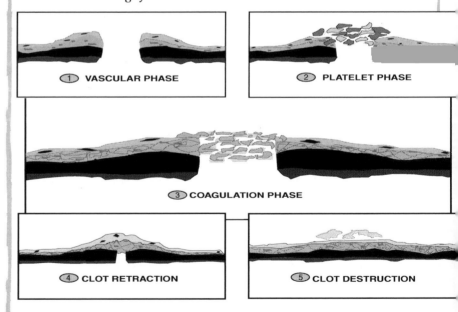

Again, in this complex system, it is argued that if one part was missing then the blood would not clot. It cannot have evolved from anything else; it cannot be reduced any further. It is irreducibly complex.

Although ID supporters accept that some systems could be explained by evolution, there are examples that are irreducibly complex and can't be explained by evolution. So, there must be an intelligence who guided evolution or who designed life.

Hinduism

There is no one Hindu creation story. Numerous stories can be found in almost all of the important Hindu scriptures. A Hindu principle states that 'Truth is One; the sages call it by different names' (Rig Veda 1:164:46). This helps to explain how it is possible for Hindus to accept so many different versions of creation at the same time. Hindus tend to see metaphors in these creation myths for philosophical and spiritual truths. The *Encyclopedia of Religion* article on Cosmogony (theories or studies into the origins or evolution of life) classifies such myths into six categories. Within the Hindu tradition, there are Creation stories that fall into each of those categories. Hinduism has thought of most of the ways that the universe may have come into existence!

A beautiful and indeed spiritual account of creation occurs in the Rig Veda 10:129. It ponders the mystery of origins and offers more questions than answers.

'Who really knows, and who can swear,
How creation came, when or where!
Even gods came after creation's day,
Who really knows, who can truly say
When and how did creation start?

Stretch and challenge

Research the Buddhist, Muslim or Sikh creation stories.

Grade boost

Do not just 'reel off' the stories. That is something that you are expected to do as a minimum at GCSE. Draw out the implications and meanings of the details given. For example, why does it make sense to leave the creation of creatures until days 5 and 6? Or, how do the stories show God's power?

Also, note down any similarities or differences between the stories of different religions. This will be useful to you for both part (a) questions which may ask you to explain similarities and differences and also when it comes to a part (b) question in the examination on whether religious and scientific views can be reconciled.

Did He do it? Or did He not?
Only He, up there, knows, maybe;
Or perhaps, not even He.'

Stretch and challenge

Look up another Hindu creation story. This variety will be useful to show diversity in an answer.

A classical Hindu creation story given below helps to explain one of the major Hindu beliefs, namely reincarnation.

This is not the first world, nor is it the first universe. There have been and will be many more worlds and universes than there are drops of water in the holy river Ganges. The universes are made by Lord Brahma the Creator, maintained by Lord Vishnu the Preserver and destroyed by Lord Shiva. Since the universes must be destroyed before they can be recreated, Lord Shiva is called the Destroyer and Re-creator. These three gods are all forms of Supreme One and part of the Supreme One. The Supreme One is behind and beyond all.

After each old universe is destroyed nothing is left but a vast ocean. Floating on this ocean, resting on the great snake Ananta, is Lord Vishnu. Some say that a lotus flower springs from his navel and from this comes Lord Brahma. And it is from Lord Brahma that all creation comes.

How does Lord Brahma create? Some tell of how he grows lonely and splits himself in two to create male and female. Then he becomes one again and human beings are created. In the same way he creates all the other living things, from the great animals to the tiniest insects. Others say that everything comes from different parts of Lord Brahma's body. All the different animals and all of the people come from his mouth, arms, thighs and feet. Everything comes from one – Lord Brahma, who is part of the Supreme One – so everything is part of the Supreme One.

For this universe, this world and this Lord Brahma like all those before and all those to come, will be destroyed by Lord Shiva. How long is the life of a universe? Its length is beyond imagination. One day to Lord Brahma is longer than four thousand million of the years that we know. Every night when Lord Brahma sleeps the world is destroyed. Every morning when he awakes it is created again. When the Lord Brahma of this universe has lived a lifetime of such days the universe is completely destroyed by Lord Shiva.

Everything disappears into the Supreme One. For an unimaginable period of time chaos and water alone exist. Then once again Lord Vishnu appears, floating on the vast ocean. From Lord Vishnu comes forth Lord Brahma of the new universe and the cycle continues for ever.

This belief in reincarnation, in the cycle of life, strongly influences the lifestyle of many Hindus. It can best be explained by the terms 'dharma' and 'karma'. Dharma is 'duty' and for Hindus, part of that duty is to respect and care for all living things. The belief that after death the soul is reincarnated in another body, not necessarily human, leads to a great respect for all life. This leads to another Hindu principle, namely 'ahimsa'. This means non-violence in thought, word and deed. Karma is the result or product of what we do, the law of cause and effect. Actions have consequences. If we do our duty, then we create good karma, since the next life we may have is directly related to the actions of our present life. To the Hindu, everything is part of the Supreme One, and thus every living thing is equally important in the great cycle of life.

Scientific views of the origins of the universe and of human life

Science offers us theories, too. The theories that follow are the best we have to date. All times shown are approximate.

Continuous creation or steady state

Often the two terms are used to mean the same thing. Others say that continuous creation is a quasi-steady state theory. This is a theory associated with Hoyle and Bondi. It says that there is no beginning or end to the universe. The universe has always been here, so there is not a single event which began it.

Further, it states that at any one point in time, the universe should basically look the same. The Universe is expanding. This theory says that new galaxies are created to fill the gaps left by old galaxies. It could be likened to a crowded train. As more passengers get on, the passengers already on it make room for newly arrived galaxies.

Today, this theory has largely been abandoned, due to the Big Bang theory.

The origin of the universe

Timeline from the Big Bang:

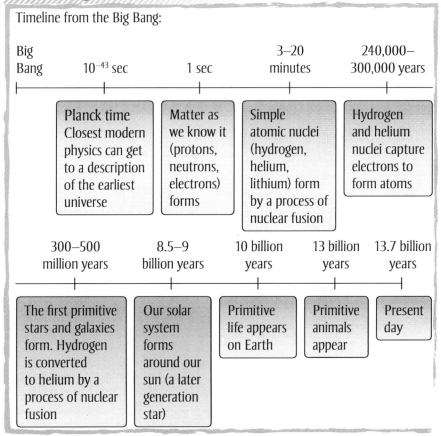

Big Bang | 10^{-43} sec | 1 sec | 3–20 minutes | 240,000–300,000 years

| Planck time Closest modern physics can get to a description of the earliest universe | Matter as we know it (protons, neutrons, electrons) forms | Simple atomic nuclei (hydrogen, helium, lithium) form by a process of nuclear fusion | Hydrogen and helium nuclei capture electrons to form atoms |

300–500 million years | 8.5–9 billion years | 10 billion years | 13 billion years | 13.7 billion years

| The first primitive stars and galaxies form. Hydrogen is converted to helium by a process of nuclear fusion | Our solar system forms around our sun (a later generation star) | Primitive life appears on Earth | Primitive animals appear | Present day |

Stretch and challenge

In preparation for an AO2 question explain how the Big Bang theory may rule out God but also how it could include God.

The Big Bang

There was a point at which the universe began, between 12 and 15 billion years ago, in an event known as the Big Bang. The current best estimate for the age of the universe is of the order of 13.7 billion years. The point at which the universe began is described as a quantum fluctuation. What emerges is an infinitely hot, infinitely dense and an infinitesimally small universe.

Within the first second, the building blocks of matter that we recognise today (protons, neutrons and electrons) form. As the universe continues to expand and cool simple atomic nuclei of the lightest elements form. These will eventually capture electrons to form atoms.

About 500 million years after the Big Bang, hydrogen is by far the most abundant substance in the universe. Due to irregularities in the density of pockets of gas, gravity causes clouds of hydrogen to collapse in on themselves. At the centre of such clouds, the temperature rises to the extent that the hydrogen nuclei have enough energy to form helium by nuclear fusion. This process releases large amounts of energy, resulting in the formation of the first stars. Gravitational attraction eventually leads to these primitive stars clumping together to form galaxies and galaxy clusters.

After 8.5–9 billion years, a later generation star forms in an outer arm of a spiral galaxy. As this star forms, the debris surrounding it grows together to form a collection of eight planets orbiting the central star, as well as assorted collections of moons, asteroids and dwarf planets. This is the formation of the solar system that we recognise as our own.

Around a billion years later, the third planet from the star at the centre of this system develops a curious phenomenon where certain complex molecules appear to have the ability to replicate themselves. This marks what scientists now believe to be the origin of life on Earth.

The origin of human life on earth

Timeline of evolution of life

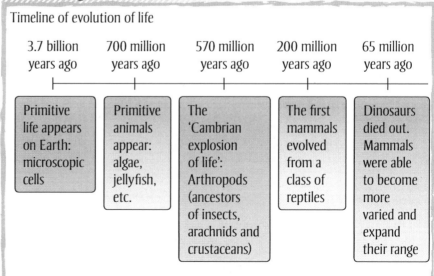

3.7 billion years ago	700 million years ago	570 million years ago	200 million years ago	65 million years ago
Primitive life appears on Earth: microscopic cells	Primitive animals appear: algae, jellyfish, etc.	The 'Cambrian explosion of life': Arthropods (ancestors of insects, arachnids and crustaceans)	The first mammals evolved from a class of reptiles	Dinosaurs died out. Mammals were able to become more varied and expand their range

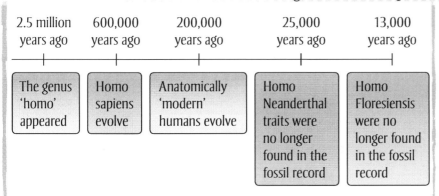

2.5 million years ago	600,000 years ago	200,000 years ago	25,000 years ago	13,000 years ago
The genus 'homo' appeared	Homo sapiens evolve	Anatomically 'modern' humans evolve	Homo Neanderthal traits were no longer found in the fossil record	Homo Floresiensis were no longer found in the fossil record

Today there is an abundant amount of life on our planet: birds, mammals, reptiles, fish, crustaceans and insects, all of which exist as many different types.

Deposits in rocks suggest that life appeared some 3.7 billion years ago. The primitive life can be termed prokaryotes (simple cells). Next are stromatolites (green plant cells). Bacteria and amoeba then appear. This is all before primitive animals appear.

The Cambrian explosion of life some 570 million years ago saw much more complex organisms appear.

The basic groundwork for Darwin's theories had been laid by Lyell and Lamarck. Lyell's work devastated religious ideas of fixity of species and the age of life on Earth. Lamarck suggested the adaptation of organisms to their environment. Darwin suggested how this happened.

Darwin (1809–1882)

Darwin wrote his theory in the book *On the Origin of Species by Means of Natural Selection* (1859). He gave the mechanism by which life developed on Earth – by means of **natural selection**.

He considered the small-scale selective breeding of a number of species that had gone on for some time. Here, breeders will select animals born with certain desirable characteristics that make it easier for them to survive. They can produce healthy, fit offspring who can, in the future, pass on the desirable characteristics to their own offspring.

Darwin said that in nature the same process happens naturally on a larger scale over a longer time span. Organisms born with particular variations of characteristics that make it easier to survive are more likely to survive long enough to reproduce, passing on the genes responsible for those characteristics to their offspring. For example, a bear with lighter fur living in Arctic conditions will have a survival advantage over bears with darker fur. Hence the organisms that are best adapted to the environment in which they live (the 'fittest') are most likely to survive. This component of the mechanism of **evolution** was entitled 'Survival of the Fittest' by Herbert Spencer.

These characteristics that are inherited will eventually be inherited by all members of that species in that particular environment. This explains how species evolve, change from one form to another or die out. Genetic

Key Terms

Evolution = the process that can trace how life has developed from its most primitive form to the present day.

Genus homo = any member of the genus that includes extinct and modern humans.

Homo Floresiensis = a species of the genus 'homo', the remains of which were found at Flores in Indonesia, and nicknamed 'Hobbit' due to its small body and small brain space inside the skull.

Homo Neanderthal = a species of the genus 'homo', which possibly evolved from Homo Heidelbergensis, the remains of which were found at Neanderthal, a valley in Germany.

Homo sapiens = the species of humans that exists at present.

Natural selection = the mechanism by which evolution occurred. It is the process that drives evolution.

Charles Darwin.

mutations (small natural changes arising naturally) offering a slight survival advantage accumulate over time until new species are formed. Those whose characteristics are not as well suited to their environment eventually die out.

Human life can be traced back to the most primitive life forms. From the most primitive life forms it is possible to trace the development of fish, followed by reptiles, then mammals and then ape-like species. Humans represent a continuation of this process of evolution.

An example can be taken from Darwin's visit to the Galapagos Islands. He noticed that each of the islands had its own species of giant tortoise. Surely God would not have created a species for each island? Darwin concluded that the species of tortoise were not fixed, but had developed from other species.

Therefore all creatures evolved and this process took millions of years. Humans evolved like any other species. Different species evolved from earlier ones, and there is scientific evidence to support this theory.

Richard Dawkins

Modern supporters of evolution are helped by genetic theory and also by modern technology. Computer simulation can be used to show how, when environmental variables are present, a species may evolve to suit that environment.

He supports evolution. He provides evidence in favour of survival of the fittest, explaining how survival chances are affected by the environment that a species finds itself in. Humans are their DNA and that is it.

In *The Selfish Gene* first published in 1976, he said that human behaviour is genetically motivated. Genes struggle to survive and humans are just the kernels in which this struggle happens. In *The Blind Watchmaker* (1986) he said that natural selection made things appear designed. In *Climbing Mount Improbable* (1991) he suggests that the apparent improbability of atoms and molecules forming complex things is wrong. As advantaged genes survive and disadvantaged ones do not, there is a gradual path up the back of the mountain. The peak of the mountain represents the fact that there is ascendancy in terms of complexity. So, far from being improbable, Dawkins says that it is inevitable that complex forms will arise.

In *Cultural Evolution* Dawkins says that humans can be moral, but not because God has put some sort of divine spark into people. Conscience is something that humans create in society in order to make that society one we can live in. Our norms and accepted practice evolve just as physical characteristics evolve. The evolution of culture makes sure that humans fit into their environment. Examples of this can be seen in the development of law making and marriage.

Evaluative issues

These are the part (b) (AO2) questions which demand a different skill from part (a) (AO1) questions. AO2 questions will always ask the candidate to consider a quotation or a viewpoint. The candidate will be asked to assess or evaluate the validity of that quotation or statement. The aim is to give a series of arguments both in favour of and against the quotation or statement, analysing and evaluating the information.

Key things to bear in mind when answering these questions appear on page 46.

What follows are some examples of how you could deal with the issues in this topic. There will clearly be material that you could use in several different questions. The material given here is for guidance only. There are other, perfectly acceptable ways to answer all of these questions. You must remember that the examiner is looking for a consideration of the issue with evaluative skills which present evidence for a viewpoint. Reasoning must be used and the conclusion reached must be based upon what you have written in the main body of your answer.

Stretch and challenge

Do the exercise suggested in the 1st paragraph below.* This will allow you to consider the pros and cons of each definition. It may even lead you to a preferred definition of your own. You will see an example given for one of the definitions: *'a miracle is a break in the law of nature by the intervention of God or gods'* in essay 1 which follows 'There is no adequate definition of miracle.' Assess this view.

An examination answer would expect you to cover the adequacies and inadequacies of a good number of definitions so your answer will comprise sets of evaluations per definition.

How adequate are the definitions of miracles?

Here, you need to remind yourself of the definitions of miracles found earlier in this guide. *The exercise you need to carry out* here is to take each definition in turn and write out a set of adequacies and inadequacies about that definition. So, you need to do this for Aquinas, Hume, Mackie, Swinburne, Hick, Holland, Wiles and a change for the better in a person. If you have looked at any other definitions you can do it for those as well.*

One issue for you to consider is whether any definition of miracle can actually be adequate. The fact that there are so many definitions may mean that no single definition will ever be one that everyone can agree with.

Our own definition is subjective and our definition will determine whether we believe miracles may happen. For example, I may define a miracle as 'a break in the law of nature' but may not believe these laws can be broken, therefore I would not believe miracles happen.

Someone may have a definition of a miracle as 'a change for the better in a person'. If a person does change for the better, then a miracle would be declared. I, however, may not define a miracle as 'a change for the better in a person' thus I would not view that change as a miracle.

There are also some *general* issues that you could consider in your analysis and evaluation of whether the definitions of miracles are adequate.

≫ Pointer

Definition of miracles

Definition too narrow?
Definition too wide?
Are 'laws of nature' set in stone?
Can 'laws of nature' be broken?
Does the scientific method (observation and repeatability) rule out miracles?
Can God intervene in the world?
Can a miracle be whatever the individual wants it to be?

AO information on this topic is on pages 58–60.

1: 'There is no adequate definition of miracle.' Assess this view.

Below is a worked example based upon the definition of miracle as a 'break in the law of nature'.

Agree

- Laws of nature cannot break. 'Law of nature' is a name given to those things which we accept as generalisations based upon our experience up until now. They are not set in stone. We accept them as a working hypothesis in order to live our lives, but hypothesis is the telling word – a hypothesis is something to be tested and it can be proven wrong. So this part of the definition is inadequate.

- It is not adequate to say that a God or gods must be involved in our definition. Many do not believe in God, so are they not allowed to have a definition without a God? Also, upon this definition it would mean that atheists could never accept any event as a miracle.

- It is not adequate to say that a miracle needs the intervention of a God. A God who intervenes is one who chooses randomly, arbitrarily and sparingly. This God would then not intervene in very many cases leaving many in distress or turmoil. Should this action then be called a 'miracle'? It seems rather inadequate (and immoral) to say that it is.

Disagree

- It is adequate to say that a miracle is a break in the law of nature as the law is the best explanation we have for the way the world has worked up until now. The law is so well established that a break of it would be extraordinary. For it to break is simply not the same as saying my hypothesis may simply change. For example, if tomorrow morning I refuse to emerge from under my duvet in case there is no gravity when I go to put my feet in my slippers then people would think me insane. If I did start to float upwards, this would be a break in the law of nature and I think I would be perfectly justified in saying 'a miracle has happened'.

- Surely it is adequate to say that God or gods must be involved? The whole idea of a miracle is that it is due to something extraordinary which has 'intruded' into the world of regularity. In order for this to happen there must be a God or gods who have the power to overcome regularity to perform this act.

- The whole point of a miracle may be that an intervention is required. If there is no 'breaking into the world' then it is not worthy of being called miraculous. Also, it is an adequate part of the definition because the reasons behind God's intervention are known by God. So there is an overall plan. An analogy is often used where there is a shoal of fish being washed up to shore. A small child has a very small bucket. She rushes over to the edge of the water to scoop up some of the fish into her bucket in order to place them back into the water. An onlooker says 'why are you bothering, you will never save them all' to which the reply came 'it's worth it as I can save some of them'. So God's pointed intervention to perform some miracles is better than performing none.

Now do the same exercise for the other definitions of miracle. A concluding section to your essay could be that no one definition is adequate as there are so many definitions. Alternatively, you may identify one definition that you find to be adequate, explaining why.

Is a belief in miracles unreasonable and/or unconvincing?

 quicKfire

⑧ What is a secondary cause?

The Specification requires that a candidate investigates whether a belief in miracles is reasonable and also whether arguments against miracles are convincing. What follows is a model of some of the evaluative points you could consider for these two issues. Some material can be used to answer *both* questions. Other material will only apply to a question on 'convincing' and some material will *only* apply to a question on 'reasonable'. In an examination you can tailor this material to the specific question.

> AO1 information on this topic is on pages 61–63.

2: 'Arguments against miracles are convincing.' Assess this view.

'Convince' = to persuade by argument or evidence

Agree

- Any claim should be based upon evidence. Our past experience has established laws of nature. We have a lot of evidence for them. We have very little evidence for miracles. As Hume said, a wise man proportions his belief to evidence. So, a wise man should believe that the laws of nature 'hold' rather than believe that miracles happen. Miracles are therefore improbable. Believing in them would be unreasonable. This argument concerning lack of evidence for miracles is therefore convincing.

- So, what do we make of the fact that people do claim miracles have happened? Hume says that their testimonies are poor in a number of ways. Firstly, they are poor as, when weighed against the amount of evidence for the laws of nature holding, the testimonies are flimsy. Secondly, the testimonies are given by people of poor quality, such as the fishermen of the New Testament or those that come from 'ignorant and barbarous nations'. It would be unreasonable to believe these testimonies. So the argument against miracles based upon poor testimony is persuasive.

Disagree

- There are some things that we can justifiably believe in with little evidence. For example, I am perfectly justified in accepting that the finger I am using to type this is my finger. No evidence needs to be given. Also, the whole point of miracles is that they are one-off events; that's what makes them miraculous. So, lack of evidence is inevitable, not a challenge to miracles. Lastly, Hume only says that miracles are improbable, not impossible. So it is not unreasonable to believe in miracles, despite there being little evidence in their favour.

- There might not be a large amount of testimony to miracles, but there shouldn't be. Miracles are relatively isolated events which may happen to individuals in private. Further, the New Testament fishermen would have been more educated in what they needed to know than many at that time. It seems to be a sweeping statement that all claims to miracles come from ignorant and barbarous nations. Where are these? Have we not heard of claims that come from 'civilised' nations? It is reasonable to cite examples of claimed miracles from civilised nations as evidence in favour of a belief in miracles being convincing.

- Further, with regard to testimony, people who claim miracles seem to abandon reason when they do so. People love superstition and wonder, and telling such tales excites them. Also, a religious person may be subjective and may report a miracle to 'promote a holy cause'. There may indeed be something to gain from it. If reason is abandoned, this testimony would fail to convince us.

- Superstition and wonder can be soaked up by other claims or by reading certain books and watching certain films. There is no need to satisfy this desire for wonder by claiming a miracle. Also, would it be reasonable to suggest that a religious person should lie, even sacrifice their life, for a 'miracle' that they knew did not happen?

- All religions claim miracles. Hume suggests that a religion's authority is grounded in its belief in miracles. As they all claim different miracles, not all can be right. Each cancels the other out. Therefore, none of them are right. This gives a 'complete triumph for the sceptic'. It would be a fairly convincing argument in every day life to say that if a person's evidence for something conflicts with the evidence of others, then that evidence is pretty flimsy.

- It is not true that the authority of a religion is based upon the truth of a miracle. Also, just because there are a number of claims to something, it does not thereby make all of the claims wrong. Five people may claim that five different Shakespearean plays are 'the best'. It does not mean that all five of them must be wrong. So, Hume is wrong when he says that religious claims cancel each other out.

- It is unreasonable to believe that the whole structure of the world has been demolished by a miraculous act which breaks the established laws of nature. God has established a structure, as the Design argument states, and this is the pattern of the universe. Once established, these laws cannot be broken. So the argument against miracles is an argument in favour of regularity. The latter is a convincing argument.

- It is perfectly reasonable to accept that a miracle can break the structure of the universe; that is why it is called a miracle. Things are designed all the time, for example cars, televisions, with the design aim that they work. However, these things do stop working. There is nothing unreasonable in this observation.

- Claimed miracles are no more than psychosomatic cures. No intervention from God has occurred; no laws of nature have been broken. All such claims are unreasonable and unconvincing as it is simply 'mind over matter', the placebo effect. Scientific evidence does not support claims, for example, faith healers, who claim miraculous cures via 'laying on of hands' for ailments such as blindness, deafness and AIDS.

- There are, however, people who claim that miraculous healings can be performed. There are stories in the Bible of Jesus curing a man born blind, for example. Today, many claim to have left crutches behind at Lourdes in France. The Pentecostal/Charismatic movement claims to have initiated miracles in its meetings. A well-known example is the Azusa Street Revival in Los Angeles, led by William Seymour. These meetings began in 1906 and continued until 1915. These meetings contained not only miracles but other spiritual experiences, such as speaking in tongues. So 'mind over matter' arguments against miracles are unconvincing.

- Many miracles are private events. They happen to a person who has no one else to confirm the claim. Their claim is therefore unconvincing as it would be unreasonable to believe something on the basis of uncorroborated evidence. This argument against miracles based upon the fact that we ask for empirical confirmation of claims, is convincing.

- Bultmann said that the stories of miracles in the Bible, including the Virgin Birth and the Resurrection, are myths. He said that once the myth is stripped away from the stories, we see the events as either the ways that people interpreted their experiences, or indeed a literary device for explaining the event the 'best they could'. So, the belief in miracles as literal historical events would be unreasonable and unconvincing.

- Another argument against miracles is that they could just be 'coincidences'. If someone has made a 'miraculous' recovery at the same time that a loved one prayed for them, it may seem to be as a result of divine intervention, but it would have happened anyway. There is absolutely no evidence that could prove that it was not a coincidence. So this is a convincing argument against miracles.

- If God is said to be timeless, then past, present and future are bound up in one. This means that God is outside of time and it is illogical and against reason to say that this God, who is outside of time, can act in time. A timeless God not being able to act to perform miracles is therefore a convincing argument against them happening.

- Other miracles have been claimed to happen publicly. Certain television channels broadcast 'miraculous' events that all can see. Newspapers report stories of multiple people having visions of the Virgin Mary at the same time. Jesus performed a number of public miracles. Surely such multiply attested (empirically confirmed?) stories could convince us of the occurrence of miracles?

- Even if miracles are myths, it does not mean that belief in them as a means by which some truths are shown is unreasonable. 'Miracle' stories in the Bible reveal something of how Jesus' contemporaries viewed him. Even if the Resurrection itself is a myth, it still describes the impact that Jesus' life had on the disciples. So, to interpret this impact in a miraculous way is a valid interpretation.

- There are some instances where the medical profession has said that people with a certain condition have no chance of survival. If they do survive, then surely it would be reasonable of us to state that their survival was miraculous. Whether the survival was the result of divine activity or not, it can reasonably be called 'a miracle'.

- Aquinas' God was a timeless God and Aquinas certainly believed that God can act to perform miracles either as Primary Cause or acting through another, a Secondary Cause. Also the notion that a timeless God acts timelessly, although hard to put into words, is still a reasonable suggestion. So saying that God is timeless, thus miracles do not happen, is not necessarily a convincing argument.

Is a belief in miracles essential for a religious believer?

A dictionary definition of 'essential' is 'absolutely necessary' or 'relating to the essence or most fundamental part'. So this question is investigating whether believing in miracles is at the very core of a faith or whether it is an element that is at the very least peripheral, at the most disposable.

Definition of 'miracle'

In order to answer whether belief in miracles is essential one needs to explain the definition of miracle one is working with. The definition being used will lead to different answers. For example, let's take a miracle as 'a coincidence that can be taken religiously as a sign' and a miracle as 'a break in the law of nature by God'. The former may be seen as something 'lucky' an event that can also be seen as a miracle. Perhaps this is not essential but rather fortuitous. However, the latter definition would be seen by some people as being essential to their faith.

Essential for whom or what?

This is another important consideration. You will be able to give a more comprehensive answer if there is consideration of the context of 'essential'. Is belief in miracles essential for the faith of an individual believer? Is it essential for belonging to a particular faith? For some faiths, accepting certain creeds is essential. This creed may well form part of worship. Is it essential that the believer accepts this creed wholeheartedly or is it enough to state acceptance as part of the act of worship?

Grade boost

In an examination answer differing definitions should be pointed out to the examiner and you should remember to state the definitions being referred to in your answer.

Grade boost

Include some of the creeds that you were asked to research in Topic 1 as examples.

Purpose

Essential is very often followed by an 'if'. For example, 'it is essential that you revise *if* you want to get a good A-Level grade'. Or 'it is essential that he eats protein and lifts weights *if* he wants to build up his muscles'. It may be helpful to you to write in this way when considering essential for whom or what. This will then give you a method of analysing information. For example, 'believing in miracles is essential for some believers *if* they want to fit in with the mainstream view of their faith'.

An example: The Resurrection of Jesus

The Resurrection of Jesus along with the Virgin Birth are arguably the most famous miracles to consider. What follows is an introduction to some key areas for discussion with regard to Jesus' Resurrection.

Essentially four views exist concerning the New Testament Resurrection stories. One is that it is a fact of history (traditional Christian view). The second is that it was an error; Christians got it wrong for whatever reason. The third is that it was a natural phenomenon re-explained supernaturally (modern rationalist view). The fourth is that it is a myth/legend, a religious idea put into historical form (modern mythical view).

Does a believer have to accept the Resurrection of Jesus as an example of a miracle? Is it fundamental, is it essential for them individually or as part of Christianity as a whole? Belief in Resurrection itself is an old belief and one which exists in religions today. It is one of the 13 principles of faith of Maimonides in Judaism, and Orthodox Judaism accepts Resurrection of body and soul. For others Resurrection is of the soul not the body. As it is an ancient Jewish belief, the claim that Jesus rose would not be out of the ordinary. His Resurrection is mentioned many times in the Gospels and in other books of the New Testament. The fact that it is mentioned many times may give it credibility. This is called 'multiple attestation'. However, the accounts do vary.

For the Church Fathers, belief in bodily Resurrection was an essential part of the Christian hope. St Paul said in I Corinthians 15 that it is because Jesus was raised that we know his followers will also rise. The ancient Christian creeds state belief in Resurrection.

Is it essential to believe that it happened as historical fact or is it simply essential to believe in the meaning of it as a myth? Some would argue that to deny the miracles of the Bible, including the Resurrection and the Virgin Birth is to declare the whole of the Bible as 'fake'. In *Religion today* Albert Mohler said Christians must face the fact that a denial of the Virgin Birth and Resurrection of Jesus is a denial of Jesus as the Christ. He said that the Saviour who died for our sins and was raised was none other than the baby who was conceived of the Holy Spirit, and born of a virgin. These beliefs are not just stand-alone. They are an irreducible part of the Biblical revelation about the person and work of Jesus Christ. With that the Gospel stands or falls. He concluded that if the Bible is regarded as being wrong in what it says about Christ, then obviously the authority of the Bible in any sense is gone.

So for many, belief in Jesus' Resurrection is essential to the integrity of the Bible and essential to the integrity of Christianity as a whole. It may even be seen that to deny the miracle of the Resurrection is to deny their faith.

Julian N. Hartt wrote in *Christian Theology* (1982): 'The Resurrection of Jesus Christ is the absolutely crucial miracle. It embraces the natural forces of life and death on the one hand, and such historical realities as the demonic pride of Israel's messianism and the imperial might of Rome on the other. In the Resurrection of Jesus Christ, the ultimate salvation of the people of God is guaranteed. The life everlasting of traditional doctrine presupposes the miracle in which soul and body are reunited.' Here it is clear that belief in the miracles of the Resurrection and the Virgin Birth is essential.

However, others do not accept the bodily Resurrection of Jesus as a miracle and do not see this as an essential part of their faith. Some look to the words of St Paul in I Corinthians 15 where it is said that Resurrection involves a transformation: 'It is sown a physical body, it is raised a spiritual body.' For some believers, Jesus' Resurrection is taken to be a metaphor for a changed state of being and so belief in it as an historical event is not needed. An understanding of the metaphor is what is needed.

Bishop Ernest William Barnes (1874–1953) attacked the miraculous elements in the Christian tradition, including the Virgin Birth and Jesus' Resurrection. In *The Rise of Christianity* he wrote, 'Ignore the miracles of the New Testament and Christianity remains that same way of life, lived in accordance with Christ's revelation of God, which through the centuries men have been drawn to follow.'

On the Resurrection he says that it is a great essential truth of Christianity, but one 'which is quite independent of the question as to whether the body of Jesus was reanimated after his death. What matters is that Christians shall feel a spiritual power in their lives, which they can rightly interpret as that of the spirit of Jesus revealing, as in his teaching in Galilee, the wisdom and righteousness of God.' Some of his fellow bishops were really not too happy with this view but he is not alone in that view.

Many Christians state that if we were to find the tomb of Jesus then there would be bones in it. This view that the Resurrection is not a historical event in which Jesus' entire body got up and walked out, does not make any difference to the belief of those Christians. Their faith does not have this miracle as an essential part of it.

Grade boost

Remember to use scholars in your answer, such as the ones on this page. Also, give your opinion of their view.

3: 'Belief in miracles is essential to a religious believer.' Assess this view.

Agree	Disagree
• Miracles show God's love and power. They show that through Jesus God's victory over death, disease and disasters is possible. Miracles show that God wants to be involved with the world and without this involvement something essential would be lost in a faith that has a relationship with God.	• God's love and power need not be shown through miracles. Without a belief in miracles a believer still sees God's characteristics and intentions displayed in other ways, such as human love and acts of kindness. In fact miracles that help some and not others may actually seem to be the opposite of God's love.
• Miracles are recorded in sacred writings, so a belief in them is essential so as not to lose the integrity of the sacred writing. St Paul writes that Christ's victory over death is our promise that this will happen to us too. To deny miracles is to deny the validity of the holy book and to deny the faith. If the miracle stories are false then so is the whole of the holy book.	• Stories in holy books need not be regarded as literally true. Miracles may be regarded as myths (just as many view the Creation stories). They could illustrate such things as God's power or the authority of the religious leader as opposed to being literal accounts. Nothing essential is lost from a faith if the miracle stories are not historical fact. Likewise it does not deny the validity of a holy book if one rejects the miraculous elements of it. A car may have one part of it that is not working but that does not mean that one must scrap the whole car!
• Some denominations require acceptance of creeds which may include reference to belief in Jesus' Resurrection. The whole point of having a faith is that one accepts certain parts of it, such as a belief in the miraculous. Being a believer and not accepting the essence of what it means to be a part of that belief is like wishing to play a game of football without a football.	• Not all faiths would require a belief in creeds and/or miracles as their core. Hence a belief in miracles is certainly not essential. Surely it cannot be essential to a belief that one thing is accepted as if that one thing contains the complete essence of that faith? Within religions there are so many component parts that make up the religion as a whole that no one thing can define it. Within Christianity, for example, belief in God, belief in love as shown in I Corinthians 13 could be considered essential, whereas a belief in miracles may not be. There is no point to miracles if I have no love, as without love 'I am a noisy gong or a clanging cymbal' (verse 1). As verse 13 says 'but the greatest of these is love'.
• Some would argue that belief in miracles is essential as they give credibility to the status of the performer of the miracle. For example, in Matthew 8 verse 17 it is claimed that the healing of the centurion's servant is to fulfil a prophecy of Isaiah 'he took our infirmities and bore our diseases'.	• Others would argue that the credibility of Muhammad, Jesus or the Buddha, for example, is not won or lost on their performance of miracles. Their credibility still remains as there are so many other wonderful deeds they performed, as well as many inspirational stories surrounding them. Indeed it should be noted that not all faiths view miracles as being important. We should also be guarded about giving special significance to miracles or signs done on demand.
• A miracle such as Jesus' Virgin Birth is absolutely essential as it gives a special and unique significance to Jesus. The event proves Jesus' status as God's son. In the time of St Augustine it was essential that Jesus was the only one to be born of a virgin as Jesus was then not tainted with Adam's sin which was passed on by the physical sexual act.	• Nothing essential is lost from Christianity if the Virgin Birth is not considered miraculous. Extraordinary births were a popular literary genre in the ancient world. Tales surrounding births of emperors and other leaders (the Buddha is said to have been born in a most unusual way!) were very common. Some therefore argue that the Virgin Birth is a myth. Many claim that it was a story made up as part of that popular literary genre in order to cover up Jesus' illegitimacy. Jesus can still be viewed as someone unique with very special significance even if there is no miraculous birth.
• Also use information from the previous text regarding definition of miracle, essential for whom or what and the information on the Resurrection in order to provide an assessment.	• Also use information from the previous text regarding definition of miracle, essential for whom or what and the information on the Resurrection in order to provide an assessment.

Key Term

Entropy = inevitable and steady deterioration of a system.

AO1 information on this topic is on pages 63–76.

Can religion and science be reconciled?

There is much information elsewhere in this guide to help you answer this question. Relevant materials could include the differing interpretations of Creation stories (literal does not leave room for reconciliation whereas non-literal does). The Big Bang theory can involve an evaluation of whether God was needed to cause it. Continuous creation may or may not involve God. The evolutionary material on Darwin and Dawkins can show a complete lack of reconciliation (but see the anthropic principle later on).

In the examination there are at least four possible questions on this topic:

1. How far can religious and scientific views be reconciled?
2. How far can religious and scientific views on the origins of the universe be reconciled?
3. How far can religious and scientific views on the origins of human life be reconciled?
4. How far can religious and scientific views on the origins of the universe and of human life be reconciled?

Depending on the actual question asked, you will be able to tailor your material to suit that question. What follows is some new material that can be included in the debate regarding reconciliation of religion and science's views on the origins of the universe and of human life. At the end of this material, you will find one question dealt with in a worked answer which includes material from across this topic.

Stephen Hawking in *A Brief History of Time* (1988) said that the universe had no beginning or end. The universe is here as a result of an infinite, cyclical series of Big Bangs and Big Crunches. So, what does this mean for reconciliation? It could mean no precise moment of cosmic origin, so no role for God. As Hawking asked, 'What place therefore for a Creator?'

But, lack of a starting point does not rule out God. There is no single point in time of Creation, but God exists outside the series of Big Bangs and Big Crunches. There is no reason for God to be involved in this cyclical process.

Roy Peacock, in 1990, wrote a considered response to Hawkings's book entitled *A Brief History of Eternity*. He said Hawking was wrong to say the universe had no beginning or end. Imagine a person bouncing a ball. They would have to start the ball bouncing. The first bounce would be the highest, then the second, third and so on would be less high. **Entropy** would take its toll and eventually the ball would no longer bounce. The universe following a process of expansion and contraction (Big Bangs and Big Crunches) would follow the same pattern. Just as the bounce of a ball needs a beginning and an end, so does the universe.

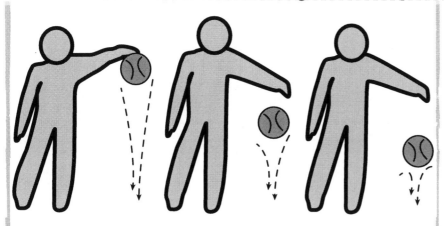

Peacock says that science does its best to look at the 'how' but with God in the system, the 'why' can be answered.

Russell Stannard's ideas can be found in *Grounds for Reasonable Belief* (1989). He said that religion and science are both searching for truth. Science's search is impersonal and looks to the intellect. Religion's search is personal and engages the whole person.

Further, he re-defines God and creation. God is not an object that exists, like an apple exists. God is the source of all things in existence. Origins and creation are two different things, says Stannard. If we ask 'How did the world start?' that is a question about origins. This is a question for scientists, the best explanation at present being the Big Bang. The creation question, though, is different. This involves questions like 'Why am I here?', 'What keeps existence going?', 'Why is there something rather than nothing?' These are questions for religion and they concern the source of all existence.

What happened at the beginning is not the biggest question. What is important is what is happening now. God's action is not to be thought of as one action that happened a very long time ago. God's action is throughout all time.

So, he does not accept the typical idea of a Creator God that some have, where God decided at one point in time to light the fuse to cause the Big Bang. But the idea of a Creator God can still exist whilst also accepting the Big Bang.

With regard to evolution, Stannard accepts that evolution appears to have no need for a designing God. But, while life seems to evolve randomly, the conditions needed for evolution to happen are so precise, they cannot be random.

⊚)》《《《 quicKfire

⑨ Does science answer questions about origins or creation?

⑩ Does Stannard allow for reconciliation of religion and science?

Anthropic principle = *anthropos* is the Greek word for man. This principle says that God designed the conditions necessary for evolution to occur.

Immanent = present within and throughout.

Transcendent = beyond ordinary experience.

Stretch and challenge

Prepare a talk on 'what religion can learn from science and what science can learn from religion'.

The anthropic principle

This is a more modern development of the design argument. It says that if the fundamental constants of the universe had been any different then the development of life would not have happened. In fact, there probably would not have been any life at all. The conditions of the universe are just right for humans. The odds of this happening through sheer chance are slim. The simplest explanation is that the universe was designed this way and, being designed this way, it allows for evolution to happen. The highest point so far in God's design is the emergence of human life.

Arthur Peacocke says that science can deepen our understanding of religious matters. He says there is not a 'blanket' separation of science (facts) and religion (moral, spiritual). Both make claims, both try to describe reality. Both should be evaluated to determine whether they are reasonable. Both should allow themselves to re-examine and change their own ideas.

Religion must face evolutionary ideas, as it should face all scientific 'truths'. But it should embrace evolution as a scientific discovery. This positive response can allow it to be consistent with religion. Science, too, must face the religious truths' of morality and spirituality that can be brought into the practice of science.

This leads to a mutual respect. Each must listen to the other. In this way, they can be seen as two approaches that work together to discover the true nature of reality. The more science can discover about the world, the more it can discover about God. Science is ongoing, just as God is still creating through the evolutionary process. God creates through the evolutionary process that science has discovered.

God's activity and the processes of the natural world are not separate. God is **immanent** in creation, yet is also **transcendent**. Peacocke uses several analogies to describe this. One is to imagine that the world is like a sponge floating on the sea of greatness. The sea is 'other' yet the sponge is part of it. This God is one who is 'other' yet as near to you as is your own breast.

Teilhard de Chardin's views can be read in *The phenomenon of man*. This was finished in 1930 and published posthumously in 1955. He wanted to reconcile evolutionary biology and religion. These would give a complete view of the universe. Evolution and a belief in God go hand in hand. The process of evolution is examined from atoms, cells, to the simple forms of life and eventually to humans. As this process continues he observes that as things become more complex they become more conscious. So where is this process leading us? There is a point at which the whole evolutionary process will have its fulfilment. He calls this final destiny of evolution the Omega point. That is the Cosmic Christ. All things would find their fulfilment in Christ. The meaning of evolution is in the life of Christ.

It was originally criticised by the Roman Catholic Church as being against Orthodox teaching. However, the Roman Catholic Church later on was more supportive of it, notably Pope Benedict XVI.

For Darwinian evolution, evolution is driven by the present into the future, from the start onwards. For de Chardin, the Omega point, the end point drives the whole process. This can almost be imagined as a magnet, where every step in the evolutionary process brings humanity nearer to converging with the Cosmic Christ.

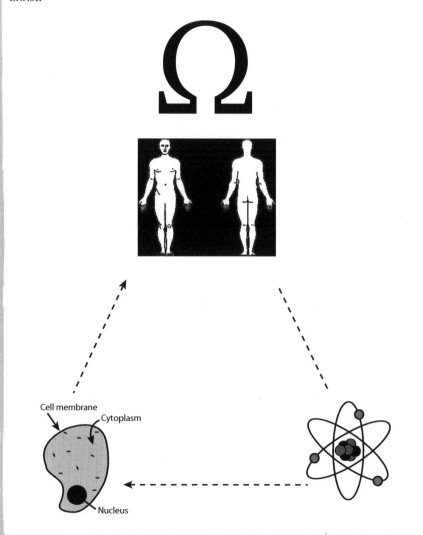

Grade boost

Remember that for the higher levels, it is important that points are not just stated. Your answer needs to show an understanding of what is being said, in this instance what de Chardin actually means. In preparation for an AO2 question you also need to consider what is convincing and unconvincing about the views that you are referring to.

4: 'Religious and scientific views can be reconciled.' Assess this view.

Agree

- If we accept a non-literal account of Creation stories then reconciliation is possible. For example, the one day of Genesis could be viewed as a metaphor for a period of time as opposed to 24 hours. It could also be seen to tie in nicely with evolution as what we see in Genesis is the development from very simple life to the end point thus far, humans.

- Many accept that the Big Bang happened but recognise that a reason for it happening cannot be given. Their explanation is that God was somehow responsible for the Big Bang and this provides us with the answer to the 'why' question.

- Their views can be reconciled if we accept that God is somehow in control of the evolutionary process. The traditional view of God is that God is creator and sustainer. This reconciles well with the anthropic principle's idea that God made the conditions necessary for evolution. God's sustaining of the universe is essentially the same as God's continual creation of it. As Peacocke pointed out, if God is the Creator of natural processes then science does allow us to discover more about God. Thus religious and scientific ideas are in harmony.

- Both religion and science show humans as being the most important species. In the Christian and Jewish accounts humans are made last, in the image of God, thus showing their special status. At present in evolutionary terms humans are the most developed and due to this one could argue, the most important species.

- They both work together to form a complete picture of the world. Religion answers the 'why' and science answers the 'how'. This shows reconciliation as they have different means of achieving the one aim, which is to give a complete picture. One without the other is of no use. Both together give us a harmonious picture.

Disagree

- However, if a literal interpretation of Creation stories is taken then no reconciliation is possible. The stories regarding Brahma, Vishnu and Shiva or the literal six days that it took God to create the earth simply cannot be reconciled with the scientific accounts of the Big Bang or evolution. They are poles apart.

- Others say that no reconciliation is possible as the Big Bang explains everything, leaving no room for God. The fact that we cannot adequately explain why the Big Bang happened does not leave us with 'God did it' as the only solution. Even if we do not know the answer to the question 'why' if we do not feel that this is an important question then there is no issue here.

- However, others would argue that evolution alone without reference to God is perfectly adequate as a theory. Darwin has explained how species have come to be as they are now and this does not reconcile with the religious ideas of fixity of species. Neither is including God in the evolutionary process necessary. It seems absurd to include another entity into a scenario when there is absolutely no need for another entity in order to explain the scenario. Also in terms of continuous creation as a scientific theory, this has now been abandoned. Perhaps the same should happen for it in its religious usage too.

- The importance of humans in both religion and science is due to very different reasons. In the religious accounts humans are given their importance by God. Without this gift they would not have a special significance. However, in the scientific sense, humans gain their importance due to the faculties that they have developed over time. This they use themselves in order to develop even further. So science and religion may 'end up' with a similar view but they have got there through very different means. So this shows no reconciliation at all.

- They answer different questions. They cannot be reconciled at all. In fact they are absolutely not supposed to be reconciled. Science and religion are two distinct disciplines. Artificially pushing them together would be like trying to make a sandwich which combines fish and custard.

- Both religion and science allow for a spiritual aspect. Many scientists would not deny the capacity of humans to feel deeply moved or a sense of awe. Some scientists believe we have a soul. Indeed there is an experiment often cited where a soul having left the body leaves the body lighter. Perhaps science can help religion in a quest for the neurological and/or physical explanations of the soul.

- Stannard makes some valid points when he redefines God and creation. These new definitions take into account modern developments in science. Religion need not shy away from science; it has nothing to be afraid of. If religion does not take scientific developments into account then not only will it get left behind by today's world but it will also lose out on its quest for and share of the truth.

- The view of de Chardin that the final destiny of evolution is the Omega point, may be a way of reconciling religion and science. His view of consciousness is becomingly increasingly popular. The view of consciousness stems from scientific understanding of the quantum world. The idea that there is a unifying field of consciousness held in being by God, the compassionate consciousness could reveal to us so much about what Jesus was and what he achieved. If we see the Cosmic Christ at the Omega point as the culmination of evolution, we could see Jesus as the one whose consciousness became completely at one with the compassionate consciousness. We could take this to mean that Jesus was one who became what we could become; one who developed everything that it is possible for a human to develop. As Jesus is a human being who is fully divine his consciousness was at one with God's consciousness. His life lived in complete awareness of God is the high point of evolution. Because the idea of consciousness and energy fields is explained to us by science, religion can be reconciled to it as de Chardin shows that a modern religious scheme needs it.

- The soul and/or spirituality in religion is an entirely different concept than anywhere else. It cannot be reconciled with any scientific explanation of it. There is no universally accepted definition of the soul across the religions, nor is its function the same. In Western religions the soul is a God-given thing which allows humans to worship God. If a soul is even accepted in science it certainly does not have this origin.

- However, is Stannard's redefinition of God and creation justified? Some would argue that definitions are steadfast for all time and just because society changes does not mean that all of religion's definitions should also change. We can redefine all we want but that does not make the new definitions correct. Stannard may be accused of making new definitions which try to fit a template that they really do not fit into.

- However, de Chardin has been criticised. Is it really true that the more complex something is the more conscious it becomes? Perhaps an adult gorilla is more conscious than a newly born baby. He has also been accused of 'gambling' everything on the future, which critics say is an inspired guess as opposed to a legitimate theory. Others argue that his work distorts Biblical eschatology in the way that he seems to give the cosmos divine attributes. Others describe this as 'divinising the cosmos' or burying the divine in the cosmos. Lastly, if the process to the Omega point is inevitable what happens to human freedom? So, religion and science cannot be reconciled as trying to explain religion in evolutionary terms simply does not work.

Summary: Is religious faith compatible with scientific evidence?

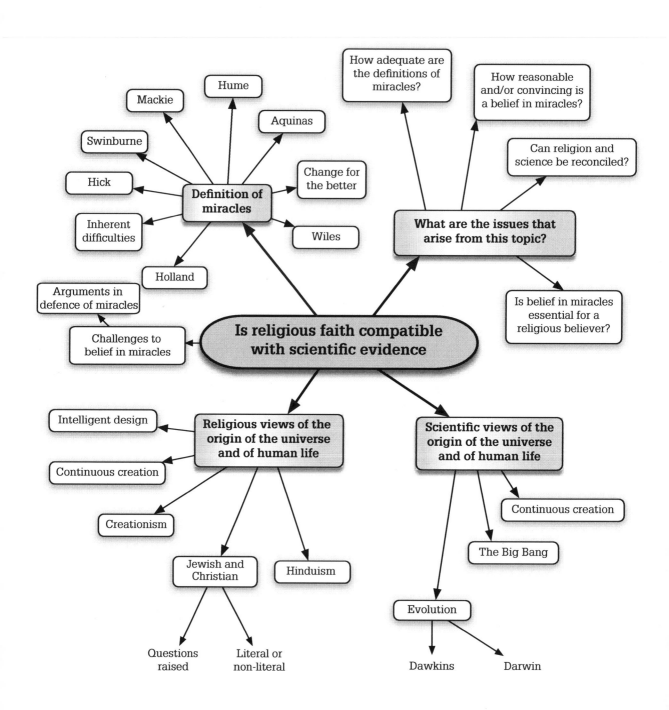

- How adequate are the definitions of miracles?
- How reasonable and/or convincing is a belief in miracles?
- Can religion and science be reconciled?
- **What are the issues that arise from this topic?**
- Is belief in miracles essential for a religious believer?

- Hume
- Mackie
- Aquinas
- Swinburne
- Change for the better
- Hick
- **Definition of miracles**
- Inherent difficulties
- Wiles
- Holland
- Arguments in defence of miracles
- Challenges to belief in miracles

Is religious faith compatible with scientific evidence

- Intelligent design
- Continuous creation
- **Religious views of the origin of the universe and of human life**
- Creationism
- Jewish and Christian
- Hinduism
- Questions raised
- Literal or non-literal

- **Scientific views of the origin of the universe and of human life**
- Continuous creation
- The Big Bang
- Evolution
- Dawkins
- Darwin

4: Are we 'free beings'?

When revising 'Are we free beings?' you should focus on the main topics and issues. You should understand the concepts of hard and soft determinism, Libertarianism and nature and nurture. Also, you should be able to investigate the religious concepts of predestination and free-will with reference to authorities who exemplify these concepts. Concepts of determinism/free-will and their relationship with religious beliefs and moral attitudes need to be studied. Finally, you need to evaluate the issues arising from these topics from a variety of viewpoints using scholarly opinion, and an informed conclusion must be reached.

Revision checklist

Tick column 1 when you have completed brief revision notes.
Tick column 2 when you think you have a good grasp of the topic.
Tick column 3 during final revision when you feel you have mastery of the topic.

			1	2	3
What is meant by determinism?	p94	Hard determinism			
	p97	Soft determinism			
	p97	Libertarianism			
	p98	Tha nature/nurture debate			
Religious concepts of predestination	p104	Texts			
	p106	Augustine			
	p107	Calvin			
Religious concepts of free-will	p110	Texts			
	p112	Pelagius			
	p113	Arminius			
	p115	Luther and Erasmus			
The relationship between concepts of determinism/free-will and religious beliefs and moral attitudes	p116	Determinism			
	p117	Free-will			
	p118	The relationship: the other way around?			
What are the main issues that arise from 'Are we free beings?'	p120	The Human Genome Project			
	p121	Genes or Environment?			
	p123	How far does an individual have free choice?			
	p127	Can predestination and free-will be reconciled?			
	p129	What influences religious beliefs and moral attitudes?			

Key Terms

Behaviourism = refers to the school of psychology founded by John B. Watson based on the belief that behaviours can be measured, trained, and changed.

Determinism = the philosophical idea that every event is causally decided by prior events.

Hard determinism = human behaviour is completely decided by external factors.

Grade boost

Get the concepts right first. There is little point in simply reeling off a list of scholars with a little bit of information about their work if you do it in a vacuum. By all means, always include scholarly views where you can show a better understanding of the concepts *through* your inclusion of them.

Stretch and challenge

Research the work of two hard determinists to include their work in an essay.

① Why is hard determinism called 'incompatibilism'?

② Why is there no moral responsibility in hard determinism?

③ Why in hard determinism is there no 'sin' in its usual sense?

What is meant by determinism?

Determinism means that an uncaused event is impossible. Cause leads to effect, so actions (effect) will have a cause that has come before. This includes the actions of humans. So, humans are not truly free. Our actions are determined by such things as our nature (our genes/the way we are 'made') and nurture (family background and upbringing, past experiences; essentially our environment). For religious determinists the actions may also be determined by God (see Predestination). We are not in control of what we do.

Hard determinism

This is also called incompatibilism. **Hard determinism** says that a belief in determinism is opposed to (or incompatible with) a belief in free-will. Free-will is an illusion. If anything must happen, then it is forced. If it is forced, it can't be free. There can also be no moral responsibility. We can't blame someone if they could not have acted differently. Equally, there is no need to praise good deeds either. The people who did them had no choice to do differently. People are different, not better or worse. In this sense, there is no 'sin' as such.

This is associated with scholars such as d'Holbach, Strawson and Smilansky, to name just a few.

Some branches of determinism:

1. **Scientific determinism** says that for every physical event there is a physical cause. This is mechanistic, the theory of universal causation. Thoughts and decisions are causally determined. Regularity means that complete prediction in our physical universe is, in theory, possible. This is associated with people such as Laplace and Newton.

2. **Historical determinism** says that there are universal laws that can allow us to predict the future direction that society will take. It suggests that societies work in a cause and effect way; that one type of society will lead to the development of the next one and so on. Some associate this with Marx but some would argue against him being a determinist.

3. **Theological determinism** says that God has determined the future. This is predestination (see work on this later).

4. **Psychological determinism** says that all human behaviour can in theory be predicted. Human behaviour is affected by heredity, society, culture and environment. **Behaviourism** would come under this umbrella term. It is a theory of learning based upon the idea that all behaviours develop via conditioning. Conditioning occurs through interaction with the environment. Behaviourists believe that our responses to external stimuli form our behaviours. These responses can be studied in a systematic and observable manner. Internal mental states play no part in this. There are two major types of conditioning.

Classical conditioning

Classical conditioning is a technique used in training behaviour. An automatic, unconditioned stimulus is coupled with an unconditioned response. Next, a previously neutral or conditioned stimulus is coupled with the automatic, unconditioned stimulus. Eventually, the previously conditioned stimulus becomes associated with the unconditioned stimulus and brings about a conditioned response.

Imagine that when you smelled pizza, you felt hungry. The smell of the pizza is the unconditioned stimulus. The feeling of hunger is the unconditioned response. Imagine that when you smelled pizza you also heard the theme tune to 'Match of the Day'. While the theme tune is not related to the smell of the food, if the theme tune were paired many times with the smell, the theme tune would eventually trigger the conditioned response of you feeling hungry. In this case, the theme tune is the conditioned stimulus.

Stretch and challenge
Make up a scenario for your own example of 'classical conditioning' along the lines of the two examples given on this page.

AO2 evaluative issues on this question are on pages 121–126.

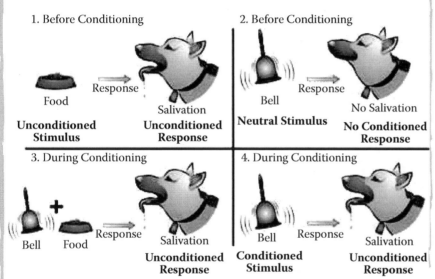

Operant conditioning

Operant conditioning is a method of learning that occurs through rewards and punishments for behaviour. Through operant conditioning, a link is made between behaviour and a consequence for that behaviour. Skinner used the term operant to refer to any 'active behaviour that operates upon the environment to generate consequences' (1953). Skinner was an American psychologist and behaviourist who read the works of Pavlov and Watson and was influenced by them. At the age of 24 Skinner enrolled in the Psychology Department of Harvard University.

Skinner conducted experiments using rats. With his enthusiasm and talent for building new equipment, Skinner constructed apparatus after apparatus. After a dozen pieces of apparatus Skinner invented the cumulative recorder. This was a mechanical device that recorded every response as an upward movement of a horizontally moving line. The slope showed rate of responding. This recorder revealed the impact of the items that were there on the response of the rats.

Skinner discovered that the rate with which the rat pressed the bar depended not on any preceding stimulus (as Watson and Pavlov had insisted), but on what followed the bar presses. This was new indeed. Unlike the reflexes that Pavlov had studied, this kind of behaviour operated on the environment and was controlled by its effects. Skinner named it operant behaviour. The process of arranging the items of reinforcement responsible for producing this new kind of behaviour he called operant conditioning.

- Positive reinforcers: imagine a student working hard at a piece of homework as the teacher will give them praise as a result.
- Negative reinforcers: imagine the last time a student did a poor piece of homework they got a long detention. So the behaviour of doing homework well has been negatively reinforced as the student has removed the need for a detention. A negative outcome has been avoided by performing a specific behaviour.

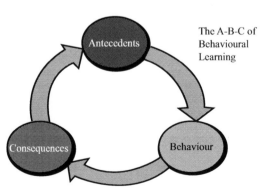

The A-B-C of Behavioural Learning

Soft determinism

William James coined this term. It is also called compatibilism. **Soft determinism** says that a belief in determinism is compatible with a belief in free-will. For a soft determinist, an act is free unless it has been forced by another person. They would argue that the choice you make will always have been determined, but if you have not been forced by a person, then it is still your free-will. In other words, all acts are *caused* but caused is not the same as forced or compelled. Forced, not caused, is the opposite of free. There are two types of cause:

1. **Internal.** These lead to voluntary acts, acting out of free-will according to what you want or do not want to do. For example, if I leave a concert because I do not like the music.

2. **External.** These are involuntary, where a person has been forced to act against what they may want or not want to do. For example, if I leave the concert because I have been ejected by security.

Unlike hard determinism, soft determinism does allow for moral responsibility in cases where the causes are voluntary. For example, if I choose not to give blood which could save someone's life, then I am morally responsible. However, if I cannot give blood to a person because I am of a different blood group, then I am not morally responsible.

Libertarianism

This is also an incompatibilist theory (as is hard determinism) but it is the complete opposite of hard determinism. For **Libertarianism** free-will and determinism are incompatible. So whereas hard determinists accept determinism and reject free-will, libertarians accept free-will and reject determinism. For Libertarianism liberty is truly real, so determinism cannot be true. Humans can choose different actions; therefore the future is 'open'.

- **The liberty of spontaneity** says that there are limits on a person's freedom in the sense that their nature or nurture makes certain choices easier or harder to make. But, they are still free to choose.

- **The liberty of indifference** is when a person is not bound by limits to their freedom such as heredity, upbringing and society. This is 'real' freedom.

There is a distinction between:

Personality: this can be known empirically by observing a person's behaviour. It is formed by genetics and environment. Our personality may *incline* us to choose or not to choose certain things. For example, a person who has had an upbringing which was aggressive and unloving may become aggressive and unloving. This has become part of their personality.

Moral self: this is ethical and 'kicks in' when we need to make a moral decision. It acts in deciding between what is our wish or inclination and what is our duty. The libertarian would say that in the above example the choice is down to the individual and the individual alone. So, they can freely choose to show aggression towards others or not. The moral self can make a causally undetermined choice to be calm and loving. So, the moral self can set aside and cancel out the personality.

Key Terms

Libertarianism = the freedom to choose – the opposite of determinism.

Soft determinism = human behaviour is determined by external factors, but free-will still exists.

Stretch and challenge

Research the work of two soft determinists, such as Hume, Ayer or Stace, to include their work in an essay.

quickfire

④ What are 'internal' causes?

⑤ What are 'external' causes?

⑥ Why is Libertarianism called 'incompatibilism'?

⑦ For libertarians are humans morally responsible? Why?

Humans are therefore morally responsible for their actions. This idea lies behind the notion of punishment. It is associated with scholars such as Lucretius, Kant and Mill.

Key Terms

Nature = that which is inherited.

Nurture = all environmental influences after conception.

Genes/nature versus environment/nurture

It is important to note at the start that there is not an accepted scientifically correct answer to the question on whether genes or environmental factors influence a human being. The beauty of the fact that influences on humans are debated is that you can research from both the nature and nurture sides and give a really interesting account, presenting the changing attitudes towards this topic. It is also very much ongoing, with new studies emerging on a daily basis. Many TV programmes are dedicated to the topic, sport analysts are intrigued by it and scientific research is homing in on it.

The aim of this section is to give you a framework within which to work, a platform to set you off on by (hopefully) stimulating an interest into this fascinating topic.

Stretch and challenge

Discuss, at the start of this topic, what characteristics you feel you have as a result of nature and/or nurture.

Definitions

Nature: this refers to the qualities that we are born with, anything determined by genes. These qualities are ones that stay the same regardless of where a person was born or raised. This includes traits that 'appear' as we mature. This is often called nativism.

Nurture: this says that at conception (as many say nurture 'kicks in' pre-natal) or birth, humans are a *tabula rasa*, a blank slate, which is then 'loaded' by our environment, which would include type of family upbringing, socio-economic status, the media and so on. (You will often read of environmental factors as being split into shared family factors and non-shared factors.) This view is often called empiricism.

Don't forget that intertwined with nature/nurture is determinism and Libertarianism. So, evaluating the relative strengths and weaknesses of determinism and Libertarianism is valid here. For example, if it is suggested that our traits are determined by our genes and/or environment then there may seem to be little room for free-will.

The history

1. In the late 1800s with the work of Darwin, it was very much nature/genetics that was regarded as the main influence on what a human becomes. In psychology, there was the work of Francis Galton in his book *Hereditary Genius: Its laws and consequences* (1869). His findings were that talented people came from talented families. 'Genius' is inherited and is the result of natural superiority. In 1883 he said that society could be improved by 'better breeding'. He said it would be 'quite practicable to produce a high gifted race of men by judicious marriages during several consecutive generations'. This became known as eugenics. In a positive sense this kind of approach could be used to try to eliminate certain inherited conditions. But abuse of it could lead to ethnic cleansing or compulsory sterilisation, both of which unfortunately have happened too often in human history.

2. In the 1920s data on human intelligence was analysed and some evidence seemed to suggest that there was a link between social class and intelligence as opposed to intelligence being inherited. So, a number of psychologists turned their attention to nurture. Hence, Watson's famous work of 1924:

   'Give me a dozen healthy infants and my own specific world to bring them up in and I'll guarantee to take any one at random and train him to become any type of specialist I might select – doctor, lawyer, artist, merchant, chef and yes, even a beggar and thief, regardless of his talents, penchants, tendencies, abilities, vocations and race of his ancestors.'

3. Nazi ideology rejuvenated the idea that there could be a master race, the Aryan race, a white race, and set about its policy to eliminate Jews, gypsies and homosexuals, to name a few. You can see the ideas of eugenics in here. Hitler's ideas, however, were embarrassed when Jesse Owens, a black man, won four gold medals in the Berlin Olympics of 1936.

4. From the 1940s this simplistic either/or choice faded. The role of both nature and nurture became the accepted norm. Different people gave differing amounts of 'weight' to each side. In 1999, Ridley said in his book *Genome: The autobiography of species in 23 chapters*:

   'Mother Nature has plainly not entrusted the determination of our intellectual capacities to the blind fate of a gene or genes; she gave us parents, learning, language, culture and education to program ourselves with.'

It may well be true to say that for some things, nature is solely responsible (certain diseases strictly identified as genetic or such things as eye colour). The same can be said for nurture (native language). But it seems that whilst gene disorders are the only cause of some diseases, for example haemophilia, the genetic part of the cause of many diseases, diabetes, for example, could be partial.

Stretch and challenge

Explain your response to the statements of Galton, Watson and Ridley.

However, the current trend seems to be that genes have to 'work in a context'. In other words the environment affects the extent to which a genetic trait will show itself. An example of this may be weight. Many would argue that weight is hereditary. Let's imagine that a person's genes are such that the person should be of a relatively heavy weight. However, let's imagine that the person loves sport, has the influence of many role models around her, has the facilities, she trains and is therefore never inactive. Would she not then weigh less that her genes predispose her to? Similarly, imagine that this same person lives in an area of deprivation, where food is of a limited kind and is not plentiful. Would the same happen?

So, gene–environment interaction may give us an alternative to choosing one or the other. The pendulum below is rather 'crude' in giving numbers to the relative roles of each but it is simply trying to show that there are degrees of influence, all of which interplay with each other.

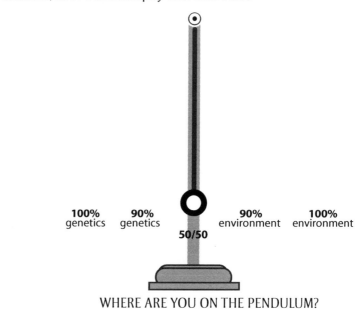

WHERE ARE YOU ON THE PENDULUM?

Grade boost

The specification asks you to discuss the issue of whether nature or nurture makes us what we are. This is a R.S. examination, so consideration should include reference to religious perspectives, although not specifically stated on the specification.

Religious perspectives

Here we find a variety of viewpoints. Some believe that a human, created by God has been given that human nature by God. This nature, some believe, is inherently good. They may be predisposed to follow a religious lifestyle, or at least have an inbuilt awareness of God as the Creator. So nature, the way one is born, affects behaviour.

Some would claim that we are predetermined to act in a certain way. St Augustine would say that our human nature very much affects our behaviour as this nature is a mass of corruption, predisposed towards doing what is sinful. In this sense, environmental factors will not be able to change what we do.

For others what 'I' am is the result of what 'I' have done in my preceding moments (Buddhism). There is no fixed human nature as 'I' am in a state of constant flux. 'I' may be influenced by anything around me which will make 'me' what I am. Karmic influences may also affect future existences.

Genes/nature

There is a hypothesis that suggests that there is what has become known as 'The God gene'. It has been identified as VMAT2 which makes a human inclined towards having a spiritual or mystical experience. The hypothesis comes from geneticist Dean Hamer, the director of the Gene Structure and Regulation Unit at the US National Cancer Institute, and author of the 2005 book *The God Gene: How Faith is Hardwired into our Genes*.

What is being claimed is that the human capacity to be spiritual is partly genetic. Being spiritual, it is claimed, gives those individuals survival advantage, as part of what it means to be spiritual is that the individual has more hope and confidence about the future. This in turn makes the individual feel happier, which benefits them physically and psychologically.

In *The New Scientist* 16 March 2005 there was an article written by Maggie McKee which said that genes contribute to religious inclination. This was based upon a US study of twins who were raised apart, which concluded that genes may help determine how religious a person is, further commenting that the effects of a religious upbringing may disappear over time. The study did not say that religious behaviour is completely the result of nature. But what it did say was that genes contribute around 40% to a person's religious behaviour.

Research by Laura Koenig, a psychology graduate student at the University of Minnesota in Minneapolis, US, has tried to tease apart how the effects of nature and nurture vary with time. Her study suggests that as adolescents grow into adults, genetic factors become more important in determining how religious a person is, while environmental factors decrease.

About a dozen studies have shown that religious people tend to share other personality traits, (although it is not clear whether these arise from genetic or environmental factors). These include the ability to get along well with others and being conscientious, working hard, being punctual, and controlling one's impulses.

Stretch and challenge

Look up studies on 'the God gene' and present a table of arguments 'for' and 'against' its existence.

A response

John Polkinghorne was asked for a comment on Hamer's theory. He said that 'The idea of a God gene goes against all my personal theological convictions. You can't cut faith down to the lowest common denominator of genetic survival. It shows the poverty of reductionist thinking.' Reductionist means 'an attempt or tendency to explain a complex set of facts, entities, phenomena, or structures by another, simpler set'. In other words, Polkinghorne is saying that the debate surrounding nature and nurture cannot be resolved by explaining it with reference to just one thing, in this case, genes.

Another response to Hamer's work was given thus: 'Religious belief is not just related to a person's constitution; it's related to society, tradition, character – everything's involved. Having a gene that could do all that seems pretty unlikely to me.' Hamer responded that the existence of such a gene would not be incompatible with the existence of a personal God: 'Religious believers can point to the existence of God genes as one more sign of the Creator's ingenuity – a clever way to help humans acknowledge and embrace a divine presence.'

The Nurture Assumption (1998, revised 2009) by Judith Rich Harris was a controversial book. She said that nurture from parents was far less important than had been thought to be the case thus far. She said that about 50% of 'how we are' is due to genetics, 50% by other factors. The 'nurture assumption' had been that this was parental influence. Harris denied this. Harris said that in evolutionary terms humans need to be a part of a group, a tribal identity. This gives humans a better chance of survival as humans can then fight off other tribes. Children, said Harris, learn this from their peers and this effect is stronger than any influence from parents.

If this is the case then a person's tendency towards being spiritual or belonging to a religious grouping will be due to their social network of friends. Of course, many disagree with this saying that if a person is raised in a religious family then they are more likely to be religious. Equally such a view would suggest that being born into a family of atheists would likewise result in the child being atheist. An interesting view on this comes from Dr. Olivera Petrovich – 'Babies are hard-wired to believe in God, and atheism has to be learned.' She continued, 'Atheism is definitely an acquired position.'

Stretch and challenge

Compile a list entitled 'what we learn form our parents' and 'what we learn from our peers'.

What does the research say?

There are literally thousands of studies out there, on identical twins, fraternal twins, adopted children, biological siblings brought up together and apart, IQ scores, personality traits and so on. The list is endless. It can't be the scope of this guide to analyse these (as that would take a library of guides!). However, it could be something that you could do. Including a summary of relevant studies and data from the fields of Biology, Sociology and Psychology can really give 'meat' to your answer.

For every argument in favour of nature, you will find one in favour of nurture. One example that I will indulge in is athletics. This is because as I write, the London 2012 Olympics are on. Very interesting research has been going on concerning the dominance of African American and Caribbean athletes. At the moment, of the 82 athletes to run under 10 seconds for the 100 metres, only one has been white (Christophe Lemaitre).

Grade boost

Include ideas from work on determinism and Libertarianism, referring to theories and scholars.

quickfire

(12) What is nativism?

(13) What is empiricism (in this context)?

(14) Galton's view – nature or nurture?

(15) Hitler's view – nature or nurture?

(16) What is the generally accepted view today – nature, nurture or both?

Michael Johnson, four-time Olympic gold medallist took part in a programme called '*Survival of the fastest*'. This was broadcast on Channel 4 5 July 2012. The aim was to discover whether the dominance of African athletes is due to their ancestry in the slave trade where plantation owners exercised hideous breeding programmes, which saw mass murder on slave ships and hence only the fittest survived. Experts on the programme concluded that this ancestry *did* contribute.

However, Johnson, speaking on the BBC on 9 August 2012, said that he felt environment was also very important. When discussing the Jamaican, Usain Bolt, Johnson said that the fact that sprinting was essentially the national sport of Jamaica, with role models being numerous and facilities being geared to sprinting, it is not surprising that children want to train to become athletes. He further commented that he felt that if a youngster grew up in an environment where there were five Christophe Lemaitres then this would be an advantage to them.

The Welsh hurdler Colin Jackson also took part in *The making of me,* broadcast on BBC1 on 31 July 2008. The aim of the investigation was whether his Jamaican heritage contributed to his ability. It was found that the 'fast twitch' muscles that enable someone to run fast were present in 80% of the white males sampled. But, they did not become world class athletes. Why? Is it because their environment did not encourage, allow or expect them to? Jackson concluded that there are many ingredients to a cake and that they all have to be put in the mix correctly in order to make the cake. He said that parents, school, facilities, your mental aspect and so on all play a part.

The religious concept of predestination and free-will

For a part (b) question in the examination you will need to consider whether both of these concepts can be accepted together or whether they are contradictory. Here, however, they will be dealt with separately, which will give you some information to use in both parts (a) and (b).

AO2 evaluative issues on this question are on pages 123–128.

Predestination

Predestination is a concept found in many world religions. Depending upon the religion, predestination will have a different meaning and a different usage. In religions that accept 'karma' predestination can be seen as that which is impersonal, that which determines the future. Others view predestination as 'fate'.

However, for theistic religions predestination is the belief that God determines all that we do. There is a causal chain that goes back to God. You may remember this idea from the Cosmological argument at AS. This means that God knows our actions in advance as God is omniscient and/or can decree our actions in advance as God is omnipotent. This applies to everything, including what happens at death. It is this concept of predestination that will be used in this guide.

Texts

It should be noted that some of the texts given below are open to interpretation. However, they are given in this guide as one of the interpretations is that they are quotations which relate to predestination. The quotations span across a number of religions to show that predestination is an idea which spans across a number of religions.

I add one note of caution though. These texts are here to simply direct candidates to areas of possible research into predestination. Candidates *must not just* write out these quotations in an examination and think that they have done enough. Such an approach would not even gain a lower level.

> 'For thou didst form my inward parts, thou didst knit me together in my mother's womb.'
>
> (Psalm 139:13)

Some people interpret this verse as showing the Psalmist's feeling of intimacy with God. This is due to the fact that even before birth he was under the control of God. God's omnipotence reflects the fact that God predestines. God is not just an observer but is in charge of a person's most 'secret' self.

It must be borne in mind though that this is certainly not the only interpretation of this verse and many would have a very different understanding of its meaning.

> 'Since his days are determined and the number of his months is with thee and thou hast appointed his bounds that he cannot pass.'
>
> (Job 14:5)

Grade boost

Research religious texts that show a belief in God's omniscience and/or omnipotence. This will mean you have evidence for such statements rather than just stating them.

Some people interpret this verse as Job showing the feebleness and frailty of humans. Human life is short; God has fixed or settled the number of days of life and these cannot be exceeded.

It must be borne in mind though that this is certainly not the only interpretation of this verse and many would have a very different understanding of its meaning.

> 'And we know that in all things God works for the good of those who love him, who have been called according to his purpose. For those God foreknew he also predestined to be conformed to the image of his Son, that he might be the firstborn among many brothers and sisters. And those he predestined, he also called; those he called, he also justified; those he justified, he also glorified.'
>
> (Romans 8:28–30)

The context of these verses is often said to be St Paul encouraging believers during severe persecution. The verses would give hope to believers in looking beyond the present, difficult time to an assurance of salvation.

Some people interpret this verse as a 'proof text' for Calvinists. They may interpret it as God predetermines the fate of every individual. Humans cannot affect their destiny. No one who is predestined will fail to be saved. Human response is not a determining factor in terms of salvation. Many Calvinists see this passage as being decisive in terms of showing beliefs about predestination to be right.

It must be borne in mind though that this is certainly not the only interpretation of this verse and many would have a very different understanding of its meaning.

Predestination is Article 17 of the 39 Articles of Faith in the Church of England: 'Predestination to life is the everlasting purpose of God, whereby, before the foundations of the world were laid, He has constantly decreed by His counsel secret to us, to deliver from curse and damnation those whom He has chosen in Christ out of mankind, and to bring them by Christ to everlasting salvation as vessels made to honour.'

> A Muslim quotation is: 'And it is not [possible] for one to die except by permission of Allah at a decree determined.'
>
> (Surah 3:145)

This is from Surah 3: Surah Al Imran. Imran in Islam is regarded as Mary's father. Many believe this chapter was revealed in Medina, possibly in the third year of the Hijra (Muhammad's migration to Medina in 622CE).

Some people interpret this verse as showing that Allah has destined a fixed term for humans which will be finished. After this fixed term is finished no one dies except by Allah's decision.

It must be borne in mind though that this is certainly not the only interpretation of this verse and many would have a very different understanding of its meaning.

> A Sikh quotation is: 'The year and moment of my death are fore ordained, come and anoint me with the oil of love.'
>
> (Guru I Gauril Rag)

Candidates should also understand that all three religions above also have a belief in human free-will. This will be seen later on in this guide. Whether these two beliefs can be reconciled will also be considered later under 'Evaluative issues'.

Stretch and challenge

Find other quotations relating to predestination. Compile them into a 'body of evidence' for predestination, for use in an essay.

Augustine (354–430CE)

You may remember studying Augustine's theodicy at AS. At the heart of Augustine's teaching is his belief in original sin. In the Garden of Eden, the first sin was committed. This was due to rebellion against God, stemming from '**concupiscence**'. This sin has been passed on through the physical act of sex, which Augustine observed is driven by concupiscence; therefore no one is free from this inherited sin. The only exception is Jesus, who did not inherit it; he was born of a virgin.

Coupled with this is the belief that humans were with Adam when he ate the forbidden fruit, seminally present, hence his guilt is ours. We are *massa peccati* a mass/lump of sin. However, we are still free. We have an 'essential human nature' (*liberium arbitrium*) which is free, but we have lost our moral liberty (*libertas*).

This means that we 'freely choose the bad'. Our sinful nature is a 'second nature' which overrides our essential human nature. So, although free, we cannot help sinning. This is a 'self-imposed bondage to sin'.

Due to this pessimistic view of human nature, we need God's grace and Christ's **atonement** to be able to do 'the good'. God chooses 'the Elect' to be saved. No-one knows who or why some are saved and some not. But, as all deserve to be punished as all are guilty, saving some shows a merciful God.

    ——— essential human nature = free
    - - - - 2nd nature = freely chooses what is bad

John Calvin (1509–1564CE)

Calvin was a Protestant Reformer who owes much of his thought to Augustine. At the heart of his views was the absolute power of God, God's election of those he chooses for salvation and predestination and the corrupted nature of humans. He denied free-will as humans are predestined in all of their choices.

Grade boost

When including quotations in your answers, remember, it is not about just learning them and writing them down. It is important that you comment on them, explaining the meaning of each. Also, consider whether predestination and free-will quotations are contradictory or whether a believer could reconcile the two beliefs.

It is vital that you emphasise that Augustine retains human freedom, God's omnipotence and God's omniscience.

quickfire

⑧ What is predestination?

⑨ What is concupiscence?

⑩ How, according to Augustine, are we free, yet will always choose 'the bad'?

Eternal reward or punishments are determined by God before birth. As Calvin said in *Institutes of the Christian religion* (1536, 1559):

'By predestination we mean the eternal decree of God, by which He has decided in his own mind what He wishes to happen in the case of each individual. For all men are not created on an equal footing, but for some eternal life is pre-ordained, for others eternal damnation.'

His 'Doctrine of Election' is also known as 'The Doctrine of the living saints'. His view on predestination is called 'Calvinist fatalism' by some as they say that his views are more fatal for an individual's fate than the views of others. Humans, said Calvin, cannot choose a good act apart from God's grace. God gives grace to those who are to be saved so God allows the Elect to have faith. This is 'justification by faith'. Humans do not co-operate as such with God's grace as this would imply they can resist it. This grace is impossible to resist. Those who have been predestined to suffer eternal damnation are called 'The Reprobates'. Election cannot be reversed. You cannot fall away (apostasy) from being the Elect; God will see to it that you persevere in your faith, nor can someone who has rejected Christ be saved. Salvation or damnation is assured.

This had implications for Ethics. The Elect were saved by God's grace and cannot be earned by human merits. If predestined to be a reprobate one would still be, even if that person lived a good life. This is because despite living a good life that person is still 'totally depraved' that is completely corrupt by nature. God's absolute power and supremacy means that God will know of this.

Later on in Calvinism believing that one was among the Elect did lead to problems for Protestants in a practical sense with the temptation being there to feel that behaviour was not important. As one cannot fall from grace, according to Calvin, it is easy to see how this view could come about.

Followers of Calvin gave 'Five Points' of belief:

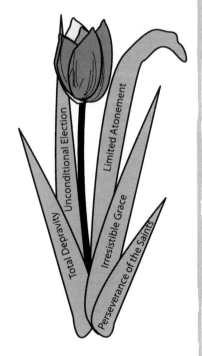

Total Depravity – humans are inherently (by nature) corrupt. They cannot choose the good.

Unconditional Election – there are no conditions attached to Election to salvation. It depends on nothing other than God's choice.

Limited Atonement – atonement means to be 'at one with' someone. Being at one with means in agreement with, in a restored relationship. To atone for something is often used in the context of making amends after an offence. In this context, Christ's death atones for the sins of the Elect. Christ's death puts the Elect back into the right relationship with God. The important point is that this is limited to the Elect.

Irresistible Grace – God's grace is given to the Elect, the ones God has chosen to receive salvation. This grace cannot be resisted.

Perseverance of the Saints – to persevere means to keep on going despite obstacles. The Elect are also called 'the living saints'. So, here Calvin is saying that God will make sure that the Elect do not commit apostasy (give up their faith). This is done via the power of the Holy Spirit.

A negative response

Bertrand Russell, a famous atheist and critic of religion, found the type of God described by Augustine and Calvin to be a 'monster' imposing its hellish will on humans. A God who punishes or rewards on the basis of God's own decision is unfair and immoral, says Russell. A good God would have chosen all to accept Jesus. This God's concern is to exercise power as opposed to being concerned about morality.

Free-will

This is a fundamental belief of many religious believers. The idea is that human free choice is vital and God-given. It is only in this way that humans can choose a relationship with God, which is the only true relationship and one in which their character can develop. At AS you may have seen this in the work of Irenaeus. Only by having free-will can humans be morally responsible for their actions.

As it stands, this may be interpreted as meaning that God does not decide people's fates or their actions. Many would argue that free-will is essential to the concepts of sin and the need for redemption. It also means that people truly are accountable for their actions on the Day of Judgement.

Free-will is found in the teachings of all major world religions. In the Eastern religions of Hinduism and Buddhism free-will is seen in the teachings of the law of karma. Humans are free to act and this will have karmic consequences.

In other religions free-will is an essential part of being created by God. In Genesis, Adam and Eve are given limited free-will. They can disobey God's instructions due to the fact of free-will. God commanded them that they may freely eat every tree in the garden except the tree of knowledge of good and evil. They were responsible for their disobedience when they chose to eat the fruit as they did it out of their own free-will.

Stretch and challenge

Find other quotations relating to free-will. Compile them into a 'body of evidence' for free-will, for use in an essay.

Texts

It should be noted that some of the texts given below are open to interpretation. However, they are given in this guide as one of the interpretations is that they are quotations which relate to free-will. The quotations span across a number of religions to show that free-will is an idea which spans across a number of religions.

I add one note of caution though. These texts are here to simply direct candidates to areas of possible research into free-will. Candidates *must not just* write out these quotations in an examination and think that they have done enough. Such an approach would not even gain a lower level.

In this section RSV is used for Bible quotations.

In the book of the Proverbs of Solomon, son of David, Wisdom is portrayed crying aloud in the streets that humans have turned away from wisdom, knowledge and instruction; they have turned away from God. So they will make their own destiny. The simple will be killed due to their turning away,

> 'Since they hated knowledge and did not choose to fear the LORD.'
>
> (2 Corinthians 9:7)

Some people interpret this verse as showing clear indication of free choice as to whether or not to follow what is wise, to follow God.

It must be borne in mind though that this is certainly not the only interpretation of this verse and many would have a very different understanding of its meaning.

> 'By faith Moses, when he had grown up, refused to be known as the son of Pharaoh's daughter. He chose to be mistreated along with the people of God rather than to enjoy the fleeting pleasures of sin. He regarded disgrace for the sake of Christ as of greater value than the treasures of Egypt, because he was looking ahead to his reward.'
>
> (Hebrews 11:24–26)

Some people interpret this verse as showing that Moses had free-will in terms of his 'refusal' and choice to be 'mistreated'.

It must be borne in mind though that this is certainly not the only interpretation of this verse and many would have a very different understanding of its meaning.

The background of the following quotation may be in Jewish Temple life. There were two chests for alms; one was for alms that had to be given. The other was for free-will offerings. Some may grudgingly give what they were told to give. Others may give lovingly out of pity for the poor.

'Each of you should give what you have decided in your heart to give, not reluctantly or under compulsion, for God loves a cheerful giver.'

(2 Corinthians 9:7)

Some people interpret this verse as St Paul saying that all giving can be done as a voluntary act. All acts can be free offerings of the heart.

It must be borne in mind though that this is certainly not the only interpretation of this verse and many would have a very different understanding of its meaning.

When Jesus speaks of his own death, which he freely chooses to give, he said,

'No one takes it from me, but I lay it down of my own accord. I have authority to lay it down and authority to take it up again.'

(John 10:18)

The 'no one' is emphatic and 'I' is said twice. Some people interpret this verse as Jesus saying that his life was his own (with the authority of God) to choose what he was to do with it.

It must be borne in mind though that this is certainly not the only interpretation of this verse and many would have a very different understanding of its meaning.

A quotation from the Quran from the Surah Al-Baqarah: 'the cow':

'Indeed, those who disbelieve – it is all the same for them whether you warn them or do not warn them – they will not believe.'

(Surah 2:6)

Some people interpret this verse as a stubborn refusal to believe which is performed out of complete free-will.

It must be borne in mind though that this is certainly not the only interpretation of this verse and many would have a very different understanding of its meaning.

From the Surah Al-Kahf: 'the cave':

'And say, "The truth is from your Lord, so whoever wills – let him believe; and whoever wills – let him disbelieve."'

(Surah 18:29)

Some people interpret this verse as saying that free-choice will be the factor which determines whether a person will believe or not, nothing else.

It must be borne in mind though that this is certainly not the only interpretation of this verse and many would have a very different understanding of its meaning.

Stretch and challenge

Apart from evidence in religious texts, list why religious believers may have a belief in free-will.

Pelagius (354–420/440CE)

Pelagius was an **ascetic**. Some refer to him as a monk but others deny this. He visited Rome where he was appalled by what he found. The life being lived there was the complete opposite of his asceticism. He found it indulgent and morally lax. He also disliked the grandeur within the Church, especially the Papacy. He firmly believed that these low moral standards in Rome were due to the doctrine of divine grace as if people had adopted an 'anything goes' attitude. On one occasion he heard a bishop quote from Augustine's *Confessions* 'Give me what you command and command what you will'. Pelagius believed that this made humans appear as mere robots, denying the traditional Christian teachings on free-will and grace. This, thought Pelagius, endangered the entire basis of morality.

Pelagius said that grace may help in achieving salvation but it is not necessary for it. Humans can resist anything, as they have free-will. His view on free-will was similar to the Stoics, which also may have been the root of his absolute belief in a practical faith and moral virtue. This may well have made him even more determined in his ascetic lifestyle.

He denied the doctrine of original sin. Original sin says that all humans are born sinful and can only be saved by the unmerited grace of God received through Christ and the Church. Pelagius found this despicable. He said that God is fair and it would be unfair to punish humans for the sins of Adam and Eve. Adam's sin affected only Adam. Human nature was perhaps modified but not corrupted by sin. Adam set a bad example, but Christ set a good example.

His view of human nature was much more optimistic than Augustine's. He denied predestination. He believed in true human free-will. His view of free-will is called Pelagianism. We have free-will so sin can be avoided. We are free to choose between good and evil thus he was freeing humans from the guilt of Adam.

Pelagius said the view of Augustine, which said that humans would go to hell for sins that they could not avoid doing, was completely against the doctrine of free-will. As we are free, we are morally responsible for our actions. Pelagius rejected predestination as it takes freedom and responsibility away. His view was seen as a **heresy**. Karl Barth, seemingly sadly, once described British Christianity as 'incurably Pelagian'. People accused Pelagius of emphasising human choice far more than human dependency on God or Christ's work to redeem humans.

Key Term

Heresy = view which is against the accepted view.

quickfire

⑪ Why did Pelagius reject original sin?

Jacobus Arminius (1560–1609CE)

Arminius was a Dutch theologian who criticised the Calvinist doctrine of predestination. He did have an element of free-will in his beliefs. Humans were affected by original sin and so could not, in *that* condition, choose God. But God gives grace that removes the taint of The Fall thus allowing humans to choose God of their own free-will. This is done via the Holy Spirit enabling those who wish to find God to do so. Arminius calls this grace 'preventing'. Prevenient grace is so called as it is grace which is available to both believers and non-believers, which is enough for salvation. It allows believers and non-believers, if they will, to be saved or not saved.

Unlike Calvin, Arminius said that the election of believers was conditional on faith. He found the unconditional election of Calvin absurd. He did accept that there was an Elect but due to the fact that humans have free-will, others could choose to have faith and achieve salvation. He extended the range of Jesus' atonement to all and also, due to the fact that humans have free-will, Arminius said that humans can resist God's grace. So there is the possibility of apostasy.

The Five Articles of Remonstrance (1610)

Arminius' followers became known as 'The Remonstrants'. To remonstrate means to oppose or to protest. So 'the Five Articles of Remonstrance' is a protest against the Calvinist doctrine of predestination. This document was condemned as heresy by the Reformed Churches at the Synod of Dort, 1618–1619.

Article 1

That God, by an eternal and unchangeable purpose in Jesus Christ his Son, before the foundation of the world, hath determined, out of the fallen, sinful race of men, to save in Christ, for Christ's sake, and through Christ, those who, through the grace of the Holy Ghost, shall believe on this his son Jesus, and shall persevere in this faith and obedience of faith, through this grace, even to the end; and, on the other hand, to leave the incorrigible and unbelieving in sin and under wrath, and to condemn them as alienate from Christ, according to the word of the Gospel in John 3:36: 'He that believeth on the Son hath everlasting life: and he that believeth not the Son shall not see life; but the wrath of God abideth on him', and according to other passages of Scripture also.

Article 2

That agreeably thereunto, Jesus Christ the Saviour of the world, died for all men and for every man, so that he has obtained for them all, by his death on the cross, redemption and the forgiveness of sins; yet that no one actually enjoys this forgiveness of sins except the believer, according to the word of the Gospel of John 3:16, 'For God so loved the world, that he gave his only begotten Son, that whosoever believeth in him should not perish, but have everlasting life.' And in the First Epistle of 1 John 2:2: 'And he is the propitiation for our sins: and not for ours only, but also for the sins of the whole world.'

Article 3

That man has not saving grace of himself, nor of the energy of his free-will, inasmuch as he, in the state of apostasy and sin, can of and by himself neither think, will, nor do anything that is truly good (such as saving faith eminently is); but that it is needful that he be born again of God in Christ, through his Holy Spirit, and renewed in understanding, inclination, or will, and all his powers, in order that he may rightly understand, think, will, and effect what is truly good, according to the Word of Christ, John 15:5, 'Without me ye can do nothing.'

Article 4

That this grace of God is the beginning, continuance, and accomplishment of all good, even to this extent that the regenerate man himself, without prevenient or assisting, awakening, following and co-operative grace, can neither think, will, nor do good, nor withstand any temptations to evil; so that all good deeds or movements, that can be conceived, must be ascribed to the grace of God in Christ, but respects the mode of the operation of this grace, it is not irresistible; inasmuch as it is written concerning many, that they have resisted the Holy Ghost. Acts 7 and in many places elsewhere.

Article 5

That those who are incorporated into Christ by true faith, and have thereby become partakers of his life-giving Spirit, have thereby full power to strive against Satan, sin, the world, and their own flesh, and to win the victory; it being well understood that it is ever through the assisting grace of the Holy Ghost; and that Jesus Christ assists them through his Spirit in all temptations, extends to them his hand, and if only they are ready for the conflict, and desire his help, and are not inactive, keeps them from falling, so that they, by no craft or power of Satan, can be misled nor plucked out of Christ's hands, according to the Word of Christ, John 10:28: 'Neither shall any man pluck them out of my hand.' But whether they are capable, through negligence, of forsaking again the first beginning of their life in Christ, of again returning to this present evil world, of turning away from the holy doctrine which was delivered them, of losing a good conscience, of becoming devoid of grace, that must be more particularly determined out of the Holy Scripture, before we ourselves can teach it with the full persuasion of our mind.

Taken from www.theopedia.com

In summary form the Articles say this:

Conditional election. Election is conditional on faith in Christ. Those people will be saved.

Unlimited atonement. All who believe will be saved.

Total depravity means we cannot achieve salvation without help from God's grace. We must be born again.

Resistible grace. We need grace for salvation but we can resist it.

Evil can be resisted. Apostasy is possible but if a person has faith in Christ it can be resisted.

John and Charles Wesley, the founders of English Methodism adopted the Arminian position. Welsh Methodists, following Howell Harris, followed Calvin.

Luther and Erasmus

Erasmus had a controversy with Luther, another Protestant Reformer. Erasmus defended free-will, which Luther had called a fiction. Luther had said that all events occur by necessity so it is not in a human's power to think well or ill. Erasmus wrote *De Libero Arbitrio* which emphasised free-will. In response, Luther wrote *De Servo Arbitrio* in which he emphasised the helplessness of humans.

Grade boost

Your own research into the views of any of the following would certainly make your answer more comprehensive: the Wesley brothers, Howell Harris, Luther or Erasmus.

The relationship between concepts of determinism/free-will and religious beliefs and moral attitudes

The degree to which the concepts of determinism and free-will influence religious beliefs and moral attitudes is a question to tackle in the 'Evaluative issues' section. Here we will address the 'relationship' question.

AO2 evaluative issues on this question are on pages 129–130.

Determinism and religion

It is clear that a strong case can be made for a relationship between determinism and religious beliefs and moral attitudes. Theological determinism or predestination is a predominant view in many religions. It has support in scriptures and also amongst leading authorities such as St Augustine and John Calvin. In scripture, the belief is in a God who has determined people's fate before they are born, a belief in a God who is omniscient and omnipotent, the almighty sovereign God who has an overall plan for Creation already worked out.

So, the concept of determinism leads to such religious beliefs as the absolute power and providence of God. Hard determinism tries to account for the fact that we feel free, but explains that this is merely an illusion.

All beliefs that we have would in fact have been determined by God, including a belief in God. In no way could it then be said that we found God; God has to find us. A secondary effect of this is that God has determined that others would either not believe or that others would not be given the chance to believe. This leads to the belief in a God who predetermines eternal damnation for some. This leads some to question a belief in an omnibenevolent God.

However, from Augustine's point of view the religious belief that stems from a God who predestines is not one who is ruthless but one who is merciful. This is because God should have let all suffer their deserved fate of eternal damnation. Instead God chose to save some through Christ's atoning death. This may lead to the moral attitude that some would do what they liked as whatever they do will make no difference to their ultimate fate. It seems that Pelagius witnessed this in Rome.

The concept of determinism could also lead to the religious belief that human free-will is an illusion. Because of their corrupt nature and the fact that God is in complete control there is no such thing as human choice. No matter what 'choice' is made the end result will be the same. This kind of fatalism may well have a knock-on effect to attitudes and behaviour.

The concept of determinism may lead to a pessimistic belief about human nature, a nature which is completely corrupt. Humans are totally depraved as Calvin said. The belief would be that humans can do nothing without the grace of God and are therefore totally reliant upon God's will and mercy.

Moral attitudes could vary here. Some may view their depravity with disgust, and see the body as something to be punished. Others may take the opposite view whereby if all has been decided by God then nothing they do will make

Stretch and challenge

Explain how you feel when you have no choice over whether you do something.

any difference. The body may be seen as something which is for pleasure only. Inappropriate actions and attitudes may be the result. St Paul had a similar problem to deal with in I Corinthians 6 where Christians were taking their 'freedom in Christ' rather too literally and were indulging in sins of the flesh. St Paul condemned this as inappropriate behaviour for Christians, 'Do you not know that your body is a temple of the Holy Spirit within you which you have from God?'

Determinism may also lead to the religious belief that sin is not a logical concept. As there is no freedom in hard determinism then there is no such thing as blame or sin in the true sense of those words. So a fundamental belief of Christianity could be questioned. If there is no sin then there is no need for redemption. This may lead some to rethink their belief-system. If humans are not to blame then this could affect moral attitudes and also the criminal justice system. If humans are not truly free then is any moral decision actually a decision at all?

Free-will and religion

Stretch and challenge
Explain how having free-will may affect your actions.

It is clear that a strong case can be made for a relationship between free-will and religious beliefs and moral attitudes. Free-will is a predominant view in many religions. It has support in scriptures and also amongst leading authorities such as Pelagius and Arminius. In scripture there are many references to free-will. It is a concept that runs through both theistic and non-theistic religions.

Free-will is a concept which can lead to certain religious beliefs and moral attitudes. If one has free-will in a theistic context the idea is that God has given human beings free-will. This may give a different view of God than the God that predestines. The God that gives free-will is a God that wants a freely chosen loving relationship with human beings. We can see much of this approach in the writings of St Irenaeus. His belief is that God is still omnipotent but God restricts that power in order to give humans a genuinely human lifestyle. His religious belief is that God could have imposed God's wishes on humans but that would be the same as forcing someone to love you, which is no love at all.

Both Pelagius and Arminius believed in free-will. For Pelagius it could be argued that his belief in free-will was related to his religious beliefs. Humans have free-will so God would not send humans to eternal damnation for a sin that they had not committed. For Arminius humans have free-will that can respond to the Holy Spirit. The fact that people can reject the Holy Spirit leads to important beliefs regarding sin and human moral responsibility.

Being created in the 'image of God' means to some that we have been created to make choices, as opposed to being programmed robots. The religious belief that humans at 'the Fall' made the wrong yet free choice shows moral responsibility. The belief which follows is that punishment is fitting. It is because of free-will that humans are morally responsible for their actions. The rules contained within religions are then seen to be those things which it is advisable to follow but there is real responsibility attached to doing so.

Related to this is the belief in sin. It is because humans have free-will and are morally responsible that the belief in sin exists. It is because of sin and the need to avoid it or get rid of it that humans need redemption. This whole framework of belief is related to the concept of free-will.

Within non-theistic religions the concept of free-will is related to karma. It is because actions are real and have consequences that a belief in karma makes sense; we reap what we sow. This is a religious belief which is fair and just. This relates to moral attitudes. The feelings that humans have regarding rules of conduct are related to the concept of free-will. We have a choice over what we consider we should do. What we choose to do will have its consequences.

Many aspects of Libertarianism are compatible with religious beliefs and moral attitudes. It is not necessarily correct to say, as some have, that Libertarianism breaks major beliefs of religion. Libertarianism is a political theory. It says that one has freedom but not the freedom to exercise violence or to infringe legitimate rights of others. The essence of it is to not to kill anyone, to not take what's not yours, to not do anyone wrong, don't stick your nose in someone else's business and don't bother anyone if they haven't bothered you. These beliefs are perfectly compatible with a religious setting. Moral attitudes of a libertarian and a religious believer can be the same.

Free-will/determinism → affects belief and behaviour

OR IS IT

Belief and behaviour → affects views on free-will/ predestination

The relationship: the other way around?

It may be legitimately argued that the relationship actually begins with the religious beliefs and moral attitudes. This then means that it is religious beliefs and moral attitudes that guide views on free-will and determinism. The extent to which one affects the other will be considered in the 'Evaluative issues' section. Here some provisional points can be made.

It could be said that it is belief in the sovereignty of God that means that one necessarily believes in the concept of predestination. If a person has a religious belief that God knows everything then nothing can happen without God's knowledge or decision. Therefore God must determine all acts.

If one believes that humans are inherently sinful, a mass of corruption, as Augustine believes, then it makes perfect sense to hold to the doctrine of predestination. Humans cannot gain salvation on their own so it is down to God to determine salvation for the Elect.

If one believes that it is important that humans come to God in a meaningful, mutual relationship then one will find the concept of free-will to be a logical, indeed necessary, concept to hold.

If one has a belief in karma, what goes around comes around, a belief in free-will and consequences is related to that belief.

Evaluative issues

These are the part (b) (AO2) questions which demand a different skill from part (a) (AO1) questions. AO2 questions will always ask the candidate to consider a quotation or a viewpoint. The candidate will be asked to assess or evaluate the validity of that quotation or statement. The aim is to give a series of arguments both in favour of and against the quotation or statement, analysing and evaluating the information.

Key things to bear in mind when answering these questions are:

- Do not just write information. That is an AO1 skill. The examiner should be able to read your work without the question in front of them and be able to tell what that question is. If you just write information, it will look just like a part (a) AO1 question and, in itself, is not worth any marks.

- Instead, use the information in order to evaluate effectively how valid, persuasive, strong (words used will differ depending on the wording of the question) and so on it may be.

- Aim to be synoptic in your answer. This means that in part (b) answers you should try to use information from more than one of the bulleted points specified for study in the part (a) questions as well as using material from other topics in the Specification. You can also refer to relevant aspects of your AS modules. The less isolated you make each bullet point, the greater scope you will be able to give to your answers.

- A conclusion must be given for the top levels. Otherwise you have not done what the question is asking you to do.

What follows are some examples of how you could deal with the issues in this topic. There will clearly be material that you could use in several different questions. The material given here is for guidance only. There are other, perfectly acceptable ways to answer all of these questions. You must remember that the examiner is looking for a consideration of the issue with evaluative skills which present evidence for a viewpoint. Reasoning must be used and the conclusion reached must be based upon what you have written in the main body of your answer.

The Human Genome Project

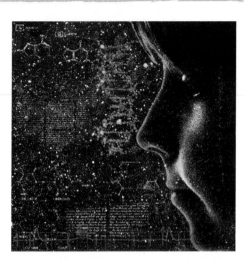

There is much interest in the attempt to trace certain behaviour to particular strands of DNA. Will we be able to locate a gene for criminality, aggression or 'the gay gene'? Will we be able to predict who will show empathy or who will develop heart disease? Gene experts say that genetic discovery will help us to understand environmental factors better.

Professor Robert Plomin said:

> 'The first message from genetic research is that genes play a surprisingly important role for almost all complex traits, whether behavioural or medical. But the second message is just as important: individual differences in complex traits are due at least as much to environmental influences as they are to genetic influences.'

It has been stated that one of the goals of the Human Genome Project is to identify nature and use this to identify nurture.

So…

Well done for reading this far – your genes or environment? You may have your blonde hair from your mother and your height from your father, but the jury is still out as to why you have your sense of humour, your love of music and your ability to do RS A Level. Perhaps the best we can say is 'God knows'!

1: 'Our genes make us what we are, not our environment.' Assess this view.

Agree

- Our genes are an essential part of what makes us the person we are. How often has it been said 'you are just like your mother'? Well, it is not surprising as her genetic make-up is part of what has made you what you are. There is this scientific component that we cannot overcome. If parents are tall, it is highly likely that the child will be. Genetic disorders may be passed from parent to child. If a parent is loving or aggressive it seems reasonable to suggest that there is a loving or aggressive gene that will be transferred to the child. We have evidence of these traits that parents and children have in common.

- Some argue that the God gene contributes to what we become. It is argued that a personality which is able to be selfless, thinking of others, with the capacity to be spiritually aware is inbuilt. We can see evidence of this by observing very young children who, before they have time to be affected by the environment just seem to be happy or unhappy, calm or disturbed. The effect that the God gene has on behaviour is that the person becomes more conscious of the feelings of others. This ties in well with modern thinking on energy fields and streams of consciousness. It would make perfect sense for this to be genetic.

- Child prodigies can only be explained by suggesting that there is a gene which gives the child a tremendous ability to write music, dance or learn a language. This gene is already carried by the parent and is passed on to the child. This is the best way of explaining how Mozart could compose as young as 6. It also explains why in a school situation teachers find that some pupils can learn faster than others. They are just the lucky ones to be carrying an advantageous gene.

Disagree

- However, genes cannot account for everything. It is arguably the case that physical characteristics are genetic, such as height or hair colour. But in many things we must accept that the environment is also a factor. Children who have fairly light hair passed on genetically may also undergo a change in hair colour due to sunlight. Research is being carried out to eliminate some genetic disorders so in the future it may be possible to say that genetics has not formed what a person becomes. A child of an aggressive parent may be aggressive, but can we prove this is as a result of nature? Is it not just as possible that this behaviour has been learned from the parent, peers or society? When it is said 'you are just like your mother' this could be because you have observed her behaviour and copied it.

- But suggesting that genes have such a large role in forming us may be too big a claim. If we are born with the God gene how is it that some people come to religion late on in life? Where was the God gene for the first 50 years of their life? Also, it suggests that without this gene a person does not have the ability to be spiritual or aware of the feelings of others. This would mean that all atheists (and Buddhists?) are pretty ruthless and lacking in feelings for others. Surely we have enough evidence of selfless acts from non-religious people? It is also the role of a family to nurture compassion by praising a child where compassion is shown and telling off a child when it is not shown. Such positive and negative reinforcers are backed up by the psychological studies of Skinner.

- Children can have a talent as the result of so many other factors. The role of the family environment cannot be underestimated. Many talents exist in children that the parents do not have, so this demolishes the genetic theory. Without support, encouragement and facilities talent cannot flourish. I may have the genetic capacity to be a pianist but without a piano I will struggle! Also, if we say that genes affect everything and environment has no effect on what a person becomes, then there would be no point in an education system, as if a child is not born with a certain gene then they can never learn. But the fact is that teachers do make a difference, which shows us that environment is a factor to be considered.

- A determinist may say that nature does have an effect on what a person becomes. There is no free-will so what we are is determined by past events, past causes. It could be argued that one such 'past cause' is our genes. This makes sense in that the parents that cause us to be must surely have an effect on us in the genetic sense. Cause and effect are inextricably linked. This genetic make-up is indelibly imprinted into what we become.

- Some would look to case studies such as the famous case won by Clarence Darrow, where he argued that the genetic make-up of people can make them do the most terrible (or good) things. There is no choice as such as they are programmed by their genes to act in a certain way. In this sense when it is said, 'I just could not help it', this is actually true. In a religious sense this could get back up from St Augustine's view that humans inherit their nature which is sinful, hence 'the cruel necessity of sinning'.

- It is all well and good people saying that in theory we can be influenced by the environment, but in practice, however, this is not true. We have a genetic predisposition to certain things, height, and weight and so on and this, in practice means that our genes determine what we are and what we do. Imagine that I have sickle cell anaemia. Sickle cell anaemia is inherited from both parents. If you inherit the sickle cell gene from only one parent, you will have sickle cell trait. People with sickle cell trait do not have the symptoms of sickle cell anaemia. This is the reality of it. This does affect us as symptoms involve very painful episodes, often with pain in the back, accompanied by fatigue amongst other things. This is definitely not the environment.

- However, a determinist could also accept that, as we are determined by past events, causes and circumstances, what we become is determined by the environment in which we happen to be. We are not free, our family, socio-economic situation, culture and so on affects our behaviour. Humans do not and cannot operate in a vacuum. These other factors are indelibly imprinted into what we are to become.

- However, others would say that this is ludicrous, almost pardoning atrocious acts and not giving praise to good acts. Humans have free-will and a moral self and so we can choose. Even if we are predisposed to act in a certain way we can overcome it. We can be affected by environmental stimuli, for example. In a religious sense it could be argued that religious teachings could influence people to act in a certain way. Such rules for living may mean that we have to act contrary to our inclination but it can certainly be done.

- But this does not cover everything as it is only dealing with genetic disorders. The point of what Hospers was trying to say in his analysis of what food we may find present in the stomach of people who have committed certain crimes is that there is a combination of factors which influence what we become. Indeed, genes may be one of them but not the only one. The fact that advertising works shows that we can be influenced by external factors. What we buy as a result of an advertising technique is evidence of this.

AO1 information on this topic is on pages 94–104.

How far does an individual have 'free choice'?

It should be noted that in this question you should explain the understanding of free-will that you are working with. This will generally be a personal view and will be open to interpretation. There is a difference between free choice in theory and in practice. It would be worth considering possible boundaries to free-will:

1. Laws of nature – there are certain established laws which will, in theory, continue to hold; they have done in practice for some time. Some things are predictable. This means there is not complete freedom.

2. Physical – the body is born with boundaries on our freedom. In theory and possibly in practice we may not be able to do certain things because of this. Of course some will argue that we can do what we wish as we can have a sex change, for example. But there are certain disabilities that cannot be overcome whatever surgery is undergone.

3. Socio-economic – where we are born and to whom, in theory, limit freedom. Again, others may argue, though, that in practice we are still free to overcome obstacles of birth and do whatever we want.

4. If we regard 'me' as being in a state of flux, that 'I' am not a permanent entity, such as in Buddhism then there is no 'I' to make any decisions, free or not.

5. God – some argue that God's sovereignty means that God predestines human life. This may impose a boundary on human free-will. Others say that free-will and predestination are compatible so there is no limit to our freedom.

AO1 information on this topic is on pages 104–115.

Stretch and challenge

For each of the 5 'boundaries to free-will' suggest specific examples, such as:

1. Laws of nature – gravity means that I cannot jump off my roof and fly, despite wanting to.

2: 'An individual has complete free choice.' Assess this view.

Agree

- There are many criticisms which can be made of all of the branches of determinism, thus allowing for free choice to be a more plausible answer. How can it be proven that we merely 'feel' free? If I feel free then surely I am perfectly justified in believing that I am free. In fact, it could be argued that when a human makes a decision believing that they are making it freely then that is what matters. Our actions are genuine ones where we genuinely feel that what we are doing will make a difference. This makes our decision autonomous.

- Predestination does not rule out free-will. God may have determined the future but the choices that we make are still very real choices. We could say that there is a predestined result of misusing our free-will but the free-will itself is unchallenged. This could be a way to view 'the Fall'. Adam and Eve were given the real choice of whether to eat from the forbidden tree but if they did, then the punishment had already been decided. This does not take away free-will, but says what the punishment will be if free-will is misused.

- An individual is free as if we were not then there is no morality and no responsibility. Relationships would be pointless without free-will. Clearly this is not how our world works. There is a framework for responsibility, called the criminal justice system, which recognises that acts are performed through choice. We do blame or praise people for their action. Why? Because they are done freely.

- Aquinas believed that humans have free-will. He accepted that there is a purpose for all humans which can be found by using reason. The Highest Good for a human is to be in a relationship with God. This can be done if our actions correspond to the purpose of humans. So, we can exercise our free-will to (hopefully) act according to reason and establish this relationship with God. Fulfilling our purpose is a possibility but so is not fulfilling it, so humans have the choice to do so.

Disagree

- Locke's analogy of the sleeping man in a locked room illustrates that freedom is an illusion. It makes no difference whatsoever that the man 'decided' to stay in the room being unaware that it was locked. The reality of the situation is that he could not have done otherwise. So an individual does not have free choice. Just thinking that we do does not make it a reality. This is confirmed by Spinoza who said that we have an illusion of free-will because humans 'are conscious of their actions and ignorant of the causes of them'. We do not ask why we made certain decisions and jump to the wrong conclusion that nothing caused our decisions.

- Predestination does rule out free-will. For God to be in total charge then nothing can happen without God's power and knowledge. So any act which may be considered to be free cannot be free in any way, shape or form. Also, the argument given regarding Adam and Eve is talking about a different issue. The fact that the punishment had already been decided was made necessary by the fact that God knew that they had no real choice. God had determined what they would decide.

- It could be argued against this libertarian approach that not all acts are done out of free-will and our criminal justice system recognises that. Some crimes are called 'crimes of passion' or done by someone with 'diminished responsibility'. This suggests that it was performed without total free-will. Manslaughter is given a different punishment than murder as the crime was not planned. A person's 'free' choice is narrowed or widened by that person's nature. For example, if a child was asked to decide whether they wanted to sing a solo on stage, then certain children would find it far easier to say 'yes'. This is the liberty of spontaneity.

- But it could be argued that the fact that purposes are already inbuilt into humans and the world suggests that humans do not have complete free choice. These goals have been predetermined, so our use of our free-will for whatever end, has already got a consequence attached to it which is outside of our control.

- Kant believed that humans have free-will. He accepts that empirical or physical phenomena/things come from determining causes. But the human mind is different. Kant said that the mind is not physical (noumenal) and is therefore not determined. Our mind can start an event which has not been caused by something else. So humans do have free choice because the mind can initiate something completely freely as the mind is free from outside influences.

- Humans have complete free choice as we see evidence of this all of the time in life. I choose to have an Indian meal rather than a Chinese meal. I choose to watch football rather than tennis. I choose the pair of white trainers rather than the blue pair. I chose to do a Theology degree rather than an Engineering degree. I chose to become a teacher rather than a bank worker. I am asked 'what do you think?' and I respond with my decision. Choice, choice, choice. We are surrounded by it and we make it.

- Dennett in his book of 1984 *Elbow Room* says that free-will is choosing to do something from a limited number of choices. So his approach is from a compatibilist standpoint and he tries to convince the reader that determinism provides 'The Varieties of Free-will Worth Having' (which is the book's subtitle). He says that free-will is unpredictable. Humans can act in a way that is not expected of them. This is convincing as we may see evidence of this in life – 'I really didn't expect.' True free-will demands unpredictability.

- Science today can accept that the universe is more random than it was once thought to be. If this is the case then it means the future is not wholly determined, leaving room for free-will. Also in the psychological field some studies show us that a positive mental attitude, chosen of one's own free-will, can help patients cope with and/or overcome some pain and illness. This suggests that the individual has complete choice over their attitude which does have a knock-on effect to a condition that may have seemed determined.

- Honderich said that the concept of free-will is meaningless. He said that we are determined in every way, including our mind. The mind and the rest of our body are not separate as physical brain activity is needed by the mind. In this sense he was in agreement with the view of Strawson. Strawson in 1986 said that free-will is incoherent as a concept as we must get to a point where something began a chain of events. With complete free-will we would be saying that nothing caused a choice. But how can a choice or a mental state come from nothing? As many philosophers have said 'nothing can come from nothing' so humans cannot have free choice as it does not work as a concept.

- Sam Harris in his book of 2012 *Free-will* set out to show that free-will is an illusion. Harris' essential point is that much of what we put down to free-will is actually not the result of us consciously thinking about something and deciding to do it. Much of it, says Harris, is due to luck. When discussing why someone may be a surgeon or a psychopath Harris says we are 'at the confluence of all the genetic and environmental causes that led you to develop along this line. None of these events requires that you, the conscious subject, be the ultimate cause of your aspirations, abilities, and resulting behaviour. And, needless to say, you can take no credit for the fact that you weren't born a psychopath.'

- However, one could argue that complete free-will does not have any limits imposed on it whatsoever. As soon as a deterministic element comes into a situation then that situation is no longer completely free. However, it could be added that free-will and determinism are not compatible. We could say that every event is caused. I am writing this guide for a reason, I go into town for a reason. All of our choices have a cause. These choices, conscious or unconscious, have something prior to them, they have been predetermined in some sense by the many happenings before the outcome. In fact, everything that takes place has been set in motion by the start of the universe.

- Scientific and psychological study shows us, though, that we can predict and control behaviour. Laplace (1749–1827) asked us to imagine a demon that could know the behaviour of every particle in the universe. So, we could in theory know exactly what will happen in the universe in the future. Psychological study has shown that free choice is certainly not complete as we can control behaviour through classical conditioning (Watson) and operant conditioning (Skinner). Human behaviour is therefore not free as it is predictable.

- Lastly, in terms of the human body itself, it seems quite natural to state that I am typing this guide now because my hands are freely typing it. I am in complete control of what keys my fingers touch. After I have finished this section I am going to go to bed where I am going to put a DVD on. Complete free-will.

- But what about human behaviour that seems to be out of the human's control? Two come to mind. The first is Tourette's syndrome. Here the person will involuntarily shout out, swear or perform involuntary movements. This person is not free. Another is alien hand syndrome. On 20 January 2011 the BBC reported on Karen Byrne. This is adapted from that report. As a result of an operation to cure her of epilepsy she was left with no control of her left hand. Both her left hand, and at times her left leg, behaved as if it were under the control of an alien intelligence. Sometimes Karen's left hand slaps or punches her and her left leg takes her in a direction she does not want to go. Her left hand has taken things from her bag and also opened the buttons on her shirt! So no, an individual does not have complete free choice.

3: 'Religious belief in free-will and predestination can be reconciled.' Assess this view.

Agree

- Religious texts contain both teachings. This shows that there is no contradiction. Both can co-exist as they appear harmoniously in texts. For example, in Genesis 2[16&17] God gives Adam free-will to eat of the fruit of any tree except one. His future, if he chose of that one, would be predetermined. Also, both concepts appear in the Book of Romans. In 2[7&8], 'Some people keep on doing good, and seek glory, honour and immortal life; to them God will give eternal life. Other people are selfish and reject what is right, in order to follow what is wrong; on them God will pour out his anger and fury.' Then in 8[28&29] 'We know that in all things God works for good with those who love him, those whom he has called according to his purpose. Those whom God had already chosen he also set apart to become like his Son, so that the Son would be the eldest brother in a large family.'

- If we consider Augustine's theodicy then we may be able to justify reconciling free-will and predestination and of course have back up from a renowned Christian thinker. Augustine's theodicy is a form of the free-will defence. It is vital to this theodicy that humans have free-will. Otherwise God would be to blame for evil, which of course Augustine says God is not. Humans continue to make the wrong choice (privation of good). As we know, Augustine was a supporter of predestination, too, so the two concepts can be reconciled.

- It has been argued that God has predestined what has happened but humans do not know what has been predestined. So, human choice is absolutely real for humans. All actions are performed by a human who is conscious that in their mind the decision will make a difference. As a result of this real decision they are still morally responsible, thus reconciling the two concepts.

- Aquinas would agree with the above point. God is timeless, outside of time. This means that God sees the past, present and future simultaneously. For such a God, past, present and future are redundant terms really as there is no time for timeless God. God has determined the future, has knowledge of it but humans have a choice of how to achieve that future. Again, the choice is a real one.

Disagree

- The fact that religious texts contain both concepts is not an argument for their reconciliation. When the concepts are in the same book of a holy book, such as in Romans, the texts are not without scholarly scrutiny. There does appear to be the issue that they are very different and perhaps the writer of the text realises that tension. Perhaps she or he has not worked out that tension in their own theology. This does not mean that they can be reconciled as concepts. Also, if we accept the writing of such texts by very many hands then the fact that both concepts are there is not surprising.

- Pelagius, of course, strongly disagreed with Augustine's views on predestination. He said that it was a most unfair doctrine and supported free-will instead. Therefore, the two cannot be reconciled as predestination does not exist. In terms of Augustine's theodicy, we can question its logic too. He wishes to assert that humans are free but that we freely choose the bad on each and every occasion. This is because our second or sinful nature overrides our essential or free nature. So, there we have it, we are not actually free after all!

- God must have the characteristics necessary to predestine. God is omnipotent, omniscient, absolute sovereign. So predestination is undoubted. What is doubted, however, is free-will. This is because as God is sovereign then nothing can happen without God's will or knowledge. If human 'choice' has already been decreed then it is no choice in the real sense of the word at all. Reconciliation is not possible.

- A criticism of this is the same as above – is this really a choice at all? Where they are going is determined, but how they get there may be rather more open. It has restrictions placed within the freedom. Also, if one believes in an everlasting God then this God is in time. One could question whether this God can actually predetermine anyway as for everlasting God, the future is yet to come.

- It could be argued that God has the capacity to predetermine but chooses to withhold that power in order to give us free-will. This is an approach that can be seen in the work of St Irenaeus. This therefore has theological backing and allows for a truly loving relationship with God.

- However, it could be argued in response that this does not fit with other characteristics of the God of classical theism. This God is omnibenevolent. A God who chooses to give humans free-will knowing the risks, does not square with a loving God. The conclusion we are led to may be that either humans are not free or God cannot predestine.

- Others look to the creation of humans by God for the source of reconciliation. As God caused humans God also caused human choice. God put human wishes and desires into humans. Our choices are not restricted but human wishes are thereby God's wishes. This is a clever way of showing how the two concepts can be reconciled.

- However, this does seem to be very much like a pre-programmed robot. If God has infused God's wishes into us, humans may make a 'choice' but it is hard to see how they could do differently. It is therefore argued that this is not free-will at all.

- It may be possible to argue that God has an overall predestined plan but that individual situations in life leave room for free-will. As an example one could use prayer. Humans need free-will in order to take part in prayer and other acts of worship. This may not mean that there is not an overarching predestination to one's life as a whole, even though there may not be predestination in all individual acts.

- This begs the question of how there could be free-will in a system which is ultimately predetermined. What if the 'free' act chosen in prayer meant that the predestined plan is ruined? Clearly that last sentence is incoherent as a predetermined plan *cannot* be ruined. Predestined as a whole also means that individual actions are decided beforehand too.

- Arminius could be used in this context. He believed that some had been chosen as the Elect and Non-elect, but humans can choose faith and with the help of God's grace can be saved. Here we see an argument that could be used in favour of reconciliation. This has the benefit of seeing a more optimistic side to human nature as well as extending the scope of Christ's atonement.

- Arminius' view, as others like Pelagius, could be seen as emphasising human freedom too much at the expense of God's sovereignty. Calvin's and Augustine's views on predestination and original sin were the Orthodox views as opposed to the heretical views of Arminius and Pelagius. So, by emphasising God's sovereignty they are accepted schools of thought, emphasising the need for God's grace and Christ's atoning death.

- Religious teachings in general include both God's sovereignty and human sin. These teachings, it could be said, stem from predestination (God's sovereignty) and free-will (sin). Hence the two religious concepts are absolutely essential and are both needed in order to present a religious system that fits together.

- Some religious teachings may include both predestination and free-will but Buddhism certainly doesn't. As it rejects the concept of a God the predestination in the sense of God determining the future is not a meaningful concept. Therefore, the two concepts are not reconciled in Buddhism.

The degree to which concepts of determinism/free-will influence religious beliefs and moral attitudes

Grade boost

For every bullet point in the 'issues' column in each of the four topics, you need, before the examination, to have written a sample part essay and, importantly, to have included a conclusion. So, for each possible part (b) question write a concluding few paragraphs to an essay, based upon the evaluative information (agree/disagree) that you have found in this guide.

There are a number of ways in which to address this issue:

- Free-will influences religious beliefs and moral attitudes
- Determinism influences religious beliefs and moral attitudes
- Free-will does not influence religious beliefs and moral attitudes
- Determinism does not influence religious beliefs and moral attitudes
- Religious beliefs and moral attitudes influence our concept of free-will
- Religious beliefs and moral attitudes influence our concept of determinism

4: 'Free-will completely influences religious beliefs and moral attitudes.' Assess this view.

Agree

- Free-will influences beliefs about death and the afterlife. If one believes that the future is 'open' then this gives rise to beliefs about reincarnation, rebirth, Resurrection or none of the above. It makes sense that beliefs are affected in this way. Free-will drives the beliefs.

- It is the concept of free-will which leads some to their beliefs about God including God's characteristics. Accepting the concept of free-will leads to a belief in a God who values free-will and wants a relationship with humans which is freely chosen.

- Pelagius' concept of free-will influenced his beliefs in the power of human choice, leading to an altogether more optimistic attitude towards human nature.

Disagree

- But it could be said that religious beliefs and moral attitudes come first. It is the type of belief in the afterlife which influences our concept of free-will. What one expects in the future is what drives the concepts. Equally it could be said that it is determinism and not free-will that influences beliefs about death and the afterlife. It is belief that the afterlife has been determined by God which influences attitudes and beliefs about God including God's nature.

- However, it could also be suggested that the relationship is the other way around. It is plausible to suggest that it is beliefs about God's nature that influence people to accept free-will. They believe in a God who wants a loving relationship and this means that they accept the concept of free-will. Equally, however, it could be the concept of determinism rather than free-will which influences our religious beliefs about God's characteristics. Accepting the concept of predestination can influence our beliefs about God's sovereignty, for example.

- In contrast however, it could be claimed that Pelagius' beliefs about God influenced his views concerning free-will. Also. His beliefs about human nature therefore meant that his understanding of free-will was influenced. Humans are not a mass of sin and so they can perform good, freely chosen deeds.

- The concept of free-will influences our religious beliefs as it forms the basis of many beliefs. For example, sin is a belief influenced by the fact that humans have free-will. Without free-will then sin would not enter into the equation. How can someone be accused of sinning if they had no choice to do otherwise? Moral attitudes are influenced by the concept of free-will as our ethical dilemmas and hence moral attitudes derive from the concept of free-will. This applies whether a person is religious or not.

- Free-will influences religious beliefs and moral attitudes towards such things as stewardship. Humans, it is believed, have been asked to perform the role of looking after the earth. They are given free-will to do this, which is what attaches responsibility to it.

- The concept of free-will could influence a religious belief such as the sanctity of life, which thereby influences our moral attitudes to a variety of moral issues. One may believe that life is special; it is in the palm of our hands. We have freedom to give life or take life. The sacred nature of life may be influenced by the fact that we have free-will to choose in issues concerning life.

- When it comes to religious beliefs and moral attitudes towards helping others it could be argued that the concept of free-will influences our beliefs and attitudes. If it is believed that one has free-will given by God then it is reasonable to suggest that this would influence our attitude towards helping others. Religious beliefs regarding our religious duty to help may then be influenced by our concept of free-will.

- But sin is a concept which exists in its own right, being completely unaffected by any other concept. It is not driven by the concept of free-will. It could be said that it stems from other beliefs such as the depravity of human nature. So the relationship is different from the one described in the question.

- However, it could be said that free-will does not influence a belief such as stewardship. Stewardship is a belief in its own right irrespective of the concept of free-will. There are also other aspects to consider that may influence such a belief anyway, such as obedience to God's will in looking after the world.

- It could, however, be said that the sanctity of life is a belief that is not affected by the concept of free-will. An inbuilt feeling that life is special is perfectly logical in its own right, a belief which is influenced by absolutely nothing else.

- However, there was a most interesting study carried out in 1973 by Darley and Batson. Basically a group of theological students were asked to take part in some research. Some of them were given the parable of the Good Samaritan to read and others were not. They were then asked to go to another area to finish the research. Some were told to hurry to their next destination, some of them were not told this. On the way, a person had been 'planted' to look as if they were in distress and in need of help. Who stopped to help? The findings were that whether or not they had read the story of the Good Samaritan made no difference at all. The people most likely to stop were the ones who had not been told to hurry. So we could argue that free-will and determinism do not completely affect moral attitudes as what affected moral attitudes here was the instruction given to the students.

- The concept of free-will may influence a belief in the law of karma. The idea that humans are free to act but with the belief that the action will have a corresponding consequence seems to be a fitting relationship. The karmic consequences may not catch up with you in this lifetime but they will. Moral attitudes towards a variety of issues are likewise influenced.

- Libertarians say that humans have complete free-will so this can be used as an argument in favour of it influencing religious beliefs and moral attitudes.

- For some, it works the other way around though. That is that it is the belief in karma which influences our understanding of free-will. The belief in the law of cause and effect gives us our perception of the role of free-will.

- However, free-will cannot completely influence beliefs and attitudes due to legal restrictions on our free-will. In practice there are things that humans just cannot do without there being severe punishment. So, free-will does not have complete influence over actions; other things are also borne in mind.

AO1 information on this question is on pages 116–118.

Summary: Are we 'free beings'?

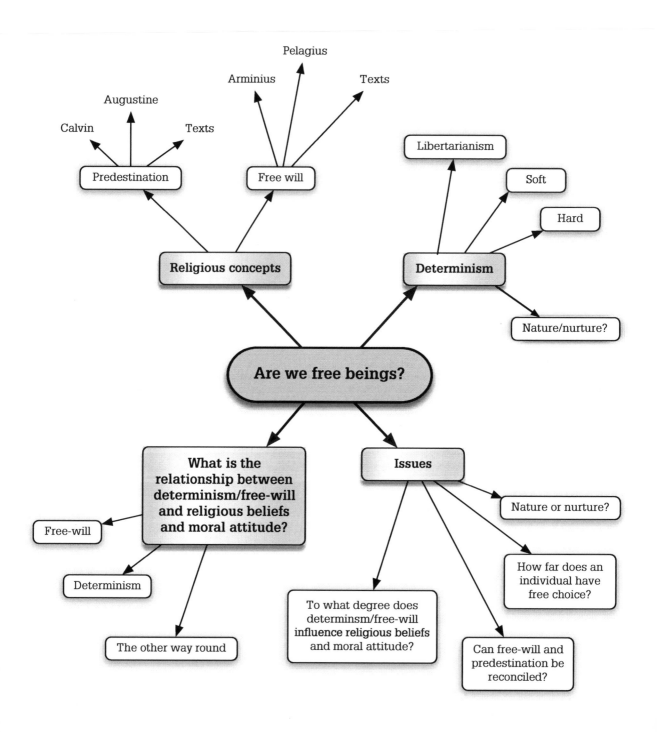

Exam Practice and Technique

Exam practice and skills

How exam questions are set

They are written well in advance of the exam by the Principal Examiner, in order for stringent revisions and checks to be made. A highly skilled academic then comments on the first submission and then the Principal acts upon these comments. After this a committee of experienced examiners and teacher representatives scrutinises each question and the mark schemes to ensure that they are appropriate to the specification and are fair to candidates.

How exam answers are marked

It should be noted that examiners are given a mark scheme which is a guide as to what we may expect in an answer. However, this mark scheme always allows for the candidate's individual manner of response and will 'credit any valid argument'. You should be familiar with the levels of response for AO1 and AO2, which will show you what aspects are expected for each of the levels.

- **Assessment Objective 1 (AO1)**
  60 out of 100 marks in the A2 module

  This tests knowledge and understanding and questions for this will be set from the 'topics' section of the specification.

  #### Knowledge

  Your writing should show that you know the information and can select what is relevant to that particular question.

  #### Understanding

  You cannot effectively learn by rote. Trying to do this shows a lack of understanding and without the understanding, revision and the writing of an essay is incredibly hard work. Information and evidence that is relevant to the question shows understanding.

  #### Grade boost AO1

  Top tips:

  1. Be concise and clear: include only what is needed. Do not include material that should be AO2 as this cannot be credited in AO1. Do not reproduce a 'here's all I know about…' answer. It is important that the question set is answered. Be aware of the trigger words such as 'explain' or 'examine'. Include examples, quotations and reference to scholars.

  2. Have a logical approach to your writing. This will come with good planning during the revision process. Each paragraph should naturally lead into the next, allowing your writing and argument to flow.

- **Assessment Objective 2 (AO2)**
  40 out of 100 marks in the A2 module

  This is analysis and evaluation. These are often called higher order skills as they involve something more than the skills needed for AO1.

  #### Analysis

  You do this when you explain what a piece of evidence shows or explain the meaning of an idea or concept. Analysis is also shown when you clearly link your information to the set question, making connections between the various points made.

  #### Evaluation

  In order to evaluate, you must understand the information. You will then be able to look at the strengths and/or weaknesses of a particular viewpoint and be able to give a reasoned conclusion.

  #### Grade boost AO2

  Top tips:

  1. Give a variety of responses to the issue raised. These could be arguments in favour of, or against, the issue.

  2. Make use of the views of scholars, making sure that you do analyse their views as opposed to just stating them, which is an AO1 skill.

  3. Always give a conclusion otherwise you are not doing what the question is asking you to do. This means 'rounding up' your analysis. It is always a good idea to keep one point back for the conclusion, possibly the most conclusive piece of evidence in your view. Independent thought is always very welcome.

Exam performance advice and where students go wrong

Good preparation is, of course, a must. With confidence in what you have done, being fully aware of what information to put into what essay, there is less of a chance that things will go wrong. Throughout this guide there are tips related to specific topics. Here follow some general points, which have been noticed over many years of marking A-Level scripts.

Poor exam answers

- Not tailoring the information to answer the specific question set.
- Showing no real awareness of the specification, which means that certain questions, although legitimately asked, seem to be alien to the candidate.
- Lacking awareness of the difference between AO1 and AO2, and therefore dividing the answer inappropriately between parts (a) and (b) of the question.
- Not using key terms (accurately).
- Not writing in a logical fashion and/or legibly.
- Not including accurate reference to scholarly views and/or not including pertinent quotations.
- Not showing independent thought.

Good exam answers

- Answer the question exactly as it is set in this paper, not as it was set on a previous paper, including only what is relevant. This will be a focused and thorough response to the question set rather than a summary of some of the relevant points.
- Show a thorough grasp of the topics listed in the Specification.
- Focus upon knowledge and understanding in part (a), and analysis and evaluation in part (b), demonstrating a range of skills. Part (b) questions should give a balanced evaluation of the issue raised rather than a one-sided answer.
- Use key terms fluently and accurately.
- Write in a logical fashion, which shows essay planning.
- Include reference to scholarly views and include pertinent quotations.
- Show independent thought.
- Use past papers and mark schemes in your revision.
- Have a thorough understanding of the level descriptions and know what needs to be done in order to achieve a Level 7.

Questions and answers

1. Is religious faith rational?

2. Is religious language meaningful?

3. Is religious faith compatible with scientific evidence?

4. Are we 'free beings'?

Topic 1

1 Examine a classical version of the ontological argument.

(30 marks)

Seren's answer:

① Anselm wrote the ontological argument in Proslogion in two forms. This can be seen as an attempt to prove God's existence. To others they see it more as him showing how obvious God's existence was to him.

② It uses a priori reasoning. It is deductive. This means that it starts with a statement or a definition and works through logical stages to come to a conclusion. This method works by the definition then leading on to more premises. If these are all accepted then the conclusion is the logical one. This kind of argument does not need any research to back it up. It just relies on the analysis of a definition.

③ As this is the case here, the definition of God is what Anselm starts with. In his first form he says that God is 'a being than which nothing greater can be thought of'. He says that everyone understands and accepts this definition even if it is to reject it. This includes the fool or the atheist. They reject God's existence but have to have an understanding of God in their mind before they can reject it.

④ He says that existence is a predicate. If God is the greatest being then He must have the predicate of existence. If He did not, He would lack something – the predicate of existence. This would mean that we could think of another being that had the predicate of existence and then this being would be greater than God. But this can't be true as he has already said that *God is the greatest being we can think of*.

⑤ Anselm says that it is greater to exist in reality than in the mind only. If I have an idea of a chocolate fudge cake in my mind then that is a lovely thought. But one that exists in reality can also be eaten and that is so much better. As God is the greatest being we can think of then God must exist in reality as well as the mind because if He did not that would be a contradiction.

⑥ In his second form, he says that God's existence must be necessary. By necessary he means that God cannot not exist. This is the opposite of contingent which is when something could not exist. It makes sense to say that necessary existence is greater than contingent existence as a necessary being just 'is' and relies on nothing else. So, God must have necessary existence otherwise there is a contradiction in the argument. Because if God was only contingent then there could be another being who has necessary existence that would then be greater than God. But this can't be true as we have already stated that God is the greatest being we could think of.

Examiner commentary:

① Sets the scene with important issues raised, which does make a difference to the argument. Descartes, amongst others, could have been an alternative classical form studied.

② Use of key terms with explanations. Perhaps these terms could have been used in the main body of the answer to illustrate certain points.

③ Flows from the previous. Seren could explain the reference to Psalm 14 and why the atheist is tantamount to a fool.

④ What a predicate is is not explained but the understanding is there as to why God needs the predicate of existence.

⑤ This is a key point and the ending really does need developing – why would there be a contradiction if God only existed in the mind?

⑥ Here is the explanation with regard to the contradiction.

Summative comment

Seren has shown understanding of many of the aspects of an argument that does demand certain skills from candidates. Her writing does have a sequence and is accurate. Had she included some more of the intricacies allowing all of the stages of the argument to be explained this would push her up to a Level 7. She scored Level 6, 25 marks.

1 Examine a classical version of the ontological argument.

(30 marks)

Tom's answer:

① The ontological argument of St Thomas Aquinas was an a priori argument. For him God is the most perfect being you can think of. The first form of his argument uses Psalm 14, where the fool says there is no God. But he has a picture of God in his mind.

② Anselm says it is more perfect to exist in reality than if something just exists in your mind. It is better to have £100 in your pocket than just thinking about £100. So God must exist in reality. This is what would make God more perfect. Because something in your mind is not as perfect as something really existing.

③ In the second form of his argument, Anselm says that God's existence is necessary. By this he means that God has to exist. If he did not exist then He would not be perfect because to be the most perfect he has to exist. Because if He could have not been then this would not be perfect.

④ It seems that Anselm is trying to explain why he believes in God rather than trying to prove God. This is because this is a prayer and is probably better for believers than non-believers.

Examiner commentary:

① Three things included in here which should have been taken separately and explained. This would easily have given body to the work and also marks.

② The key point for all candidates is to take Anselm's use of 'perfect' as meaning 'having all perfections'. Then they would be able to understand that to be perfect one must have all perfections, one of which is the perfection of existence (all premises of course, but these are the intricacies of the argument).

③ The same applies as to 2. Tom needs to say that necessary existence is a perfection, as is contingent existence.

④ This does contribute to explaining its purpose but not the argument itself.

Summative comment
Tom has given a 'partially adequate treatment of the topic'. It is better than a bare outline but his knowledge is fairly 'basic'. He scored Level 4, 15 marks.

Q & A

2 'The strengths of the ontological argument outweigh the weaknesses.' Assess this view. *(20 marks)*

Seren's answer:

① On the positive side, the ontological argument is a very logical piece of thinking. It has clear stages, with one part of the argument leading on to the next. It starts with the definition of God that surely people would universally accept.

② It is true that to reject something you have to have a picture or an idea of it in your mind. For example, if someone asked me my view on something if I said I did not like it, I can only say this because I can picture it in my mind (prawns). Or I can only say I do not believe in the tooth fairy because I have a concept of what this would entail in my mind (little girl, wings, ability to move pillow with someone's head on it).

③ So, if we accept the definition of God and the premises of the argument that follows, to reject the conclusion(God exists) would be a contradiction as if God is the definition that everyone would give to Him, then He must have the perfection of existence or else He would not be the most perfect conceivable being. The argument is a wonderful example of word-play that it is hard to deny.

④ Anselm is surely right to say it is better to exist in reality than in mind alone. However, I could say against this that some of the things in my mind can be as good as, if not better than some things in reality.

⑤ However, the weaknesses have been pointed out by a number of scholars. Kant said that existence is not a predicate. If I gave a long list of things they are only predicates if they tell me about what something is, such as my car is white, six-speed gearbox, tinted windows. Exist does not do that.

⑥ Frege discussed first and second order predicates. The cats are black is a first order predicate as it adds to the description of the cats. There are many cats is a second order predicate as it adds nothing to their description. Frege says that Anselm uses exists as a first order where it should be a second order predicate. Exists tells us nothing about the description of something. It just tells us that there is such a thing. 'A cow has udders' tells me something about a cow. 'A cow exists' does not. So, 'God exists' tells us nothing about the description of God so it is not a first order predicate.

⑦ In conclusion I believe that the ontological argument has more weaknesses than strengths as a proof for God's existence. It still seems to me to 'beg the question'. It starts with an assumption and gives premises that are persuasive but by no means necessarily correct. So the play on words is a method that can easily 'take us in'. The case, if you like, has already been decided. I'm with Hume who said that we can't establish the truth of something just by analysing it.

⑧ But, if we say that it is not a proof of God's existence but rather an intellectual explanation of why Anselm believes and what he thinks about God, then that is a different matter. If someone already believes, then his work has many strengths; it is a masterpiece.

Examiner commentary:

① Seren comments on the nature of the argument which is useful as its nature is what drives it.

② She analyses part of the argument. She is not just repeating it. Her own examples show her understanding.

③ The contradiction is explained as opposed to just saying there is one.

④ She gives a point for and against, together. This leads her nicely onto the opposite viewpoint.

⑤ She refers to a scholar. Her explanation is succinct, with examples.

⑥ As 5. Also alludes to Russell.

⑦ A conclusion which is appropriate is needed for Levels 6 and 7. This is given and it is not just a passing comment. It refers to the circular nature of the argument; it gives a different piece of evidence (Hume) and also cleverly suggests that the answer to the essay question may depend on the purpose of Anselm's work.

⑧ Here, Seren explains what many believe is the original intention of Anselm's work.

Summative comment

This is 'focused... mature... different views... schools of thought... evaluated', matching the Level 7 descriptor. There is evidence of independent thought. Seren got Level 7, 20 marks.

2 'The strengths of the ontological argument outweigh the weaknesses.' Assess this view. *(20 marks)*

Tom's answer:

① There are many arguments for and against this statement. Gaunilo, a monk, gave the example of the perfect island. He said that it is the most perfect island that can be thought of. What would it have in it? Maybe all of my friends and family, dead or alive, favourite celebrities, a place where you need no money to survive. According to Anselm's logic, this island must exist in order for it to be the most perfect island. So, after I finish my A Levels I should be able to go there. If only.

② Kant also said that we can't get beyond this world of phenomena (things) so any proof of God's existence is going to fail anyway. God is in the noumenal world. Existence is not a predicate in his view either.

③ Anselm said that God is a special case and so Gaunilo's view is not valid. This is because God and islands are completely different.

④ Overall, I do not think that the argument is a successful one because of all of the criticisms that I have outlined.

Examiner commentary:

① It is the explanation as to why this island must exist according to Anselm's logic that needs explaining. Time and time again I am sure that candidates really do not understand Anselm's use of 'perfect'. Tom here needs to say that existence is a perfection that you can have or lack. To be 'perfect' you need all perfections. Therefore to be the perfect island it needs to have the perfection of existence (in reality – making sure he says in reality is better than in mind alone).

② Two weaknesses shown by Kant that need developing.

③ Again this needs some more explanation of phenomena and noumena as well as explaining what existence as a predicate would mean.

④ The conclusion is not an integral part of the essay; it does attempt an 'assess' but it gives you nothing more.

Summative comment

Tom has been aware of some of the weaknesses of the argument and uses some technical words such as 'noumena' but here his answer shows 'some limited attempt at analysis or comment'. His answer lacks sufficient evidence so it fits with 'issues only partly understood'. Tom scored Level 3, 8 marks.

3 Explain **two** theories of the nature of faith. *(30 marks)*

Seren's answer:

① The first theory comes from Pascal. He believed it was unreasonable to be an atheist. Pascal believed that you should assume God exists in order to find the way of life God wishes us to lead. He said you must 'Hear God'.

② He put forward his ideas in his famous 'wager'. If I believe that God exists, if God does exist I receive eternal life. But if God does not exist there is annihilation (nothing) but I do not know about it. On the other hand, if I believe God does not exist, if God does exist I receive damnation for eternity. If God does not exist I receive annihilation, but do not know about it. So, it is too risky to be an atheist. If you are a theist then you have the best chance of an afterlife.

③ Pascal may be criticised for assuming that God will reward or punish with an afterlife or damnation. If God does not do this his argument is weakened.

④ Much of his thought is based upon mathematical workings out. This is where the idea of his wager has force. If you had to place a bet on something you would surely place your money on that which gave you the surest chance of a win. He is saying that it makes no sense to place your money on something that can never win.

⑤ Another theory is that of Kierkegaard. He had three arguments, certainty, commitment and cost. He said that faith is like 'floating on 70 000 fathoms of water and not being afraid'. This shows that grounding faith in reasoned argument is useless. Reasoned argument would tell you to be afraid!

⑥ His first argument was certainty. A religious believer is convinced they are right about God's existence. Reasoned argument can only suggest that there may be a God. The believer wants to give a complete affirmation.

⑦ The second argument is commitment. When arguments against faith are presented, then faith remains strong. Arguments in favour of faith could fail, so he would say that instead we must take a leap of faith. Faith remains when arguments die out.

⑧ The third argument is cost. Faith based on reason is 'religiously undesirable'. This is because the believer needs faith to be improbable. This is almost like the thrill factor of doing something risky. If you are allowed to do it then you do not really want to. Risk or cost gives faith its value. This contrasts with Pascal who said that the reasonable thing is the thing you should do.

Examiner commentary:

① A short introduction which often settles candidates. The reference to hearing God could be developed.

② The wager is present in a nutshell. Candidates need to go beyond this in order to deal with Pascal comprehensively. Using information in this guide on his theory of faith will help.

③ Not needed in part (a). Seren will gain no credit for this here. This is evaluation.

④ Shows Seren understands the reasoning behind the wager.

⑤ A good introduction which sets the scene.

⑥ She explains this succinctly.

⑦ As point 6 but an explanation of 'leap of faith' would be welcome.

⑧ It is useful to compare and contrast points. Seren needs to be aware that there is, however, a difference between saying that something is not based on reason and saying that something is unreasonable.

Summative comment

Seren's work addresses the question. She shows understanding of the two theories and some apt quotations are used. She does need more information for each theory in order to reach a Level 6. So, she scored Level 5, 24 marks.

3 Explain **two** theories of the nature of faith.

(30 marks)

Tom's answer:

① William James wrote the *Will to believe* where he gave his theory of faith. He said that you can almost make yourself believe in God, it is your choice, your will. This means it is based on a Voluntarist view of faith. It has to be your choice because you have all of the evidence that you are ever going to get. We can't sit on the fence; that would be pointless because no more evidence will come to give us that 'push' to one side or the other.

② I will to believe as there is nothing more I can do. As my decision is not based upon evidence, it has to be based on something else. James says that it is based on 'passional' grounds, meaning I decide according to what best fits with my emotions. This would mean that I would choose what is best for me.

③ He does not see this as a problem. It is not as if not having evidence to seal the issue is devastating. He just says that's how it is, just decide, in fact you have to decide.

④ Pascal's theory is based upon the idea of a wager or a bet. He said belief in God is a good wager. He then sets out to explain why. If I believe, then there is a complete win–win situation. If I do not believe, then it leads either to complete loss or at best, no change. If I believe in God and there is one, there is a big gain – eternal life. If I do not believe in God and there is one, there will be big trouble. If I believe or if I do not believe, if there is no God, well, nothing really.

⑤ So, it is much safer to believe. This is a very reasonable decision and it is worked out on the basis of probabilities, which shows how belief in God is completely rational.

Examiner commentary:

① Tom does get the point across that we simply must decide on the basis of the evidence we have. However, his point about sitting on the fence could be developed – James would say that sitting on the fence is the equivalent of saying you do not believe as you are unwilling to decide that you do.

② Key term, 'passional', used but others such as 'momentous' and 'forced' are missing, which would be needed for the higher marks. 'Choosing what is best for me' should also trigger James' pragmatic theory.

③ Recap.

④ The bare bones of the wager are presented.

⑤ This draws the wager in to the faith and reason debate.

Summative comment

Tom has dealt with the question in a partial fashion. The information given is 'mainly accurate', but the understanding is 'patchy', which is exemplified by the bare bones of the wager and especially his lack of reference to the key terms in James' work which then needed explaining. He scored Level 4, 16 marks.

Q & A

4 'Faith cannot be based upon reasoned argument.'
Assess this view.

(20 marks)

Seren's answer:

① Some would agree with this view. For example, Karl Barth believed that God transcends us. Human reason was corrupted at the Fall and so our reason cannot help us at all. We cannot in any way find God for the reasons just given. Trying to use our reason would be fruitless. This means that God has to find us, God has to reveal. Luther added to this by commenting 'that whore reason'.

② If God then has to reveal, faith must be based upon certain types of revelation. God can reveal through miracles, supernatural experiences, texts and many other ways. Many would consider that revelation could be the basis of faith, as well as build up a faith. It can give things to humans which human reason cannot access. Human faith can then be seen as coming from accepting the revelation.

③ Kierkegaard would support this view. His arguments all show that reason leads us down blind alleys. Reason only gives us probability, it is not a risky business and we cannot commit to it. So, faith cannot be based upon reasoned argument. In fact, faith is an unsupported leap, so it does not have the support of reasoned arguments. I think that this a good piece of evidence in favour of revelation. There are some things that we have to just go for that perhaps our reason tells us not to or our reason does not help us decide.

④ St Augustine commented that faith comes before reason; 'we walk by faith and not by sight'. His divine illumination shows that God must light up human minds. This shows the supernatural element of faith. To me it also shows that faith is not blind faith; revelation does form the basis of faith. It is not therefore human reason that lights up minds in the first instance. So, reason cannot be the basis for faith. However, for Augustine it should be remembered that faith is still seeking understanding.

⑤ However, it may be argued that faith can be based on reason. We as humans are rational beings so surely we can work out our beliefs? Also, if our reason is God-given then surely God gave us enough logic to be able to find Him?

⑥ Thomas Aquinas believed that both reason and revelation are needed. He managed to combine what most would separate. For example, we can use our reason to work out God's existence (Cosmological argument) but need God's revelation for other things that our reason cannot work out, such as the Trinity. So it is not faith or revelation, but both. Although, if it came to the crunch, I would say that he would go for revelation. This is because after years of writing, he had an experience of God. He then said that 'everything I have written seems like straw compared to what has now been revealed to me'.

⑦ Hick said that believing in God is reasonable and it is perfectly rational to believe, just as it is rational to not believe; it all depends on how we see the world.

⑧ To conclude, I believe faith can be based on reason, but I feel that revelation complements faith too. Perhaps some believers would base faith on revelation, whereas others would base it on reason. It all depends on your life experiences. Perhaps someone who is not a believer, on 'hearing' God, may begin to believe. Whereas another person who has never had any experience of God may wish to work things out for themselves, using their reason. But overall, I would say that for the majority of believers faith comes from reason as all experiences have to be interpreted.

Examiner commentary:

① Scholarly views mentioned. Luther could have been developed.

② The variety of types of revelation could be used to good effect but it was here just mentioned.

③ Seren has given her opinion of Kierkegaard rather than just stating. This is very important for the higher marks.

④ Augustine has been mentioned and she does get to grips with using him rather than just stating his view. There is understanding here and, although some sentences could have been in a different order to make her points flow more, it does appear that she sees reason and revelation in Augustine's views.

⑤ Useful points made. Perhaps the rhetorical questions could have been answered.

⑥ A very succinct presentation and analysis of Aquinas.

⑦ This could link in to seeing-as, experiencing-as.

⑧ Independent thought in the conclusion.

Summative comment

Different views have been given which abound with scholars. It has reasoning and the evidence is plentiful. Seren has clearly revised the works of important scholars in relation to specific aspects such as revelation, which has allowed her to not only present their views, but also to give her view of them. She scored Level 6, 18 marks.

4 'Faith cannot be based upon reasoned argument.'
Assess this view.

(20 marks)

Tom's answer:

① Some would say that faith can't be based on reason because as we all have reason, that should mean that we all believe in God. If this reason has been planted into us by God, then it would be used to believe in God. Obviously not everyone does, so faith cannot be based on reason.

② Also, sometimes our reason can be wrong. I may think that something is right but it is not.

③ Others would say that our reason is the best we have.

④ On the other hand, revelation is really clear. It tells us what God is and wants and so this is the best thing to base our faith on. In the Bible, it tells us that God wants us to be stewards. This is very clear.

⑤ But, on the other hand, what if we see something and interpret it differently? Maybe we will misunderstand God's revelation. This can be the case with picture puzzles where we look at the same thing, but one person sees an old lady in the picture and another sees a young lady.

⑥ To conclude, I think faith is an individual thing. Someone may believe and have had no revelation from God. Some may only believe because they have had a revelation, maybe through prayer.

Examiner commentary:

① The first sentence only makes sense with the addition of what follows.

② This is useful but needs expanding. Giving an example and then relating this to faith would have boosted Tom's marks.

③ Same as point 2.

④ Many would say that this is true for propositional revelation (which his example is), but not so with non-propositional. Tom is showing he may not understand the difference between these forms of revelation.

⑤ This is where Tom could have referred to non-propositional. It is a useful inclusion but would have been used to better effect if he had given an example where people could interpret a possible revelation differently.

⑥ The conclusion is stunted, but there is one and it does give something new.

Summative comment

Tom has given an argument which does contain evidence. He has understood the main issue at stake. On some points, analysis is limited but his answer does have a structure and it is better than simplistic or basic. Tom scored Level 4, 12 marks.

Q & A

5 Explain **two** concepts of revelation.

(30 marks)

Seren's answer:

① One concept of revelation is propositional. This says that revelation is found in statements or propositions. God shows important facts to humans and these important facts are then said or written down, for example. The things that are revealed are things that humans could not work out themselves. This does mean that those words or statements are certainly not human words. They are God's words and therefore the truth of them is established without question.

② Holy books are therefore of the utmost importance. So, it can now be understood why some people say that their holy book is their main guide and why it should not be questioned. Of course humans physically wrote the words down but they are written down as a result of a direct revelation from God.

③ So, literalists (people who believe the words in their holy book are word for word true) have very good reasons for that belief. It makes complete sense that God would reveal and that there has to be a place for these words to be found. This can be seen in Islam where the Quran is seen to be the direct revelation of God, unchanged from the time it was revealed to Muhammad (pbuh). When he was told to recite, that is what he did and this recitation is what is found in the Quran.

④ Some would also accept that as well as holy books there are other places where we can find the direct revelation of God in the form of propositions. It may be believed that prophets in the past, such as Isaiah, were the divine mouthpiece. These people may have had a communication from God which they then relayed to others word for word.

⑤ The same can also be said for people within the religion today. So, when the Pope declares something about perhaps a moral or political issue, that proposition may be accepted as being absolutely infallible as it has come directly from God.

⑥ Other statements of belief, such as creeds and so on, could also be seen in the same way.

⑦ A propositional theory of revelation is accompanied by a propositional faith. This means that a person's faith is saying 'yes' to the words, just accepting them as being true. This is very similar to voluntarist theories of faith where basically the person chooses to believe, they say 'yes'.

⑧ A second concept of revelation is non-propositional. This theory does not lay importance on words or propositions. In many ways the words are actually not important at all. It does not mean that holy books are useless or not to be respected, though, as they do contain the events, which is where the revelation is found. There are also important values or morals contained in the books. This would be more of a non-literal approach.

⑨ The events are there to be interpreted. Take the event of the Israelites leaving Egypt at the time of Moses. Non-propositionalists will say that the revelation or disclosure from God is found in that event. God comes into that event in history and sows a seed to possibly allow people to see Him in that event. The words written about it and found in the holy book are not the direct words of God. They are human words, they are fallible. Some will see in that event the saving acts of Yahweh. Others will see it as an event in history. Others will see it as a very lucky incident.

Examiner commentary:

① A good introduction with implications of this theory.

② This shows an understanding of why people have certain views.

③ As point 2 with a particularly pertinent example.

④ This takes propositional beyond books alone, which is what is going to be needed for the higher levels. It's a pity Seren did not look up some quotations from Isaiah.

⑤ A Papal declaration would have been useful.

⑥ So too with a creed.

⑦ Fantastic! This shows 'connections between elements of the course of study'. Not only does it refer to voluntarist faith but it also links revelation to faith. A very astute demonstration of what candidates need to do.

⑧ A good contrast shown as well as implications for holy books.

⑨ An example which shows the non-propositional idea of different interpretations of the same event.

⑩ This is very much like Pascal's 'hidden God'. God gives just enough of Himself so that if humans choose, they can have faith – knock and the door will be opened unto you, seek and you shall find.

⑪ A non-propositional theory of revelation has a non-propositional faith. A person can become aware of God in an event (although the next person may not) and then that person freely responds and has faith.

⑩ The same comment applies as in point 7 regarding 'connections'.

⑪ Links revelation to faith.

Summative comment

I'll say straight away that Seren got Level 7, 30 marks! Yes, there are some things in points 4, 5 and 6 that she could have added in, but the rest is focused and highly accurate. No answer could, nor does it need to, include absolutely everything. Examiners are aware of time constraints.

5 Explain **two** concepts of revelation.

(30 marks)

Tom's answer:

① Two concepts of revelation are propositional and non-propositional. Propositional is when a person receives messages from an outside source. They tell us deep truths about things like God's nature or will.

② As with most other religious experiences, it can be frightening or strange. Caroline Franks-Davis outlines five features of revelation that she says are common to them. She says that they are sudden and short. They tell you something. They are hard to put into words, but key for propositional they are received with complete conviction. Many of these features can explain propositional but they are not so well equipped to explain non-propositional.

③ A good example is Muhammad. He got a message from an outside source and he wrote this message down word for word.

④ Non-propositional can give a message just as deep as propositional. This is known as realisation or enlightenment. A good example is the Buddha. He had a revelation after he saw four sights. He sat under a tree to find the answer to the meaning of life and had a revelation. His questions were answered and he felt that he had to pass them on. From this, Buddhism developed.

⑤ This experience came from within, unlike the propositional revelation. Some people may not have this realisation even if they have the same experience.

Examiner commentary:

① Basic, not really showing an understanding of the importance of the words as the mode of God's revelation.

② Tom is straining to use aspects of work on religious experience in this essay at times where it cannot fit. He has, at least, alluded to the idea that propositional faith is complete conviction.

③ Pity he did not develop this.

④ The 'realisation' part is OK. I could see how such an experience could be used, if used correctly, particularly the passing on of the experience. But, without a belief in God then it is hard to see how the Buddha's experience can be used as a means through which God was shown. He could have made something of the propositions in terms of teachings of a religion.

⑤ This does show the ambiguous nature of non-propositional. But the 'within' aspect is confused in relation to non-propositional.

Summative comment

I felt that Tom did give an 'outline answer'. He is just beyond the 'glimmer of understanding'. He does have 'limited understanding'. Had he not tried to make unsuccessful links to religious experiences then he could have explored other points further. He scored Level 3, 10 marks.

Topic 2

6 Explain the problems of religious language.

(30 marks)

Seren's answer:

① Religious language deals with the metaphysical, mysterious and transcendent, all ideas that are beyond our experience. This is one of the problems. If we say that 'God is timeless', how can we possibly understand what that means? Some of this language is also quite abstract and hard to understand. The ontological argument is a good example in my opinion!

② Another problem is that we are using words to describe God that we use every day. Surely this is either inappropriate or inadequate. Nothing can properly explain exactly what we want to say about God and the end result is that it does not really do it justice. There are many examples of this. I could say that 'God is wise', but so is my teacher. This does not convey what I want to say about God. 'I worship God, she worships Manchester United'; this is an inappropriate comparison. God is meant to be so 'other' that all words may be doomed to failure anyway.

③ If I do try to describe God using the words I have at my disposal, then there are still problems. For example, 'God is loving'. What does loving mean when applied to God? A related problem is that I may end up anthropomorphising God, giving God human qualities that are misleading. For example, 'God was with me during that difficult time'. Does this imply that God has a physical presence? Does it mean that God is a larger version of my best friend with a mouth to speak words that helped me? This is not what many believers would want to picture God as.

④ Within religion, words are used that are words that we may also use in everyday life. They may mean completely different things so confusions may arise. This is another problem for religious language. Spirit in religion is different from team spirit and also an alcoholic spirit.

⑤ Some religious language is confusing, possibly even paradoxical. The Trinity is one example; how can something be the father, the son and the Holy Spirit, all at once? Also if we say that God is all powerful, He should be able to do anything. What if we then say that God has the power to create an environmental disaster that He cannot prevent from happening? But, if God has complete power then there should be no disaster that He cannot prevent.

⑥ The Vienna Circle presented further problems for religious language. They said the meaning of a statement lies in its verification. They said that a statement is only meaningful if it is analytic or synthetic. So, it either needs analysis or its needs empirical testing. This is a huge problem for religious language as it is neither of these two categories. Statements like 'God in heaven' or 'God loves me' are neither analytic (like $4 + 4 = 8$) nor can we empirically test it (like I can test if my teacher is wearing a tie today).

⑦ A.J. Ayer said that a being that is non-empirical is nonsensical if referred to in statements. There is no sense experience that would allow me to test statements about God (is God wise?) and so they are meaningless. He did distinguish between strong and weak verification. But, religious language is still meaningless under both of these.

Examiner commentary:

① This is packed with ideas that could be developed; for example, why may timelessness be hard to understand?

② Seren draws out the two separate problems of inadequate and inappropriate well and gives examples to show her understanding.

③ Two problems are mentioned here. An allusion to work on analogy in relation to what 'loving' means is given and anthropomorphising is understood.

④ The equivocal use of language and consequent problems is mentioned, again with an example.

⑤ Confusing or paradoxical language is an excellent inclusion here and the examples clearly show that Seren fully understands this material.

⑥ The problem of verification is seen as one amongst many. It is succinctly put with two religious statements as examples.

⑦ Perhaps she could have explained why 'strong and weak' and why religious language fails under both of these categories.

⑧ A. Flew's work presented a problem for religious language. He said that only statements that could be falsified are meaningful. Flew said that all religious language cannot be falsified, will not be falsified by believers and so it is meaningless. He gave an example of a believer saying that God loves us like a father. Then, a child dies of throat cancer and it seems that God does not care. Flew says that a believer ignores this evidence against God's love and qualifies it by saying 'it is a different kind of love'. They qualify their first statement so much that it 'dies a death by a thousand qualifications'.

⑨ So, there are many problems in religious language. One is the work of Ayer and Flew and there are many other general problems. These have meant that philosophers have tried to respond by showing that the problems of religious language can be overcome.

⑧ Flew is explained well, with the use of an example and what this means for religion is stated.

⑨ Simply rounds it up.

Summative comment
This deals with many problems, presenting an answer of breadth. Effective use is made of examples and the understanding is thorough and mature. She shows that verification and falsification are not the only problems for religious language. That can be a whole question on its own. It seems that Seren has taken quite a broad view of aspects of religion to come up with these ideas. She scored Level 7, 29 marks.

6 Explain the problems of religious language. *(30 marks)*

Tom's answer:

① For humans it is hard to use our words to describe God, as God is a superior being. If we say 'God is love' we diminish God's superiority.

② The main problem is that humans are trying to understand something we have no understanding of. If we say 'God is all knowing' how do we know this is true? Religious language describes God as He, but we only know this from the Bible.

③ If we were made in God's image then this does not keep the boundary between God and us which is needed.

④ A.J. Ayer said that language is only meaningful if it can be verified. For example, 'a ball is round' can be verified. Also, a statement like 3 × 3=4 is meaningful. It is not right but I can show that it is wrong. Religious language gets into problems because some non-cognitive statements (no factual evidence) can still be meaningful as it is meaningful to the individual. For example, 'God is my saviour'.

⑤ Religious language also uses symbolism when talking about God. When symbols are used there is still the potential for the meaning to be lost and so the symbol does not really describe anything.

Examiner commentary:

① This is OK but marks will increase if some more body is given to the point made.

② The same point applies as for point 1.

③ This is similar to the problem in point 1.

④ This could be 'taken somewhere' but Tom does seem confused in terms of the point he would like to make. He needs to explain why some religious language may be considered as non-cognitive and why some would say this language is meaningless. The example is stated and not used.

⑤ The problem of symbol is fine, drawn in from another area of topic 2. Again, examples would help his marks.

Summative comment
This was very borderline Level 3 and 4. Because the first three paragraphs were brief and did contain some repetition, the number of problems was limited as was their understanding. Tom scored Level 3, 14 marks.

7 'Religious language is meaningless.'
Assess this view.

(20 marks)

Seren's answer:

① A.J Ayer's strong verification principle (that you have to in practice verify) has been criticised for being so rigid that it makes meaningless many statements that we would consider meaningful. Examples of this would be events from history or stories about historical figures. I cannot in practice prove that Columbus discovered America but it is still a meaningful statement. So, if the principle that is used to class religious language as meaningless is flawed then perhaps religious language does have meaning after all.

② Also, there are many things that we may talk about that do not fit into the verification principle's categories that we still class as meaningful, for example expressing an opinion or emotions.

③ A crucial flaw to the verification principle is that it fails its own test. The principle is not a tautology nor can it be verified by appeal to the five senses. So, this flaw means that it is not a good tool to use to criticise religious language, so that language may live to fight another day.

④ Hick says in his eschatological verification that religious language is meaningful. This says that when we die the truth of God/religion will be there to be confirmed. But, this still means that in this life religious language is meaningless. However, as the conclusion that we can verify after death is based upon the verification principle, which may itself be invalid (due to flaws in it) then this could make eschatological verification invalid.

⑤ There are also criticisms of falsification, which, if successful, allow religious language to be meaningful. R.M. Hare suggests that a belief may be meaningful even if it can't be falsified. He illustrates this in his parable of the paranoid student. This student is convinced that his teachers want to murder him. His friends present him with the kindest teachers, but attempts to falsify his belief fail. The man thinks they are showing 'diabolical cunning'. This belief has considerable influence on the student's life and so is meaningful.

⑥ This is a 'blik' and Hare says that religion is a 'blik', too, a way of seeing life. If we follow the result of the parable then religious language is meaningful even though it cannot be falsified.

⑦ Other philosophers have argued that religious language is meaningful. Wittgenstein, for example, in his later work argued that the meaning of a word can be found in its use. We can only find out the use of a word by observing its use in its language game. He said that religious language is meaningful when used within the religious language game. To back up his view, we can see evidence of this if we observe religion – people in that game are a community and have a shared understanding of the words.

⑧ Science may class religious language as meaningless but under Wittgenstein's theory, this conclusion is wrong. It is meaningful and to see it as otherwise is to misunderstand the function of language.

⑨ Other philosophers, such as Braithwaite, say that religious language is meaningful. Religious statements, like moral statements, have a function – to refer to a way in which you intend to behave. As they have a use they are meaningful.

Examiner commentary:

① Analysing the logic and effectiveness of the verification principle works well here.

② Specific examples of different types of non-cognitive language could be included here but the point made is valid.

③ The fact that the verification principle does not fit into its own categories is explained.

④ Seren has referred to Hick's ideas and has effectively analysed and evaluated from more than one perspective.

⑤ The parable is explained well and starts the paragraph by linking it to the question regarding meaningfulness.

⑥ This, crucially, applies the usage of the parable's 'blik' to religion.

⑦ A concept of religious language is introduced which allows Seren to broaden the scope of her answer.

⑧ The implications for religion are made clear.

⑨ Another scholar included. Perhaps this could have been included with information from paragraph two in order to 'tighten' this.

⑩ In conclusion, the arguments given by the Logical Positivists are fairly strong and do make us think about what we class as meaningful. However, there are flaws which weaken the force of their conclusions. I think that the different philosophers who say that religious language is meaningful have a much stronger case. As Swinburne said, we may not be able to verify or falsify whether toys move when no one is looking. But, I understand this statement, it still has meaning. In terms of religion, I may not be able to verify or falsify, 'God loves us' but I certainly understand what this sentence means, it is not meaningless.

⑩ A conclusion, with some independent thought and the inclusion of fresh material to make her point is a good technique.

Summative comment
This gives 'different views, including...scholars'. It is 'strongly supported' and 'an appropriate conclusion is drawn'. Information revised is related to the question asked. Seren scored Level 7, 20 marks.

7 'Religious language is meaningless.'
Assess this view.

(20 marks)

Tom's answer:

① A.J. Ayer, a logical positivist was influenced by the Vienna Circle. He said that for language to be meaningful it had to be confirmed empirically. So, 'Wendy's house has four bedrooms' is meaningful as we can check whether this is true or false. It does not matter if she has three bedrooms; it is still meaningful.

② Religious statements cannot be verified. We cannot go and check if God is Trinity or if God is omnibenevolent. So, religious language is meaningless.

③ But, the verification principle has come under fire as things like 'the Battle of Hastings took place in 1066' would be meaningless; we cannot check up on it ourselves now by seeing it. This would be the case under the strong principle. The fact that Ayer developed the weak principle shows the problems with the strong form.

④ But Ayer says that religious language is still meaningless under the strong and the weak because we also do not know how to verify any religious statements. At any point in life, I cannot go to where God 'lives' to check things.

⑤ David Hume developed 'bliks'. His story is about a student who thinks that all of his dons are out to kill him. This shows he has a belief that he cannot prove but it is still a meaningful belief. The same can be said for belief in the existence of God.

⑥ Wittgenstein said that religion is a language game and is meaningful because it has use. But, people have criticised him by saying that religion and other parts of life are not separate; someone could be a scientist, who is quite good at plumbing and is also a Christian lay minister. That person is involved in many language games, so they are not as isolated as Wittgenstein made out. But, on the other hand, he does make sense in that during a service the minister would probably not shout out 'water leak' nor would the scientist say in the laboratory 'I baptise you'.

⑦ I do not agree with the statement.

Examiner commentary:

① This is correct but Tom needed to do two things to increase the evidence in this paragraph. First, he needed to explain why it is still meaningful if false. Secondly and importantly reference to the analytic side to the work of the logical positivists would give the 'full' picture.

② Paragraph one's point is related to religion.

③ Tom needs to refer his line of argument here to the question.

④ The difference between strong and weak has not really been explained and then analysed.

⑤ At A2 we do expect students to know the correct names of scholars. If you are unsure (like Tom here) it is better to leave the name out. Also, Tom has not understood the application of Hare's parable is to falsification rather than verification. However, the general point he makes is relevant to the question.

⑥ Some useful assessment of Wittgenstein, with an example that I have never read before!

⑦ This is certainly not classed as a conclusion. The question asks the candidate to 'assess'. Giving one sentence like this is not really any better than no sentence at all.

Summative comment
Tom's lack of conclusion, whatever the main body of the essay is like, already imposes a self-inflicted ceiling on his marks. It is clear that he has revised some of the necessary features but he has not always been able to give more than limited analysis as he has not made the most of the information in terms of applying it to religious language. Tom scored, Level 4, 11 marks.

8 Explain **two** different concepts of religious language.

(30 marks)

Seren's answer:

① I will be looking at Analogy and Language games. Both of these concepts are used in order to show that we can speak meaningfully about God. There are some who say we cannot make meaningful statements about God at all. Followers of the verification principle such as A. J. Ayer, for example, would say that whatever statement we make about God cannot be verified and is meaningless. Both of my concepts are ways of talking about God with meaning.

② In Analogy, St Thomas Aquinas claims to provide a way to construct meaningful statements about God and avoid misrepresenting Him. There is a grave danger that we misrepresent God if we talk about him univocally which means using one word in two statements where the word means the same thing. This could reduce God to the human level as it may then seem that when we say 'Lisa is kind' and 'God is kind' that they are exactly the same. Also our language is finite and inadequate to directly relate to God.

③ However, if we refer to God equivocally, which is to use the same word in different senses such as 'bat in the cave' as opposed to 'a cricket bat' we learn nothing about God as God is then completely different from humans.

④ An analogy is a comparison between two things which in other ways are dissimilar. Speaking analogically, says Aquinas, allows us to use the same word for 'different' things but to find a point of comparison between them. In this way we can make meaningful statements about God.

⑤ He breaks down analogical statements into two categories. The first is attribution and the second is proportion. Attribution statements are shown in the statements: 'the bull is healthy' and 'the bull's urine is healthy'. Aquinas says this kind of idea can be applied to God.

⑥ There is a connection that Aquinas believes exists between God and His creation (just as the health of the urine is attributed to the health of the bull). So, for example, we can know that God is kind as He is the cause of the kindness of Lisa, in my previous example.

⑦ Proportional statements mean that all created things possess a nature. God possesses a nature. Therefore, what it means to be 'a kind lady' and 'a kind God' is different as they possess different natures. But they have kindness in proportion to the creature that they are. We can say that because Lisa is kind, God is kind as God must possess what is necessary for a person to be kind. He caused us, so must have had kindness to cause it in others.

Examiner commentary:

① This introduction puts the essay into a context which is useful and many candidates feel that this is necessary. There is, however, not the time to do more than Seren has done.

② This explains where analogy fits in to other types of language.

③ As point 2. It is useful that she understands the possible dangers with equivocal and univocal and how analogy may help when talking about God.

④ A definition, which could have been accompanied by an example.

⑤ There could have been a further development of the thinking behind the healthy bull and urine.

⑥ The causal link is of supreme importance to include.

⑦ Proportion is dealt with, no problem.

⑧ This does not mean that we know what God's kindness exactly is. We can just know that he has kindness and has it in proportion to being God.

⑨ Language games says that we can talk about God meaningfully without having to verify our statements. Verification belongs to a different language game. It is not part of the religious language game. The religious language game is not a 'physical things' game and therefore verification does not apply.

⑩ We associate Wittgenstein with this view. He said that all games have rules. These rules only work when the game is being played. In other words, words are there to be used. People in a different game cannot criticise the religious language game; it is just playing its game with its rules. He used the example of a soul. It applies to the religious language game but not the science game.

⑪ He said that words are like tools, just like a drill and a hammer have different functions. An author would not take them when she sits down to write a book, but you would not criticise her for not doing so. The same is true of religion. Religious people take their own tools into their game and use them in a way that is appropriate to them.

⑫ 'Do not ask for its meaning, ask for its use.' Wittgenstein said that if we look at words with no context to surround them then we are going to get things wrong. If we see how they are used in a form of life then they do have a function. For example, 'pass' would mean something different in the football game and in a quiz.

⑬ So we can talk about God using these concepts.

⑧ This is drawing out the concept of analogy.

⑨ Seren puts language games into a context, too.

⑩ There is a lot of information here. It could be taken apart somewhat, but there are time limits that we are aware of.

⑪ The example is drawn back to religion.

⑫ Shows understanding. Ideally, I would like to see some more quotes with links to religion.

⑬ Some disagree of course!

Summative comment

Seren has given a fairly full answer. She has stuck to the 'firm favourites' in terms of Aquinas and Wittgenstein. There is no compulsion to do otherwise but it does give candidates another string to their bow to look at more contemporary scholars. Analogy was more comprehensive than Language games and it did flow better. Had Language games been of a similar standard I feel she could have got full marks. She scored Level 6, 26 marks.

Q&A

8 Explain **two** different concepts of religious language.

(30 marks)

Tom's answer:

① First, I will look at symbols. There are many symbols in religion. They are often the first thing you learn about in R.E. in school – the Christian cross, the Hindu 'aum' amongst others. There are also symbols such as water and the dove that are used all of the time. Many would say that using symbols is the best way for religious language as it allows us to get rid of any possible confusion that may arise from words, for example.

② Paul Tillich said that symbols allow us to discover what may not be discovered by looking at something or hearing something alone. Symbols, he said, open up our souls. Symbols point us to meaning that is inspirational and really allows us to 'see' in the understanding sense.

③ He said that symbols help bring understanding about God. He said the religious language is a kind of poetry. When people use it, he says they are trying to 'interpret' or 'communicate' a religious experience. This is what symbols allow a person to do.

④ He said that there is a difference between signs and symbols. A sign is something that can point you in right direction, like a road sign or it tells people about something, for example a no smoking sign.

⑤ But, a symbol is much more than this. A sign does not really mean anything to you. It does not make you emotional, whereas a symbol can do these things.

⑥ A symbol participates in what it points to, like the Star of David.

⑦ Another concept is Via Negativa. This says that, since part of God's nature is unknowable it is impossible to make a statement about what God is. So, Via Negativa says we must say what God is not. So, 'God is not a physical thing' could be used here.

⑧ This concept may be used as it stops people from thinking they can know everything about God. It shows the difference between God and humans. This God seems rather awesome as we can't pinpoint exactly what God is like.

⑨ I do not like this concept as to me it makes God really impersonal and what would He be like anyway?

Examiner commentary:

① Fine as an introduction. Gives us a little information as to the use of symbols.

② There is knowledge of the opening up of the soul; I am not convinced there is sound understanding though.

③ Again, key words used but are they really understood?

④ Necessary to show the difference.

⑤ Why can a symbol do these things? An example?

⑥ Participates, yes, but does Tom know what this means in relation to symbols? His example does not illustrate this.

⑦ Not one stated on the specification, but perfectly acceptable. However, the material is sparse.

⑧ The purpose of it is getting a little close to evaluation.

⑨ This is evaluation. This suggests that Tom is not completely aware of the demands of AO1 and AO2.

Summative comment

Tom has given this a go and I feel he has tried to learn some things that he did not really understand. Hence he displays 'basic or patchy understanding' shown by quotations that are not explained and examples that are either lacking or not developed. Tom scored Level 4, 16 marks.

Topic 3

9 Examine philosophical issues raised by the concept of miracle.

(30 marks)

Seren's answer:

① There are a number of issues raised when discussing the concept of miracle. One is that there is not only one definition of miracle. There are so many; such as an extraordinary event, an act of God, a transformation in a person or situation, or an event that 'beats the odds'.

② Because of this great number of definitions, there are issues raised. This is because working with so many different definitions leaves us with confusion as to whether or not a miracle has happened. For one person with one definition a miracle may have occurred. But for a person with a different definition a miracle may not have occurred as the event does not fit their definition. We are then left with the issues of how to judge that event. It seems problematic to have no definitive judgement on the matter. This is an issue raised by different definitions of miracle.

③ Related to this is the issue as to whether there is only one 'answer' to the question of what a miracle actually is. If there is, then the problem is that we are declaring all of the other definitions wrong.

④ A realist would agree with this view and say that there is only one answer to every question. They accept that they may not know what that answer is at the present time, but there still is only one answer. If then a person says a miracle is 'a change for the better in a person', they are only right if this corresponds to the truth. This is an issue as it does not allow for individual interpretations of what a miracle is.

⑤ Linked to this is the issue that if realists are correct in their view, truth or falsity does not depend on the individual, the society we live in or our own definitions. This is an issue as it forces people to adopt certain definitions of miracle that they may not agree with.

⑥ Another philosophical issue is that witnesses to miracles may be unreliable. Often the witness may be religious in the first place so may believe that they saw a miracle or may report a miracle to promote their religion. The witnesses may be fanciful in their ideas, determined to make wondrous claims for the drama of it. Hume pointed this out.

⑦ Another philosophical issue is the problem it raises concerning an interventionist God. Surely such a God demolishes the structure of the universe that the Cosmological and Teleological arguments establish for the universe. Intervention is a haphazard thing. This randomness is at variance with a designed world.

⑧ Also, this randomness portrays a God who prefers to help some rather than others, who decides on a whim who to spare. This God is not a morally just one.

⑨ The last philosophical issue raised by the concept of miracle is that it is impossible to determine whether something is a miracle or merely a coincidence. How do we know if a person who had a 'miracle' cure would have improved anyway? Maybe the person who escaped a crash 'miraculously' could just as easily have the situation explained by a normal set of circumstances. In Holland's train example, the driver fainted due to a medical condition that can be explained. It was an extraordinary set of events, happening just at the right time, but the issue is, when, if ever, does a coincidence become a miracle?

Examiner commentary:

① This prepares the groundwork for the next point.

② The issue regarding different definitions is a real one and it warrants comment. Perhaps using specific examples of definitions here would further the point being made.

③ The whole question of one or many 'truths' allows Seren to refer to 'realist' and 'anti-realist'.

④ The correspondence and coherence theories of truth are not regular features of essays but are welcome additions. They do allow for an extra component in an answer.

⑤ As point 4.

⑥ Tying in the issues raised by Hume with regard to testimony to miracles shows Seren using material wisely. This certainly does raise a philosophical issue.

⑦ The problem of an interventionist God is used here. She has in this point raised one issue regarding such intervention. She has used material from AS also.

⑧ Here is another issue concerning an interventionist God. Maybe reference could be made to Wiles.

⑨ Holland's definition of miracle is addressed and some exemplification is given.

Summative comment
Seren has drawn in a variety of material and has touched upon most relevant points. Her answer fits 'presented with accuracy and relevance, along with clear understanding' giving her a Level 6, 27 marks.

153

9 Examine philosophical issues raised by the concept of miracle.

(30 marks)

Tom's answer:

① There are issues raised by the concept of miracle. Wiles says that if some people are saved from enemies but others are not, then this lays God open to some serious questioning.

② Another scholar says that miracles are just coincidences. If the sun rose and set in the opposite direction to what is usual, then this is just a coincidence. We would just need to re-write the law of nature to suit this new situation.

③ The laws of nature present an issue in itself. If laws of nature cannot be broken, then a miracle cannot happen. This is because some will say that the 'laws' are only based upon what we know already, up to the present time. There is no saying that this 'rule' will last for ever. We do not know what will happen tomorrow, so if something happens that hasn't happened so far, we have just found out something new.

④ Some miracles seem to be pointless. If there is no real reason for it happening, nobody benefits, then we can question whether it really is a miracle.

⑤ Aquinas mentions three types of miracle, such as God doing what nature can't do, God doing what nature can do but nature does it in a different order and God doing what nature can do but without using nature. This is an issue.

⑥ There could also be misinterpretations. Some say that Jesus did not really die but was in a state of coma, so there was no Resurrection as such.

⑦ Another philosophical issue is that it may be that there are just no miracles as such, just new discoveries. What may seem a miracle today could happen all of the time in 200 years' time. No doubt 2000 years ago our technology would have been seen as a miracle, so perhaps we are giving an incorrect term to something that is just scientific advancement.

Examiner commentary:

① Wiles' moral rejection of miracles could be developed here. This could then draw out what the issue is.

② Tom has conflated two ideas here, that of coincidence and the laws of nature. He should have dealt with these separately as there is much to write about both.

③ Laws of nature are dealt with here which leaves coincidence rather untouched.

④ This issue could really have been made apparent with the inclusion of some examples.

⑤ The question is raised as to why this is an issue. A point made always needs to be backed up with evidence.

⑥ Tom is alluding to the Resurrection as a miracle and thereby suggesting that if there is doubt over Jesus' death then there is doubt over the miracle. But, he does not state this and marks cannot be awarded for allusion only.

⑦ This is related to Tom's point 3. Perhaps these points would go well together.

Summative comment

Tom has touched upon a number of issues that miracles raise. However, in order to raise his marks he needs to draw them out more as opposed to just stating some of them, which he does on occasion. Breadth or depth is allowed; Tom makes some broad points at times without adding accompanying evidence. He scored Level 4, 18 marks.

10 Outline differences between religious and scientific views of the origins of the universe and of human life.

(30 marks)

Seren's answer:

① The first difference is that religious views on both of these things are within a very short period of time. In the Genesis story, the start of the universe and human life happen within the space of a week. However, the scientific account has a substantially larger timescale. Between the origin of the universe and the origin of human life, there are billions of years. The Big Bang and Evolution are two distinctly separate events, whereas in Genesis they are more or less part of the same event.

② This ties in with another difference. In the religious accounts, humans are part of the process at the beginning. They were created on day 6. They are part of the original purpose of Creation. However, in the scientific accounts humans are not part of the process at the start. Life on earth is a considerable amount of time after the Big Bang and human life is a considerable amount of time after the start of life on earth.

③ Another difference is that the Big Bang appears to be an 'accident'. It could be conceived that it had not happened as it is a random event. The explanation for its occurrence is not universally agreed upon. However, this is in stark contrast to the religious accounts. Here, Creation is a deliberate choice, a plan, the explanation for which is quite clear; God wanted to make the universe and life on earth.

④ This leads to a related difference. The scientific accounts have no deeper or spiritual meaning to them whereas the religious accounts are steeped in meaning. Everything is here because God wanted it to be.

⑤ The religious accounts (apart from Buddhism) include a god or gods. In science a god is not needed so this is a difference.

⑥ According to religion, God created *ex nihilo* (out of nothing) whereas the scientific account has everything coming about as the result of an explosion where things came into being due to the coming together of certain elements.

⑦ In religious accounts of Creation humans are 'special'. Humans are made in God's image, they have an elevated status, and they are created to be the high point of Creation. In science, we have a different story. We may be, right now, the most evolved species but we were not at the beginning. We are not special in this sense, nor are we made in God's image. Neither are humans the last species necessarily in evolutionary terms. We are not special in the religious sense that we were made to be stewards.

⑧ Darwin's theory of Evolution states that humans are the result of a natural process of survival of the fittest, without reference to a designer God. We are as we are now due to small changes that happened over a long period of time, with us having evolved from apes. This is very different to the Genesis account of all species, including humans being made in their current form. The religious account needs an intelligent designer to arrange this. Science does not.

Examiner commentary:

① Seren starts with the reference to the obvious differences in timescale. She could, perhaps, have quoted what happened on certain days in Genesis or looked at other religions.

② She draws out purpose by referring to humans inhabiting the world early on in the Genesis account. Again, quotations would be welcome.

③ This leads her on to the idea of purpose deriving from the idea that the universe was the conscious choice of God. Perhaps listing some of the purposes stated in Genesis would have been a good addition.

④ The spiritual aspect of religious accounts is interesting and could be taken further.

⑤ Perhaps here is the point at which I really expected an account other than Genesis. This would give breadth to the answer.

⑥ Seren could have drawn out the idea of God's omnipotence here.

⑦ Again, here was the time for some quotations, but the difference stated is still very valid.

⑧ Fixity of species as opposed to evolution is used here.

⑨ In terms of the *age of the universe*, science says it is some 15 billion years old. This is very different to a literal interpretation of Genesis that says that the universe is a maximum of 10 000 years old.

⑩ Science has evidence for its theories of the Big Bang and Evolution. Science can track what happened seconds after the Big Bang happened. They have evidence for Evolution, for example in fossil records. However, religious accounts are found in sacred texts and rely on faith. It has no 'proof' as such, unlike science.

⑪ If we accept the Steady State theory, then this provides another difference. This theory has no need for a God, unlike the religious accounts. The theory states that there is no start to the universe. The religious accounts have to have a starting point.

⑫ Another difference is the different questions they seem to answer. Science deals with the 'How' it all happened, the physical process. However, religion deals with the 'Why' looking at the reasons behind the process. This gives us a different focus.

⑬ This means that scientific accounts are practical accounts, dealing with the use of reason. Religion is different. It deals with the aesthetic side to life, with faith and looks to the deeper significance of these events.

⑭ Scientific theories are not really open to interpretation. The Big Bang is presented as it is, an account that seems to fit the facts available. It does not change. What science today says happened 5000 years after the Big Bang is what science will say in the future. Religious accounts are different. There are different interpretations of Creation stories and as time goes on there will probably be more in order to take account of new findings.

⑮ I think that the biggest difference is that the religious accounts delve deeply into what it means to be human. Scientific accounts are just cold and stark. Religion is warm and personal.

⑨ Use of material regarding the age of the universe is presented and shows a stark difference. There is scope for even more key dates to be put in to emphasise the difference further.

⑩ Whilst this is a contentious issue, Seren is justified in suggesting this as a difference.

⑪ Good use of theories other than the Big Bang allows for a wider scope.

⑫ This is a commonly identified difference. Seren explains in a basic form what this means. She could link it to the information earlier on 'choice' versus 'accident'.

⑬ The debate regarding 'reason' from Topic 1 could be used to good effect in this question.

⑭ There are, of course, different interpretations of scientific findings, too, but Seren does make a valid point nevertheless. She is showing that the religious accounts do divide believers in terms of interpretation.

⑮ The cold logic of Athens could never understand what happened at Jerusalem. Seren has stumbled upon a philosophical gem!

Summative comment

Seren has done what has been asked of her. She has not just given accounts of what religion and science say. She has drawn out the differences. She has included reference to very many of them too. Some would like to see other Creation stories referred to; however, there is no compulsion to do this in order to secure the top grades. She scored Level 7, 30 marks.

10 Outline differences between religious and scientific views of the origins of the universe and of human life.

(30 marks)

Tom's answer:

① Religion and Science have very different views. It has been a subject of great debate for many years. Religion will point to Genesis for the answer. This says that God created the world in 7 days, which shows God's omnipotence.

② However, some religious people in the modern age would look at Genesis in a non-literal way. They could suggest that each day God created something represented a period of time, not 24 hours.

③ It is general knowledge in science that the universe was caused by the Big Bang, a massive explosion millions of years ago. This created the universe. Science may even say that there have been lots of Big Bangs throughout the years. As far as we know, this is the only one to produce intelligent life.

④ Darwin came up with the theory of Evolution which said that animals have adapted to their surroundings. He suggests humans are direct descendants of apes. This disagrees with the religious claim that humans are made in the image of God. We are just better developed animals according to science.

⑤ He backed up his claim with fossil records, showing small changes over time. Also, he looked at different types of creatures that were adapted to their environment.

⑥ Other Creation stories have a God in them who made the world. This happens in all main religions apart from Buddhism.

Examiner commentary:

① 6 days! He could also say that other religions may not look to Genesis.

② This does not show a difference between religion and science as such.

③ Here Tom states a scientific account. What he needs to do in this question is to show the difference between this and a religious account. This can be done very simply by phrases such as 'in contrast to this' or 'the scientific account says something different'. Also, change millions to billions! Some question whether the Big Bang can be referred to as a creation.

④ Tom has shown a difference by a turn of phrase. He could make more of the Genesis account in general and more specifically what it means to be made in the 'image of God'.

⑤ Yes, but not relevant if simply recounting a fact, as opposed to drawing out a difference.

⑥ Same as point 5. It's a pity Tom did not say 'science is different as it has no God in its account'.

Summative comment

Tom has mainly stated facts as opposed to explaining differences. His account is narrow in its restriction of facts. He scored Level 3, 12 marks.

11 'Arguments against miracles are more convincing than arguments in their favour.' Assess this view.

(20 marks)

Seren's answer:

① For some this statement is true. This is because they believe in a timeless God. Such a God exists outside of time and this God cannot act in time. So, miracles as interventions into time to make a change cannot occur.

② However, others who may accept a timeless God would still say that miracles as a result of God's intervention can occur. Such a person would be Aquinas. Here we must understand the principle of double agency. This is when God acts through another to bring about God's will. So, this is an argument in favour of miracles; God the primary cause acts through secondary causes. This could allow us in today's world to see medical 'wonders', for example, conducted by surgeons, to be an act of God.

③ Some believe in an everlasting God. This God is in time so can obviously act in time to bring about a miracle. So, there is no issue with regard to miracles happening here. However, some would say that a God, in time, who acts sometimes rather than always, is a concerning issue. A God who seems to cause a bizarre miracle yet fails to help starvation in Africa brings great philosophical issues. So for some, this is an argument against miracles happening. So, arguments against miracles are here convincing. Surely, it is said, God cannot perform miracles, because if God could and does not then God would not be 'worthy of worship' as Wiles puts it.

④ However, I see Wiles' argument against miracles as unconvincing. This is because Wiles then goes on to say that God has performed a miracle; the World as a whole. There is a contradiction here in my eyes. Either God can or cannot perform miracles. Full stop.

⑤ The scientific arguments against miracles are strong. The scientific method will not allow for miracles to occur. The method requires observation, hypothesis and testing which a miracle cannot satisfy. Also, if a miracle is termed a 'one-off', Science will never accept it as for scientific validity, an event needs to be repeatable, which by definition, a miracle cannot. Lastly, if a new finding occurs, Science will not declare a miracle but will simply amend the law of nature to include the new finding. I think this is perfectly justified as we find new things out all of the time. Why should we declare all new things to be a miracle?

⑥ However, on the other hand, the scientific method does not make arguments for miracles completely unconvincing. This is because it doesn't really make sense to amend the laws of nature when we discover something that appears to break them. As Swinburne said, this would be 'clumsy and ad hoc'. It may be better to say that an unusual event has occurred and that it breaks the laws of nature. Therefore, a miracle has occurred. In fact, in a philosophical sense, the simplest explanation is often the best one. So, to say the laws of nature have been breached is the simplest.

⑦ For many, an argument in favour of miracles is that a change for the better has been witnessed in a person. This is a convincing argument as this can be seen empirically. There are many whose lives have been transformed both physically and spiritually as a result of a miracle and there is no better proof of its validity than that.

Examiner commentary:

① It is useful to dip into the various descriptions of God. This can make a difference to the ease with which miracles can be ascribed to God.

② Seren has cleverly worked double agency into her evaluation.

③ Again, she has looked at another description of God and used it well here. She has linked it to Wiles' moral rejection of an interventionist God.

④ This shows that Seren has considered his argument and, although her objection would not be universal, it can certainly be a valid one to use.

⑤ There are essentially three points being made here (the method, one-off and incorporate findings). These are all very useful to this question and Seren would do well to expand upon all of these. Here she has used breadth but depth could also apply.

⑥ Here she has looked at the third of the points made in the previous paragraph and tied it in with the view of a scholar. There is scope for assessing how religion could, in fact, fit into the scientific method.

⑦ There is an allusion to this here. If we witness the change for a better in a person then that could fit the scientific criteria of 'testing'.

(8) Hume has given some very convincing arguments against miracles. For example, he said that we have a huge amount of evidence that the laws of nature do not break, but little evidence of any quality that miracles happen. Therefore, it is unlikely that they do happen.

(9) However, I think that Hume may be missing the point. Of course miracles do not have a huge amount of evidence or testimony for them. A miracle may be a private event or at least one that cannot be shown to others. That is the whole point of an extraordinary happening. Otherwise it would not be extraordinary. Just because there are not many witnesses to something does not mean that an occurrence has not happened. Nor does it mean that the people are lying.

(10) John Hick would say that miracles which show an awareness of God do happen. I think this is a convincing argument as it allows for interpretation of an event and it does not need the law of nature to be broken. Surely if an event such as a beautiful sunset or the birth of a baby brings to some an awareness of God then that is personal testimony. We cannot argue with that.

(11) But on the other hand, this could be accused of being an unconvincing argument in favour of miracles as it brings too much subjectivity into the situation. How do we distinguish fact from fiction? If it relies on how an individual receives an event then there is already so much personal interpretation brought into the debate.

(12) In conclusion, I would say that arguments against miracles are not more convincing than arguments in their favour. Arguments against them are heavily overlaid with bias and scientific reasoning which Religion should not have to face. Miracles do not fit into the scientific method but they should not have to. This would be like saying that a scientific experiment has to be a one-off event, which has to be verified by Religion.

(13) I do think that the definition of miracles has a big part to play in this question. After all, your definition determines whether or not you believe in them. But, as there are a variety of definitions, this must mean that there is not only one which is the 'correct' one. Therefore, if a person has a particular definition of a miracle and an event fits this then a miracle has happened. So, there are convincing arguments for it.

(8) Of course, there is scope for doing many of Hume's criticisms. She selects a few of his points.

(9) It is good to see a candidate who does not just accept scholarly views but does analyse for coherence.

(10) Mention of a scholar with some analysis. This aspect is drawing out the various definitions of miracles.

(11) Objectivity/subjectivity is a very useful tool to bring into many philosophical questions.

(12) Seren alludes to religion being a separate 'game' here. Perhaps there is scope for bringing more of Wittgenstein's ideas into this debate.

(13) This makes perfect logical sense!

Summative comment

Seren has dealt with this topic in a very broad fashion. We must take into account that this is perfectly legitimate in terms of level descriptors. It is 'focused' on the question and it is 'highly accurate and relevant'. On this basis she was awarded Level 7, 20 marks.

11 'Arguments against miracles are more convincing than arguments in their favour.' Assess this view.

(20 marks)

Tom's answer:

① There are lots of arguments against miracles. David Hume is someone who criticised miracles a lot. He said that miracles come from people and nations that are ignorant. This means that he doubts what they say about miracles. Also, people who claim miracles have a lot to gain if they are believed to be true.

② Hume also said that people who claim miracles have happened do so because they love what is fantastic and love the excitement caused by miracle claims.

③ Another criticism of miracles is that some people say that they are breaks in the laws of nature. The criticism here is that laws of nature are not set in stone so they cannot be broken. Going from that definition of miracle then a miracle cannot happen.

④ Some people say that some definitions of miracles are just too vague. So, it is better to say that a certain thing is not a 'miracle' but instead it should just be described as 'a change in a person which was for the better'.

⑤ Some may believe that a miracle has happened, a healing or a cure, for example, but it could all be in the mind. Such a psychosomatic event is well known in medicine where the placebo effect makes a person feel better but actually no change or miracle has happened. This seems convincing to me as often if it is, say, a pain for example, we cannot tell if a person really has still got that pain. In fact, maybe the person cannot really tell either.

⑥ But, some say that miracles do happen and these arguments can be convincing. It could be said that if there is a God who is all powerful, then this God can do anything that God wants. This can include interrupting the law of nature to bring about a miracle.

⑦ Many miraculous acts can be seen to be done out of God's love for humanity. The fact that not everyone is helped does not matter. It is better to help some than none at all.

⑧ I feel that arguments against miracles are not as convincing as arguments in their favour. God created the world and so God can come into that world to bring about a miracle.

Examiner commentary:

① There are basic references to Hume which are correct. Tom could have expanded upon Hume's accusations regarding testimony to give his statements 'body'.

② Similarly the point made with regard to wonder could have contained more information.

③ Tom deals with what is generally the most common definition of miracle and gives a criticism of this. The point is a valid one.

④ Again he looks at the adequacy of the definitions of miracle and suggests that some are simply not adequate.

⑤ The whole issue of placebo is a interesting one and he touches on part of it. Tom may like to introduce the concepts of objectivity and subjectivity, as well as perhaps considering whether 'feeling' better is actually good enough.

⑥ It is useful to consider the characteristics of the God of classical theism in order to discuss miracles. Here it is done for omnipotence.

⑦ Here it is done for omnibenevolence. The notion of 'it is better to help some' is an interesting one and further discussion of this would be welcome.

⑧ Although the conclusion is 'unexpected' in the sense that Tom wrote much more about unconvincing aspects, at least there is a very brief one.

Summative comment

Tom has understood the main point of the issue. He does present an argument and his support is partial in that it is there but underdeveloped. He scored Level 4, 12 marks.

12 'Religious and scientific views cannot be reconciled.' Assess this view. *(20 marks)*

Seren's answer:

① Many will say they cannot be reconciled as they are so different. One must be chosen over the other. Scientific accounts directly contradict Creationism in so many ways. These cannot be reconciled. Creationists say that God created the earth, God is the sustainer of the earth and many Creationists say that the earth is quite a young one. This cannot combine with the scientific account which says there is no need for a God to create or sustain and the universe is very old indeed. One is right, making the other one wrong. They cannot be reconciled.

② Richard Dawkins says that the universe has the appearance of design but it is not designed. He argues that any suggested God is a blind watchmaker and the universe has come about through chance. This cannot be reconciled with religion's design argument which says that the universe is far too intricate to have come about through sheer chance. In fact, says Dawkins, saying that the universe has an intelligence behind it is like teaching 'flat earthism'.

③ Some scientists may say that the universe does not need a 'starter'; it may have occurred spontaneously or may just always 'have been'. This is in direct contrast to religious accounts which need a start. This is true in the Cosmological arguments which must reject infinity. There is the need for a 'starter' and this starter has to be God.

④ Clearly the 6 days of Creation in the Bible and Creation at the decree of Allah in the Quran cannot be squared with the scientific Big Bang accounts. They are entirely different. One is right so the other must be wrong.

⑤ Many will say that the theory of Evolution has completely disproved the religious accounts. So, Evolution is right, religion is wrong. There is therefore no reconciliation as Evolution can explain everything without reference to a God. Species developed to what they are now. They were not designed that way by a God some 10 000 years ago.

⑥ However, others will say that they can be reconciled. They are both asking different questions so can complement each other to form a larger picture of the origins of the universe and human life. Science tells us how this was done and religion gives us the reason behind it. So they may be saying different things but that is to be expected. They are answering different questions. Put together, they go well. It is like asking 'how do you make a cup of tea?' and 'why do you make a cup of tea?'

⑦ However, some say that this last point shows they cannot be reconciled. This is because the different questions that they answer show that there is absolutely no reason for them to go together. They are two theories answering entirely different questions. Why should they be reconciled?

Examiner commentary:

① Seren has included a number of relevant points in her opening paragraph which forms a strong start.

② Reference to Dawkins, pointing out lack of reconciliation flows well from point 1.

③ Seren could here have referred to Steady State theory and/or the Big Bang in order to give more substance to her answer.

④ She continues with her point that one excludes the other.

⑤ Again she is not just stating the theory of Evolution but is making her point with regard to lack of reconciliation.

⑥ The how and why point is used well.

⑦ Here, it is turned on its head. This is not the usual way of using it but it is valid.

⑧ But Polkinghorne says religion and science can be reconciled. He says that there must be an intelligence to account for the universe as it is. It cannot be blind chance as the likelihood is just too remote. Any tiny change in the basic building blocks of the universe would mean that life would not have formed. So he says that God's guiding hand was needed in order for Evolution to take place.

⑨ Many also say that one day in the Genesis account can be a large period of time. So religion and science can both be accepted as the religious account is basically portraying Evolution. This would be accepted by many Christians today and they see no incompatibility between their faith and scientific findings.

⑩ A Ford says that they can be reconciled. He said this because he believes that everything is due to God's will. He sees early religion as hinting towards scientific findings even before science discovered these things.

⑪ I do believe that they can be reconciled. I think that religion began as an early attempt to explain the world. At this early stage, humans had a low level of consciousness. This had to be coupled with a basic explanation. They cannot be held accountable for this today. Nor can it be used to then say that religious views cannot go with scientific ones. There are so many religious views that this is too sweeping a statement. Maybe some of the religious views do not fit with science but some can. I would also add that I do not feel that they need to reconcile. They can have their own role to play in the lives of humans if kept apart. I like football and weightlifting; why would they need to be merged? It's the same for religion and science. They can satisfy different aspects of a human being's search for truth. The truth may be out there. We may not know what it is. It would be better to 'live and let live' and allow everyone to follow their own path to that truth.

⑧ The anthropic principle is referred to.

⑨ A non-literal interpretation of the religious story is commonly used.

⑩ Here we find reference to Ford's 1986 work *Universe: God, man and science*.

⑪ There are some extremely interesting points made in the conclusion. The idea of evolving consciousness is becoming popular and I loved the very personal analysis of how both religion and science have a role to play. Seren's sentiments would lead to a delightfully peaceful world.

Summative comment

She gives an argument which contains a number of views. Some points could be developed (can't they always with unlimited time?) but the impression is that she knew a lot and wanted to get a range of ideas in. The material is organised clearly and coherently. She scored Level 7, 19 marks.

12 'Religious and scientific views cannot be reconciled.' Assess this view.

(20 marks)

Tom's answer:

① There are very few successful attempts in modern day science or philosophy that support both religion and science.

② However, one of the most successful comes from de Chardin. He was a priest and a scientist. He said we have a physical drive to something better. Everything has radical energy which is a kind of consciousness. The more developed the creature, the more conscious it is. This will eventually mean we will reach the Omega point, a kind of 'Christification'.

③ A good point in my opinion is that for God to have made the universe would be amazing. But for God to make a species capable of improving and adapting to its environment is even more amazing.

④ It has also been suggested that although there is evidence for the Big Bang, Science does not show what caused it. Many believe it was God.

⑤ However, there are many who do not want to reconcile religion and science. Some say we are just better developed apes.

⑥ Most attempts at reconciliation come from science. There is still a chance for them to be reconciled. Both will have to compromise, to avoid arguments.

Examiner commentary:

① Best to keep evaluation until the end.

② Of course reference to de Chardin is valid and Tom does state it as an attempt to reconcile. But what he needs to do is to make it clear that de Chardin is saying that evolution is part of God's plan. This will then show reconciliation.

③ It is a good point but the issue is the same as in point 2. The examiner will have an idea what Tom is trying to say but it could be clearer whether he means that God made the world (no science) or God allowed evolution (religion and science).

④ Again Tom needs to say that this reconciles religion and science.

⑤ The use of 'however' and 'reconcile' is exactly what is needed. But Tom's next sentence is not one developed in a mature way.

⑥ We may or may not agree with the first sentence. He should have said how they could be reconciled and what sort of compromise is needed.

Summative comment

The main point is understood and an argument is attempted. But Tom has given a rather naive answer. He has the bare bones here which if 'beefed up' could creep up by a few marks. He scored Level 4, 11 marks.

Topic 4

13 Explain the main features of Libertarianism and 'hard determinism'.

(30 marks)

Seren's answer:

① Libertarianism says that humans have complete freedom. Determinism is not true. Only we make the decisions. We are to blame or to praise for our actions.

② It is important to separate personality and moral self. Personality is not predetermined; it is shaped, developed by human freedom. No-one can be excused from blame as all actions are freely chosen. Our personality may, due to our upbringing and wider environment, incline us to act in a certain way. Take, for example, Anders Behring Breivik, who killed 77 people in attacks in Norway in 2011. He said that he was concerned about multiculturalism and immigration. He felt that there was to be an Islamic takeover of Norway. He had radical right-wing views and belonged to a neo-Nazi internet forum. His actions, he said were done out of good not evil. So, his personality had been shaped by political influences. But, does that excuse his actions for Libertarians? No.

③ This is because of the idea of the moral self. This can be linked to Kant. He said, 'ought implies can'. This means that we can act freely therefore we ought to. It is our duty to do so. So, whatever our personality inclines us to do, when we need to make a decision as to what to do, our moral self is what decides. This may mean that our moral self decides against what our personality inclines us to. Breivik, whatever his political influences, if sane, could still decide that killing people is wrong and could refrain from the killings.

④ Hard determinism does not agree with the Libertarian view on freedom. It says that free-will is an illusion. Libertarians do think that the personality is affected by genes and/or environment but hard determinists feel our actions are completely determined by such things. Therefore, in opposition to Libertarianism, hard determinism says that as we are completely determined to act in a particular way, nothing can change the outcome. The act is caused and so is not free. This means we are not morally responsible for our actions and therefore we can't be punished for them.

⑤ There are some famous cases that show hard determinism. In 1924 Clarence Darrow successfully defended Loeb and Leopold from the death penalty for having murdered Bobby Franks. He basically said that the actions of these boys had been determined by their upbringing and environment. He said that: 'Nature is strong and she is pitiless. She works in her own mysterious way, and we are her victims. We have not much to do with it ourselves.' The boys had been born into extreme wealth and born into bodies that were determined to think and act in certain ways. It was not their fault.

⑥ Another case is that of Mary Bell who had a terrible upbringing. Her mother was violent and forced her to engage in sexual acts. The hard determinist says that this completely explains why she murdered two boys in 1968.

⑦ There are many types of determinism, such as theological, biological and scientific. Psychologists, such as Skinner and Watson, say that actions can be explained by us learning certain behaviours. So, free-will is an illusion.

Examiner commentary:

① The basic idea in a nutshell. Such concise summaries are really useful for revision.

② Personality is well explained by using an example.

③ The same applies to the explanation of moral self but Kant's work could have been developed further.

④ Comparing and contrasting with Libertarianism is a useful technique, showing the candidate's understanding of both.

⑤ A specific example is given, not just for the sake of it but to actually show a hard determinist view.

⑥ This could have been developed in the same way as paragraph 5.

⑦ If time permitted, perhaps this route could have been explored. But it does show the important point that she has started with explaining the concepts, which is a must, rather than spending too much time on case studies alone.

Summative comment

Overall, Seren's answer shows good knowledge and understanding of the two concepts. It is 'fairly full... presented with accuracy and relevance'. There is some use of evidence and examples. To push her marks up further she could have used the work of a key player such as Mill to give body to her explanation of Libertarianism. This would cover the demands of including scholarly opinion. Level 6, 27 marks.

13 Explain the main features of Libertarianism and 'hard determinism'.

(30 marks)

Tom's answer:

① Libertarianism is the idea that free-will is not an illusion. They reject anything affecting a person such as genes or environment. Humans alone make the choice and they are to blame.

② But if someone is forced to do something then they are not to blame. Such as if a person had to choose which Siamese twin to save or else both would die. The parents have to use their free-will to choose.

③ Our personality can be overcome by our moral self. This means we may not choose what our personality would do.

④ Hard determinism says that we are not free. We do what we do because of our nature or nurture. Psychologists have much to say about this, for example Pavlov says we can condition people into acting in a certain way so behaviour is not free. This was shown in the Little Albert experiment too. Watson thought that if he was given a dozen healthy infants then he could make them into anything.

Examiner commentary:

① The first and last sentences are fine, but the middle one is confused. Libertarianism does take into account that these things affect personality.

② Confusion. If they are forced it is hard to see why this example is given for Libertarianism (there is the subtle difference between the liberty of spontaneity and liberty of indifference which needs introducing here).

③ Personality and moral self have not been explained.

④ It is fine to give examples and these can legitimately be used. But here there are references but no real explanation of them nor, importantly, why they are referred to in this context.

Summative comment

Tom does give an 'outline answer'. He does have some basic knowledge of both concepts but there are some key elements missing. To increase his marks he needs to show more understanding of them, which will see confusions ironed out. Level 3, 12 marks.

Q&A 14 Examine the religious concepts of 'free-will' and 'predestination' with reference to authorities that you have studied.

(30 marks)

Seren's answer:

① Free-will is important in religion. This is because it is important that humans have the choice to believe in God or to do what is right/wrong. Only then can we be morally responsible and only then can we enter into a true relationship with fellow human beings and with God. In Genesis, Adam and Eve were given the choice whether to eat the forbidden fruit. They were told not to, but ultimately, it was their decision.

② For many, having free-will explains the presence of moral evil in the world. It is the basis of many theodicies. God is not responsible for evil as it is due to human choice. Augustine believes that our free-will can also explain natural evil as this is due to the work of fallen angels. This is very important as if we are not free then perhaps that may leave God open to some of the blame for evil.

③ Libertarians completely agree with the concept of free-will. Complete moral liberty means that all acts are truly free and this allows for the religious concept of sin. There can only be sin and the need for redemption if we have freely chosen to act contrary to what is right.

④ Mill believes that being free is part of what it means to be human. Stopping people from having free-will is despotism. But, he is aware that there are limitations on freedom as people must not make a nuisance of themselves in society.

⑤ Another religious authority I have studied is Arminius. He believed the Holy Spirit would be sent to 'woo' humans to follow God. In his view, people could choose to follow God. There are people who God has elected and therefore others that have not been, but all can exercise their free-will to believe or not believe. In this sense, God's grace will not necessarily be effective. People may reject it. This shows his belief in free-will.

⑥ In Buddhism and Hinduism free-will is a necessary part of their systems. That we have free-will, which results in the accumulation of appropriate karma, is fundamental in these religions.

⑦ Predestination is the idea that God has determined the future. God has determined who will be saved and who will go to Hell. St Paul accepts this idea, which we see in his writings: 'those God foreknew He also predestined to be conformed to the image of his Son'.

⑧ Augustine believed this too, saying that the potter has authority over the clay. Some clay the potter makes for salvation, others for damnation. This is an analogy for God predestining us (his creations) for Heaven or Hell, belief or non-belief.

Examiner commentary:

① A source for the belief in free-will and also the rationale behind free-will are given showing a sound start.

② Another reason for the acceptance of free-will is given. The reference to theodicies shows that Seren is looking at religion as a whole, connections are being made. This is a very good thing to do to enable marks to be boosted. (It also shows that AS notes should not be disposed of!)

③ The question asks for the religious concepts and Libertarianism could, if it had not been connected to sin, take the candidate into an unnecessary tangent. Here though, this inclusion is valid.

④ This does basically express a view of Mill. It is better to stick to free-will in its religious sense, as the question demands.

⑤ I loved the idea of the woo! Seren could have developed the idea that the Holy Spirit helps those that wish to find God. An authority in the Specification is Arminius, but any relevant authority would be valid.

⑥ It is a strength to see inclusions from a number of religions and Seren has picked up on an interesting angle here. It does not refer to a person as an 'authority' but this does add to the religious concept of free-will.

⑦ Seren adds breadth to her answer by including a further authority, with a quote.

⑧ The same as for point 7 with the analogy explained.

⑨ God can predestine as He is all knowing and all powerful. Everything that happens is known by God and all that happens only happens as it is within the realms of God's power.

⑩ The main religious authority I studied regarding predestination is Calvin. Humans are inherently sinful. This began with Adam and Eve. This sin has led to people being propelled into all sinful acts. We are not in this sense free. I see this as quite like Augustine's view that we are just one big lump of sin, meaning that we simply always sin.

⑪ From Calvin's ideas came five important points: T U L I P. Total depravity, meaning that basically, we have had it! We are not free to choose as we have such a depraved, sinful nature. Unconditional election, meaning that God chooses (predestines) the Elect. It is unconditional, that is no strings attached. Limited Atonement, meaning Jesus' death puts the Elect into the right relationship with God. Irresistible grace, meaning God predestines who He will save; it is God's choice, not humans. Humans cannot resist it; they will 'give in' when the Holy Spirit works on them. Perseverance of the saints, meaning God through the Holy Spirit gives the Elect the strength to help them keep going, to do the right thing, to have faith.

⑫ So basically, God decides who will be saved, who will have faith. People who have faith will go to Heaven if they are truly sorry for their sins and start afresh. This is 'justification by faith'. This issue is seen a lot in the writings of St Paul; justification by faith or by works? For Calvin, who will have this faith is predestined by God as without God's help people would be unable to have this faith.

⑬ So, it is clear that free-will and predestination have major parts to play in religion. For some, one is more important than the other. For others, the two are equally as important. For some, both can be believed whereas others say that only one of them can be believed in.

⑨ The reason behind the logic of predestination is explained.

⑩ Calvin is cited as an authority and there is also evidence of independent thought.

⑪ Seren has not just reeled off TULIP, but she has actually tried to give short explanations of them too.

⑫ Here she sums up her findings on Calvin.

⑬ There could be scope in this part essay to express ideas about these concepts but she must be wary of straying into evaluation which would suit a part (b) question regarding whether free-will and predestination can be reconciled.

Summative comment
Seren has shown that she understands the two concepts. She understands why religions may have a belief in them. She does look at authorities in a fairly broad fashion. Perhaps more quotations from sacred texts and/ or her authorities, for example, would allow her to get an extra few marks. She scored Level 7, 28 marks.

14 Examine the religious concepts of 'free-will' and 'predestination' with reference to authorities that you have studied.

(30 marks)

Tom's answer:

① Free-will is seen in the Torah in the story of Adam and Eve. God did not force His will upon them. Yes, they were told not to eat from the tree of knowledge of good and evil, but this was for their own good. This is similar to our parents advising us against something but they let us make our own decisions. If it goes wrong then we pay for it, as Adam and Eve did. There was no physical constraint put upon them to prevent them from eating the fruit.

② They were the first people and so the story is showing us that clearly God created them with free-will. This must mean that this is what God wants for humans. Our conscience may be a guide to choosing what is right. Some say this is God's voice giving suggestions, but there is no force in it. Conscience can be seen in the Bible, where people seem to be guided in their decisions.

③ It is surely better that a relationship with anyone is as a result of choosing that relationship. So, it makes sense that God gave humans free-will so that they can choose to follow Him or not. An example of this is given by Vardy. A king could force a peasant girl into a relationship with him, but doesn't as he knows that this is no 'real' relationship at all. This is the same for God. He could force us to love Him but what would be the point in that?

④ Predestination is a belief also found in religions. This is the idea that God decides our fate and also decides what we will do. A person who believed in this was Augustine. He said that due to the first sin, all humans are born with this sin. God decides to save some, even though no-one deserves it. God sends Jesus to atone for sins. This means that Jesus allows things to be repaired or put right again. Who is saved is unknown. Why those who are chosen are chosen is a mystery (but maybe not to God).

⑤ Some say this is unfair as it is random. If we are all guilty then we should all get the same treatment. If our fate is predestined then what about our free-will?

Examiner commentary:

① A decent introduction with the reference to parents showing an understanding of the notion of free-will.

② Again, this is not knowledge alone; understanding is evident. There is scope for developing the conscience idea. It's a pity that Tom did not back up his assertion about the Bible with his evidence.

③ This analogy is one we see typically at AS in Irenaeus' theodicy but it works here, too. Tom has here shown a connection which is useful. However, reference to the major 'authorities' is missing completely.

④ This is a basic description with a little about Augustine, but at least this shows Tom is referring to an 'authority'.

⑤ This type of analysis is AO2.

Summative comment

Tom has been able to explain the concepts in a partially adequate fashion. He has referred to Augustine rather briefly, but this is the only authority given. The question does expect a secure knowledge of the concepts first and foremost, but Tom needs to show a wider awareness of his authorities in order to address the demands of the question. He scored Level 4, 17 marks.

15 'Our genes make us what we are, not our environment.' Assess this view. *(20 marks)*

Seren's answer:

① Some would argue that our genes make us what we are and support this statement. If we look at the Darrow case of the 1920s it could be argued that it was the genes of the boys that resulted in them becoming murderers. They were not morally responsible as they were 'always going to do it', they were born in such a way that they were victims of the causes that came before them.

② We can see so much of our parents in ourselves, both physically and emotionally, that this statement makes perfect sense. If a person is born with a certain inherited genetic defect then that is unavoidable and that shapes their life. Also, if both of my parents are tall then it is highly likely that I will be, too. I am then more likely to be good at the high-jump than if I had been born to shorter parents.

③ However, others argue that it is the environment that makes us what we are, not our genes. Our genes give us certain characteristics, perhaps, but they have to have a 'ground' in which to grow or not grow. We must be affected by who brings us up and where. If parents give a child attention, take us to music lessons or teach us a sense of right and wrong, then that shapes what we are able to become. If environment plays no part then there would be no point in Education, as that would be like saying that if you do not have the right genetic make-up then you can never make progress. I, however, do think that my R.S. teacher has made a huge difference to me. If I had a different teacher who could not get me to understand as well then I do not think I would be sitting here today. So, my environment has made a difference.

④ Some may argue that it could be both genes and environment that make us what we are. They suggest that there may be a combination of factors that make us who we are. This could be a particular gene as there is some evidence that there may be a certain gene which makes people aggressive. But, this can only show itself in certain environmental conditions. You are less likely to be aggressive in a room full of Dalai Lamas than in a room full of hooligans!

⑤ One scholar said that we could look at a murderer who, prior to committing the offence, ate tuna fish salad, peas, mushroom soup and blueberry pie. We may then look at other murderers and find this food present in all of them. This may sound absurd but it may be possible to find certain factors which 'cause' people to do certain things.

⑥ Libertarians say that our moral self can act freely and so it is neither genetics nor environment which makes us what we are really. Each act is a free one which is taken independently of any factor other than what our duty is. But, you could argue 'Where do we get our sense of duty?' Surely the answer is to be found either in our genetic make-up or what our environment tells us?

⑦ In contrast to this, the Libertarian idea of personality may suggest that our environment makes us who we are. Surely, it is said, that someone brought up in an environment of violence will be more violent than someone who was not? This is all they know and it is a system that will keep on going in successive generations due to the type of parenting that people learn.

Examiner commentary:

① A view in favour of the quote, using an appropriate example from the course of study.

② The same viewpoint but with an awareness of how to make an individual response.

③ The reference to the need for an environment to nurture genes is made well.

④ This has a slightly different slant to it than the point made in point 3. In all of this, the examples really illustrate Seren's understanding of what she has revised.

⑤ Here Seren should draw out why she is using this example and state whether it points to genes or environment in order to link it to the question. Hospers was alluding to a combination of factors that could lead to murder.

⑥ She uses Libertarianism as evidence and within the same paragraph analyses its claims and offers an alternative.

⑦ Here she homes in on the personality and, for her purposes here leaves out any reference to the concept of the moral self overriding personality.

(8) Sartre said that neither genetics nor environment makes us who we are. People are creative and can rise above genetics; otherwise humans would be no better than animals. Humans make their own lives. He sees this as a burden, not a privilege.

(9) Some say, though, that environment causes regularity and uniformity. Based upon this we can make predictions. For example, based on environmental experience, I know that when my friend visits, she will not steal from me. I also know that my house will not fall down.

(10) But on the other hand, my friend may have a genetic inclination to steal that she has so far kept hidden. Or, she may desperately need what she is stealing, a matter of life or death. That is environmental. Also, there may be an earthquake which knocks my house down.

(11) To conclude, I disagree with the statement. Of course there are some genetic things which do make me 'me'. 'I' would be different if I had a different skin colour or size and shape. Different things would be open or closed to me. But, I cannot deny that my upbringing has had a huge influence in my life. If my parents had not been prepared to take me on a 20-mile round trip twice a week to my violin teacher then I would not be applying to university to do a music degree. But, if I had not had my mother's determination (genes) I probably would not have spent so many hours practising in order to pass my grades. So the person I am today is the result of both genes and environment but I think that environment has played a slightly larger role.

(8) Again she draws from scholars to enhance her answer.

(9) There is an attempt to give evidence for environmental influences but it is not made clear how these things make a person what they are. For example, it could have been added that this experience makes a person more trusting and so on.

(10) There are some aspects that could be promising if developed, but I get the impression that here is a good candidate who is running out of time. Rather than trying to include all of the points that you know and risking not making the point in some, it is better to consolidate fewer of them.

(11) She has come to an appropriate conclusion with some personal comments which also show independent thought.

Summative comment

Seren has gone through a number of possibilities in her answer and has thus shown a breadth in her awareness of the issues. There is much evidence of individual thought and the personal anecdotes do illustrate her points rather well. She is able to refer to some scholars but has clearly decided to approach this part-essay in her own way. She scored Level 7, 19 marks.

15 'Our genes make us what we are, not our environment.' Assess this view. *(20 marks)*

Tom's answer:

① Some may argue that it is our genes that make us who we are. This is a scientific view as genes do determine part of our physical appearance and health.

② On the other hand, environment plays a part. People who live in warm countries will have their skin colour change and they will be subject to doing different things than if they were born into a cold country.

③ Also, we looked at research in class which showed that schizophrenia was often evident in people who got mixed messages from their parents. This was often if parents were separated but not always.

④ Hard determinists, I think, are determined by their environment. This is because if you are brought up with hard determinist parents then you are more likely to be a hard determinist. But, the question is still open as to whether this comes through genes that 'make' you a hard determinist or the environment/type of upbringing that your hard determinist parents give you.

⑤ Others say that you cannot have only genes or environment affecting you, but that both have an effect. Recently people have been arguing that there may be a 'fat' gene or a 'gay' gene, which determine what you grow up to be. However, you could argue that if you have the 'fat' gene then through certain decisions such as avoiding certain food then you can make sure that you turn out quite differently. Or can you? Are there just some people who will not lose weight whatever they do? But, the basic rule is that if you burn off more than you put in then you have to lose weight. So I do not accept that such genes cannot be controlled.

⑥ Free-will plays a big role in who we become. This can mean that genes and environment are not the only things that make us what we are. With free-will the future is open and so, in a way, I make myself through choices. In a simplistic sense, I can change myself by changing the hair colour I was born with. Maybe I am affected by the hair colour or style of a certain celebrity. This is my environment.

Examiner commentary:

① The reference to the scientific view is something which could be developed by referring to scholars. This would add 'meat to the bare bones'.

② It would have been useful if Tom could have given examples of how activities may differ depending on the countries we inhabit. For example, I am more likely to ski in Austria than I am in the Sudan.

③ A case study is included. Tom needed to clearly make the point here though; is he trying to say that the parents genetically had mixed messages to give which were passed on or is he trying to say that the environment affected the child? I took it to be the latter. He could make a case for both, so it would not matter which as long as he does make the point.

④ Here Tom does 'flirt' with various ideas, which is quite legitimate. It would be the expansion of these rhetorical questions into solid arguments that would help to increase his marks.

⑤ Here he does go a step further. He presents some ideas, reflects upon them and does conclude.

⑥ The reference to the role of free-will could allow an answer to go in a different direction. If only Tom had then done something else with his example. He could perhaps say that genes give us part of our appearance, but some decisions are affected by our environment. However, the choices we decide to make may also be affected by our genes and so on.

Summative comment

'The main point of the issue is understood.' More than one view is evident and he does provide limited analysis. In some parts of his writing he just needed to drive home the point he was trying to make. There is no conclusion. Tom scored Level 4, 11 marks.

16 'A belief in predestination cannot be reconciled with a belief in free-will.' Evaluate this contention.

(20 marks)

Seren's answer:

① This statement is saying that a person can only believe in either predestination or free-will, not both. That is, they are incompatible. Believing in one means that the other one cannot be held to be true.

② On the one hand, this can be said to be true. If God has predestined humans then they absolutely, in no way have real freedom. How can they? No decision actually makes any difference in real terms. In fact, that decision, although we may think we have made it, we have not. That decision has been predetermined by God in advance of it happening.

③ If God is all-powerful then no decision can be made without His will, nor can a decision be made against His will as He has the power to enforce any decision He would like. If God is all knowing then no decision is unknown to God so therefore any action or decision that we may think is free is known by God. As God is all-powerful, too, as said earlier, He has the knowledge and then the power to enforce any end result He chooses.

④ We could also say that if God is omnibenevolent, a belief in predestination cannot be reconciled with a belief in free-will, as God loves us and does not want us to use our sinful free-will. Using this would only mean that we do what is wrong and therefore He removes free-will from the equation. So, predestination is actually done out of love for human beings. It does result in some being saved and others being damned, but if we made decisions based upon our sinful free-will, then we would all be damned.

⑤ There is biblical back up for this. After the first man sinned, humans were from then on predestined to be alienated from God, without the capacity for real free choice. Sin had entered the world and enslaved people to sinful acts. If we are enslaved then there is no free choice. It is like being imprisoned. There is no real free-will as you cannot get out of the confines of the prison, so all acts are done under constraint.

⑥ In fact, for God to be sovereign, then there cannot be free-will. A sovereign has to make rules and God, by predestining everything, is laying down His rules which humans cannot break by having free-will.

⑦ We could look at it in another way though. We could say that only free-will exists and predestination does not. Equally, this means that they cannot be reconciled as only one can exist. To give evidence for this we could say that God has given us true free-will in order for us to enter into a relationship with Him. For this to be a loving one it cannot be forced, nor can the outcome of the relationship already be established. Therefore, God does not predestine.

Examiner commentary:

① It is fine to give a brief reworded account of the question; it steadies many candidates.

② A logical implication of predestination is given.

③ Here it is explained in terms of God's nature.

④ Normally in answers candidates refer to omniscience and omnipotence in relation to predestination. So her use of omnibenevolence is novel and shows evidence of independent thought.

⑤ She can clearly source these ideas and she also gives an analogy with prison which works.

⑥ God's sovereignty is used well as a reason why the two concepts cannot be reconciled.

⑦ Showing the absence of one of the concepts does indeed show that they cannot be reconciled. It is not the orthodox way of answering this question but it does in fact answer it.

(8) Another argument in favour of them not being reconciled as only free-will exists, is that if actions were predetermined then we would not be responsible for our actions. Surely it would be very unfair if we were not responsible for our actions. In fact, that does not match up to the real world where we are punished for what we have done. We cannot appeal to 'but it is God's fault'. Also, it would be a very dubious God who sent us to Hell for something that He had determined.

(9) However, we could argue they can be reconciled. If God has created humans and given us free-will, then this free-will may also be God's will. So actually God has predetermined that our free-will is exactly the same as His will. So both free-will and predestination are true.

(10) Also, within sacred writings we do see evidence of both. For example, Adam and Eve are given free-will but the result of the wrong choice is already predetermined – they will die. They will be expelled from the garden. Adam's descendants will have to work hard for a living and Eve's descendants will have pain in childbirth. We can see this kind of idea at work in life. We are given the free choice in school as to how to behave but the result of misbehaving is predetermined. So, the world can work with both of these concepts co-existing.

(11) Anyway, as humans do not know what God has predetermined, then human choice is still free. We make our decisions in time but if God has predetermined then this is outside of our time. So there is no difficulty in accepting that we make real choices in the here and now even though God knows what these are going to be.

(12) In conclusion, I feel that a belief in free-will and predestination cannot be reconciled. I see them as completely logical opposites. We may constantly feel that we are making choices but God's will has already predetermined what those choices will be. This means that free-will cannot exist. To people who say that God would not predestine, I would say that this is not the sort of God that we are presented with in many accounts in the Bible, for example. In the Old Testament there is a God who decides a person's fate. If He deemed that the Israelites would suffer a particular fate, then that is what happened. They could not have free-will as well as God's will being enforced.

(13) There is evidence for both of them in Scripture but that is because Scripture has been written by a number of hands through the ages and each of those writers had a different view or a different story to write. So, it is not surprising that we see references to both. This does not make them compatible. In fact their presence in these writings highlights their incompatibility.

(14) So, I feel that you can only believe in one of them. Personally, I believe in predestination as I think that God would not leave us up to our own devices. If there is a final plan for this world then it has to be already determined. Otherwise, if it was left to human free-will this plan may never come to fruition.

(8) The implications for human and divine responsibility are laid out well. This shows that Seren has thought beyond the facts and discovered what a belief in these concepts may mean in real terms.

(9) This makes sense, that humans can be created with the divine will as part of their own will.

(10) An example is given where she tries to show that in the same story the two ideas run side by side. This is convincing.

(11) The use of timeless God is a good inclusion. It shows how reconciliation may be possible by the use of the two 'modes' of time.

(12) She has used evidence again which consolidates her opinion. This is just another example of looking wider and searching for information that can be used.

(13) Textual criticism would back this up and Seren has done well to bring in a connection with another area of study.

(14) This is a very fitting culmination to her 'final plan'!

Summative comment
Seren has covered this from a number of angles. She has shown that she has analysed the concepts and in her answer she shows an awareness of the issues raised. Her answer cleverly looks at the adequacy of both concepts (so that by ruling one concept out they thereby cannot be reconciled) as well as looking at reconciliation from the perspective of them both existing. She has certainly given a 'comprehensive and mature response' and so she scored Level 7, 20 marks.

16 'A belief in predestination cannot be reconciled with a belief in free-will.' Evaluate this contention.

(20 marks)

Tom's answer:

① Predestination is the belief that your future has already been decided. God has selected individuals for salvation or damnation. This cannot be reconciled with free-will as in order to have free-will, the choices that are made have to be your own. If you are determined for salvation or damnation then God has determined your choices, good and bad.

② If your future is determined then what is the point in doing the good? If you lead a good life you will be punished for it.

③ It works the same the other way. Those heading for salvation may not bother doing what is good. They will know that they could do the bad and still get salvation.

④ It is not logical that both beliefs can exist together. If there is any kind of limit on my choices then that choice is not really free. If God has complete power then God could overpower people and their decision would not really be theirs.

⑤ If God has complete power then surely He would want to predestine human life; that is a show of power, so humans cannot have free-will.

⑥ Therefore, a belief in both predestination and free-will is impossible. If the first one exists then the second one cannot. Because I feel that God must predestine then I do not think that humans are free.

Examiner commentary:

① This sets out the dilemma, but at the end it could have been developed with the key point, 'therefore, what we may think is human free choice is only an illusion'.

② This is more an evaluation of the concept of predestination. This needs extra elements if it is to be used to answer this question.

③ As point 2.

④ There are two separate points in here – the limit on choices and God overpowering. However, neither really makes a point specific enough to warrant higher marks.

⑤ Brief, but the point is made.

⑥ A round up but it is limited.

Summative comment

Tom has made a 'limited attempt at analysis/comment'. His reasoning is 'basic'. His essay has the feel of a partial awareness of the issues and this has resulted in minimal evidence. He scored Level 3, 8 marks.

Quickfire answers

1 Is religious faith rational?

① An unmarried man.

② Omniscient, omnipotent, omnibenevolent, eternal, etc.

③ These three attributes are said to belong to the God of classical theism.

④ There is an endless number of ways that things could have been.

⑤ Faith is what is actual; belief is what could be.

⑥ Otherwise nothing would be discovered.

⑦ We may take the risk and not discover what we had hoped for.

⑧ I volunteer/choose to take this faith-venture.

⑨ No more empirical evidence is going to come.

⑩ It is better to do something that is useful for me, fitting in with my hopes.

⑪ The effect can be seen in people's lives.

⑫ He is the God who comes to humans, rather than humans finding God.

⑬ Revelation.

⑭ Reason.

⑮ Yes.

⑯ It is grounded in our experience not evidence.

⑰ One that needs no justification or proof.

⑱ God lights up the human mind.

⑲ Facts that God has guaranteed to be true.

⑳ Human attempts to discover God using reason.

㉑ Reason has been corrupted due to 'the Fall'.

㉒ I-Thou is a relationship with a person; I-It with an object.

㉓ A way of seeing life that is not open to verification or falsification.

㉔ My dog is brown.

㉕ It adds nothing to the description of that thing.

2 Is religious language meaningful?

① Non-cognitive.

② As we cannot verify it conclusively.

③ We know what would have to be done to verify it.

④ A sign has no connection to what it represents, a symbol does.

⑤ And participates in that to which it points.

⑥ All tools are used for a purpose.

⑦ 'Look and see.'

⑧ They are playing different games, using different rules.

⑨ To see him read or write philosophy!

⑩ The principles are neither analytic nor synthetic.

⑪ Flew says believers do not take into account things that seem to go against their beliefs; Mitchell says they *do* take them into account.

⑫ We know what we would need to do to verify historical statements which include many religious ones.

3 Is religious faith compatible with scientific evidence?

① Something like: 'a break in the law of nature by a decision of the divine or by the stepping in of something unseen'.

② Timescale and deeper significance.

③ As laws of nature do not break; new findings are incorporated into them.

④ Evidence.

⑤ The claims of many religions to miracles cancel out all of them.

⑥ Two.

⑦ Looking after the world on behalf of God.

⑧ God acting through a human to bring about an effect.

⑨ Origins.

⑩ Yes.

4 Are we 'free beings'?

① Determinism and free will are incompatible.

② People can't be blamed as their actions were determined.

③ People just act differently, rather than being right or wrong.

④ Your own, voluntary free acts.

⑤ Where a person is forced to do something by an external force.

⑥ Free will and determinism are incompatible.

⑦ Yes. All acts are done freely.

⑧ The belief that God has determined the future.

⑨ Turning away from God to man.

⑩ Essential human nature, which is technically free, is overridden by our sinful nature, so that we freely choose what is 'bad'.

⑪ God would not punish humans for the sins of others.

⑫ The theory that what makes us what we are is our genes.

⑬ The theory that what makes us who we are is our environment.

⑭ Nature.

⑮ Nature.

⑯ Both.

Index